HOMOSEXUALITY IN COLD WAR AMERICA

NEW AMERICANISTS *A Series Edited by Donald E. Pease*

HOMOSEXUALITY

IN COLD WAR AMERICA

Resistance and the Crisis of Masculinity

Robert J. Corber

Duke University Press Durham & London

1997

© 1997 Duke University Press

All rights reserved   Printed in the United States of

America on acid-free paper ∞

Typeset in Berkeley Medium with Monotype Twentieth

Century display by Keystone Typesetting, Inc.

Library of Congress Cataloging-in-Publication Data

appear on the last printed page

of this book.

FOR KENT *"adhesiveness"*

CONTENTS

ACKNOWLEDGMENTS

I want to express my gratitude to the American Council of Learned Societies and the Tanner Humanities Center of the University of Utah, both of which provided generous financial support for this project. The director of the Tanner Humanities Center, Lowell Durham, and its staff deserve praise for creating an atmosphere that was unusually conducive to scholarly work. While at the University of Utah, I benefited from discussions with many members of the faculty. I am particularly grateful to Gillian Brown and Howard Horwitz, whose rigorous engagement with my work reminded me of why I wanted to become a scholar in the first place. I am also grateful to Marcia Klotz and Lee Medovoi for discussing the politics of queer theory with me. Jane Chance and Peggy Pascoe deserve special thanks for their friendship and encouragement.

I presented some of the material in this book as talks, and I want to acknowledge the audiences at Dartmouth College, the University of Utah, Rice University, and the University of Toledo; their comments and criticisms gave me much to think about. I am particularly grateful to the American Studies and Mass Culture Workshops at the University of Chicago, whose members asked probing questions about film noir and its relation to hard-boiled detective fiction that helped me to clarify my argument in part 1 of this study. I would like to thank Andrew Hoberek and Paul Young for arranging my visit to the workshops.

Sam Gill, Archivist Emeritus of the Academy of Motion Pictures Arts and Sciences, allowed me to examine the production files for *Laura* and *Crossfire*. Maurice Rapf shared with me his reminiscences of the period of the blacklist in Hollywood and provided useful information about Vera Caspary and Richard Brooks.

Many friends and colleagues have commented on parts or all of the manuscript. I would particularly like to thank Dana Polan and Robert Caserio, whose comments helped me rethink the project at a crucial stage of its development. Reynolds Smith, my editor at Duke University Press, arranged unusually helpful reader's reports and provided much-needed support and encouragement from the beginning. I am deeply indebted to Jonathan Arac and Donald Pease, whose continuing support of my work I hardly know how to acknowledge. Finally, I would like to dedicate this book to Kent Sargent as a small token of my appreciation for his unwavering support in both good and bad times.

A version of chapter 5 appeared in *Western Humanities Review* 68, no. 1 (spring 1994): 30–52. I want to thank Barry Weller, editor, for granting me permission to reprint it.

INTRODUCTION

I'm Really a Queen Myself

You see, she would tell him, I'm really a queen myself. I mean it's the same
difference, honey, I like and do the same things.—Cora in Tennessee Williams's
"Two on a Party" (1954)

In the 1950s, even supposedly progressive critics denied the importance of
gay male writers, claiming that their criticisms of postwar American society
were insufficiently political. Leslie Fiedler, for example, interpreted the
popularity of gay male writers not as a sign of the emergence of a new form
of politics but as an indication that left-wing intellectuals had abdicated
their political responsibilities. In "The Un-Angry Young Men," an essay that
first appeared in *Encounter* in 1958, he complained that left-wing intellectuals had created a political vacuum that had allowed gay male writers to
emerge as "the staunchest party of all."[1] According to him, left-wing intellectuals had failed to provide a satisfactory critique of postwar American
society because they remained committed to an outmoded form of politics.
They did not realize that postwar American society threatened "not exclusion and failure but acceptance and success" (390) and thus could not be
understood in terms of the categories adopted by Popular Front writers and
artists in the 1930s. Fiedler dismissed their cultural politics as an "empty
piece of mimicry" (390) that did not adequately take into account the
changes that had occurred in American society since the Depression. Their
failure to develop an oppositional politics that accurately reflected postwar
conditions was particularly disturbing because it had enabled homosexuality to become "the last possible protest against bourgeois security and
the home in the suburbs where adultery is old hat" (406). Gay male writers
had been able to supplant left-wing intellectuals because their explicit

treatment of gay male themes shocked middle-class heterosexual readers, thereby making their work seem more progressive than it really was.

Despite his complaint that left-wing intellectuals had abdicated their political responsibilities, Fiedler had no desire to promote left-wing political activity. Rather, he sought to contain the emergence of homosexuality as an oppositional practice by comparing it unfavorably to traditional forms of left-wing politics. Clearly threatened by the way in which gay male writers politicized domains of experience that he assumed were apolitical, he refused to acknowledge that homosexuality could provide the basis for a political identity. According to him, gay male opposition to the political mentality known as the Cold War consensus represented a debased form of politics that bordered on exhibitionism. Exaggerating the visibility of the gay male subculture, he argued that homosexuality had become "the purest and truest protest of the latest generation, not a burden merely, an affliction to be borne, but a politics to be flaunted" (405). Fiedler tried to explain the emergence of homosexuality as an oppositional practice in terms of the marginal position gay male writers had traditionally occupied in American letters. Unlike England, he explained, America did not have a "tradition of fiction asserting (behind the most perfunctory of disguises) homosexual responses to experience as the cultivated norm" (405). Gay male writers who dealt openly with gay male experience were mistakenly seen as engaging in a "conquest of new areas of feeling, an opening up" (405). Insofar as it tried to contain the emergence of a distinctly gay male literary tradition by assimilating it into the dominant paradigms of American fiction, Fiedler's essay was complicit with the Cold War construction of "the homosexual" as a national security risk. Like the discourses of national security, which exploited fears that gay men were virtually indistinguishable from straight men, Fiedler's claim that gay male fiction merely provided another example of the homoerotic character of American letters rendered gay male writers invisible.[2]

At first glance, Fiedler's claim that homosexuality had become a politics to be flaunted seems not only homophobic but a serious misrepresentation of the postwar political climate. As I have shown in *In the Name of National Security,* Cold War political discourse tended to position Americans who protested the rise of the "organization man" or who rejected the postwar American dream of owning a home in the suburbs as homosexuals and lesbians who threatened the nation's security.[3] Far from the last possible protest against bourgeois security, homosexuality was understood as a form of psychopathology that undermined the nation's defenses against Communist infiltration. The politicization of homosexuality was crucial to the consolidation of the Cold War consensus. The homosexualization of left-wing political activity by the discourses of national security enabled Cold War liberalism to emerge as the only acceptable alternative to the forces of reaction in postwar American society. Despite the government's massive attempts to marginalize and suppress the gay male subculture, however, there is some truth to Fiedler's claim that gay male writers had become "the staunchest party of all." Many gay male writers treated homosexuality as a subversive form of identity that had the potential to disrupt the system of representation underpinning the Cold War consensus. Their explicit treatment of gay male experience contributed to the dismantling of the signifying practices that naturalized the production of gender and sexual identity in the postwar period.

One of the purposes of this project is to clarify this aspect of postwar gay male cultural production by examining the work of Tennessee Williams, Gore Vidal, and James Baldwin in the context of the national common sense that emerged in the 1950s in response to the threat Communists, homosexuals, and lesbians allegedly posed to the nation's security. I have chosen to examine the work of these three writers less because it is representative of postwar gay male cultural production in general than because of what it can tell us about the operations of power in postwar American society and the modes of resistance those operations both enabled and precluded. By foregrounding Williams's, Vidal's, and Baldwin's opposition to the Cold War consensus, I try to establish the importance of a group of gay male writers whose cultural politics have been misunderstood.[4] Progressive postwar critics such as Leslie Fiedler, Irving Howe, and Stanley Edgar Hyman complained that Williams, Vidal, and Baldwin focused on issues of gender and sexual identity in order to shift attention away from the material conditions of existence, but I argue that they did so because they understood that such issues were crucial to understanding postwar structures of oppression. These writers sought to broaden the definition of the political by extending it to issues of subjectivity that, according to the Cold War consensus, transcended politics. They realized that the homosexualization of left-wing political activity provided Cold War liberals with a mechanism for containing the demands of women, African Americans, and other historically disenfranchised groups for greater access to the American dream in exchange for their contributions to the war effort.

But I also try to show that the work of these writers provided an alternative understanding of gay male experience, one that called into question the minoritarian, or subcultural, model of homosexuality pioneered by postwar gay rights activists. The gay male writers examined in this study tended to treat homosexuality less as a category of identity resembling other categories of identity such as race and ethnicity than as a form of oppositional consciousness.[5] They rejected models of political solidarity that were patterned on kinship relations. Insofar as such models required the constant policing of borders to determine who did and did not legitimately belong to the gay and lesbian communities, they hindered the formation of the broadly based coalitions that were needed to overcome the racist, sexist, and homophobic structures of postwar American society. These writers stressed the construction of gay male subjectivity across multiple axes of difference, thereby promoting a model of political solidarity that was rooted in a collective experience of oppression rather than membership in a particular community.[6] For this reason, their work should be understood as anticipating the gay liberation movement of the 1960s.[7] Like Herbert Marcuse, Wilhelm Reich, and Norman O. Brown, these writers conceived of sexuality as an emancipatory force that had the potential to disrupt postwar relations of power. In their work, gay male identity is defined less by sexual preference than by resistance to the dominant political and social order—hence Cora's claim in Williams's short story "Two on a Party" that she is really a queen herself. Unlike mainstream gay rights activists, the writers examined in this study were not interested in establishing that homosexuality constituted a fixed minority identity but looked forward to the end of "the homosexual" as a category of individual.[8]

Williams's, Vidal's, and Baldwin's refusal to treat gay male identity as a form of ethnicity is one of the reasons I have chosen to focus on their work and not that of other postwar gay male writers. Given the present historical conjuncture, in which the Christian Right has been able to exploit divisions among gays, lesbians, feminists, African Americans, and Latinos over the implementation of multicultural curricula and AIDS education programs in New York City and elsewhere, recovering these writers' work from the sort of institutional forgetting to which it has been subjected has struck me as a particularly urgent task.[9] Their emphasis on the overdetermination and multiplicity of gay male identity can teach us a great deal about forms of community and political solidarity that do not depend on fixed notions of identity or membership in homogeneous communities. Although they recognized the importance of affirming the practices and modes of subjectivity (gay male camp, the gay macho style, and so on) which gay men had created in response to their exclusion from mainstream American society, these writers also stressed the political interests gay men had in common with women, African Americans, and other disenfranchised groups. For them, the discourses of national security had created a common context of struggle in which racism, homophobia, and sexism were structurally linked. Thus it was in the interests of straight women, African Americans, gays, and lesbians to join forces in opposition to the Cold War consensus.

Moreover, the writers examined in this study realized that the understanding of homosexuality as a subcultural form of identity threatened to reinforce the dominant construction of "America" as a melting pot in which different racial and ethnic groups coexisted harmoniously and enjoyed equal access to the American dream of upward mobility. Unlike mainstream postwar gay rights activists, they were not interested in establishing that gay men could be easily assimilated into mainstream American society. For them, the primary source of gay male oppression was not the inaccessibility of the American dream but the regulatory fictions that governed the production of gender and sexual identity. They foregrounded the construction of gay male subjectivity across multiple axes of difference because they wanted to encourage a mobility in solidarity. Perhaps the most progressive aspect of their work was the way in which it promoted identifications across racial, class, and gender lines. Insofar as such identifications destabilized the series of binary oppositions that governed the production of the Cold War subject (male vs. female, white vs. black, straight vs. gay), they were subversive.

To establish the importance of Williams's, Vidal's, and Baldwin's opposition to the Cold War consensus and the minoritarian model of homosexuality it promoted, I locate their work in the postwar crisis of masculinity precipitated by the emergence and consolidation of a Fordist organization of production and consumption. Cultural historians have shown that in the 1950s a model of masculinity that stressed domesticity and cooperation gradually became hegemonic.[10] Men were no longer encouraged to show initiative or to exert their independence from the domestic sphere. Rather, they were expected to define themselves through their identities as consumers—an expectation hitherto confined to women—and to take an active role in childrearing. Medical experts issued dire warnings about the potentially pernicious influence women exerted over the domestic sphere and urged men to counteract it. Moreover, men were discouraged from competing aggressively with one another and were expected to submit to corporate structures in exchange for obtaining a secure place in the organizational hierarchy. As sociologists C. Wright Mills, William Whyte, and David Riesman showed in studies of the "organization man" which have since become classics, the successful negotiation of the corporate hierarchy depended less on personal ambition and individual initiative than on respect for authority, loyalty to one's superiors, and an ability to get along with others—all qualities traditionally associated with femininity.[11] Despite the loss of independence it entailed, most men consented to the domestication of masculinity because it enabled them to achieve a higher standard of living than their fathers had enjoyed and to participate in the consumer culture of the postwar period. Several surveys conducted in the forties and fifties showed that men tended to derive greater satisfaction from providing for their families than from their careers.[12]

Insofar as it promoted the mass consumption of durable goods such as automobiles, televisions, and refrigerators, the rise of the "organization man" facilitated the transition to a Fordist regime of capital accumulation.[13] It displaced forms of male identity, such as the independent, self-reliant entrepreneur, that were more compatible with an earlier stage of capital accumulation in that they encouraged self-discipline and deferred gratification. The dramatic increase in consumer spending in the postwar period helps to highlight the role the domestication of masculinity played in the reorganization of the economy along Fordist lines. In the five years following the end of World War II, expenditures on household furnishings and appliances rose 240 percent. By 1949, Americans had purchased 21.4 million automobiles, 20 million refrigerators, 5.5 million stoves, and 11.6 million televisions. Housing starts grew from 114,000 in 1944 to an all-time high of 1,692,000 in 1950. By the mid-1950s, the increase in the gross national product was due almost entirely to consumer spending on durable goods and residential construction.[14]

Promoted by both the culture industries and a set of government programs designed to encourage suburbanization, the domestic model of masculinity gradually became hegemonic. Popular television shows such as *Father Knows Best* (1954–62), *Leave It to Beaver* (1957–63), and *The Adventures of Ozzie and Harriet* (1952–66) instructed men in the responsibilities and pleasures of middle-class fatherhood and were part of a network of discourses that encouraged mass consumption as recompense for corporate jobs many men found monotonous and unrewarding. Moreover, signaling a retreat from the New Deal, with its vaguely social democratic commitment to public housing and mass transit, Congress passed legislation that all but enacted the domestication of masculinity into law. This legislation included the Servicemen's Readjustment Bill of 1944, or GI bill of rights, which provided grants to returning veterans who wanted to enter vocational training programs or to attend college. The importance of this legislation cannot be overstated, for the nearly eight million veterans who received free college educations were able to enter the professional and managerial classes.[15] Equally important was the Interstate Highway Act of 1956, which in capitalizing the massive highway construction of the postwar period helped to make the suburbs accessible by car to millions of Americans. Combined with a government-sponsored system of credit that included federally insured home loans and tax deductions for mortgages, this legislation did not just encourage the domestication of masculinity, it subsidized it.[16]

Although government programs that subsidized the domestication of masculinity improved the standard of living of white lower-middle-class and working-class families by enabling them to buy homes in the suburbs, they did so at the expense of racial minorities and the urban poor. Such programs hastened the decline of the inner cities and reinforced the racial and class segregation of the suburbs, the consequences of which did not become fully apparent until the urban uprisings of the sixties and seventies.[17] The policies of the Federal Housing Administration, which insured home loans, were racially discriminatory and promoted the dispersal of white middle-class families to the suburbs. The FHA discouraged the repair of existing structures by offering unattractive terms and made it cheaper for families to buy new homes than to modernize old ones. It also refused to insure loans to families living in neighborhoods with "inharmonious racial or nationality groups" and declared whole areas of cities ineligible for loan guarantees through the practice of redlining.[18] The Housing Act of 1949, which funded slum clearance projects and low-income housing, only compounded this potentially explosive situation by further concentrating racial minorities in the inner cities.[19] The Housing Act did not require municipalities to provide the poor with low-income housing but relied on local initiative and responsibility for creating housing agencies. In allowing municipalities to determine when and where public housing would be built, the Housing Act reinforced racial and class segregation. Moreover, only municipalities where substandard housing already existed were eligible for the program. To receive federal assistance, municipalities had to raze one unit of slum housing for every unit of public housing they built.

At the same time that the FHA's racially discriminatory policies contributed to urban decay and reinforced racial segregation, however, they also helped to contain opposition to the Cold War consensus. The concentration of African Americans in the inner cities contributed to the decline of labor militancy by discouraging worker solidarity across racial lines. Federal subsidies made it cheaper for ethnic minorities to buy than to rent and thus facilitated their assimilation into mainstream American society. Working-class ethnic families who took advantage of federally insured loans by abandoning the inner cities for the suburbs increasingly defined themselves in terms of their race rather than in terms of their class or ethnic background.[20] Thus the FHA's racially discriminatory policies insured that class struggle was refracted through the lens of race. The high unemployment rates of inner-city African Americans were increasingly understood in racial rather than economic terms. The deterioration of inner-city schools and neighborhoods was attributed to the breakdown of the black family, dependence on welfare, food stamps, and other so-called government handouts, and an erosion of the work ethic.[21] Rarely was it linked to government programs that were designed to insure the racial and class homogeneity of the suburbs.

Despite government programs that made it financially beneficial to submit to the domestication of masculinity, the rise of the "organization man" encountered considerable resistance. Masculinity remained a contested terrain throughout the postwar period. Some middle-class men registered their opposition to the reorganization of masculinity by refusing to settle down in the suburbs and raise a family. Although these men continued to pursue careers in corporations and often successfully negotiated their structures, they settled in urban areas in order to participate in the "swinging" lifestyle promoted by magazines such as *Playboy*, which began publication in 1953. Such magazines positioned their readers as consumers but did not require them to restrict their sexuality to the domestic sphere, nor did they link consumption to fatherhood and homeownership.[22] Other men protested the rise of the "organization man" by joining motorcycle and other types of gangs that contributed to the spread of "juvenile delinquency," which became a national obsession in the fifties. Such gangs allowed them to recover forms of male homosocial bonding that were actively discouraged because they conflicted with the Fordist organization of production and consumption. Still other men fashioned an oppositional form of masculinity from different aspects of the beat movement, rock 'n' roll music, and African American and working-class ethnic subcultures.[23] Such men rejected the relative security of corporate life and were often active in the New Left and the counterculture of the sixties.

Film Noir and Popular Resistance to the Domestication of Masculinity

To help situate the work of Williams, Vidal, and Baldwin in relation to the postwar crisis of masculinity, I have divided this study into two parts. The first part examines film noir as a potentially emancipatory form of mass culture. Although the relevance of film noir to the issues I have been discussing may not be readily apparent, I use it to establish the importance of Williams's, Vidal's, and Baldwin's project to broaden the definition of the political by extending it to issues of gender and sexual identity. Film noir was fairly explicit in its opposition to the postwar reorganization of masculinity. The typical noir hero is a hard-boiled detective who expresses nothing but contempt for the domestic sphere. Film noir was one of the few forms of mass culture that continued to bear the marks of the influence of the Popular Front on the culture industries.[24] Many of the directors and screenwriters responsible for developing the distinctive visual style and narrative techniques that define film noir had been members of the Communist party in the thirties and were blacklisted following the 1947 hearings of the House Un-American Activities Committee on alleged Communist infiltration of the film industry. They were drawn to film noir as a potentially subversive form of cinematic discourse that allowed them to address controversial issues and to treat realistically a neglected stratum of postwar American society. Because they were primarily low-budget productions that were not star vehicles, films noirs could express skepticism about the American dream without attracting the attention of the Breen office which was responsible for enforcing the Production Code. Abraham Polonsky, who wrote and directed *Force of Evil* (1948), has speculated that film noir could express criticism of postwar American society while escaping censorship because "the intellectual content is absorbed into what people think is a dark criminal type of picture anyhow and so there's an acceptance of it."[25]

Another reason film noir is important to my overall argument is that it can be used to show that the politicization of homosexuality was crucial to the economic restructuring of the postwar period. Film scholars seem to agree that although film noir does not constitute a genre, it does name an inflection or tendency within classical Hollywood cinema that is marked by the use of low-key lighting, flashbacks, and voice-over narration.[26] As Richard Dyer has shown, however, in identifying the set of elements that distinguishes film noir from other forms of classical Hollywood cinema, film scholars have tended to overlook the unusual presence of characters who are explicitly marked as gay.[27] Film noir developed a distinctive iconography for representing gay male characters that drew on the traditional signifiers of male homosexuality in classical Hollywood cinema (upper-crust accent, effeminate mannerisms, impeccable taste, and so on).[28] In film noir, the gay male characters are linked iconographically to the femme fatale who lures the hero to his ruin. Like her, they are fastidious about their appearance, wear expensive, well-tailored clothes, and are identified with luxurious surroundings (antique-filled apartments, richly appointed nightclubs and casinos). By contrast, the hard-boiled hero frequently appears disheveled and unshaven and is identified with coarse surroundings (shabby, unkempt offices and rooming houses).

This mode of iconographic representation, which translated into visual terms the differences between the hero and the gay male characters, distinguished film noir from other forms of postwar cinematic discourse. As I have shown elsewhere, postwar film in general tended to ratify the homophobic categories of Cold War political discourse. The discourses of national security tried to exploit fears that there was no way to tell homosexuals from heterosexuals.[29] These fears can in part be traced to the publication in 1948 of the Kinsey report on male sexuality, which provided scientific evidence that gay men did not differ significantly from straight men.[30] Shattering the stereotype of the effeminate homosexual, Kinsey and his colleagues reported that 40 percent of the men they interviewed had engaged in homosexual activity and that "persons with homosexual histories are to be found in every age group, in every social level, in every conceivable occupation in cities and on farms, and in the most remote areas of the country," a finding that added new meaning to the phrase "from sea to shining sea."[31] One of the ways in which the discourses of national security tried to contain the impact of these findings was by using them to justify the construction of homosexuality as a security risk.[32] If gay men did not differ significantly from straight men and were to be found in every level of American society, then they could infiltrate the nation's cultural and political institutions and subvert them from within. This helps to explain why in so many postwar films the gay male characters appear virtually indistinguishable from the straight male characters.[33] The possibility that gay men could escape detection by passing as straight linked them in the Cold War political imaginary to the Communists who were allegedly conspiring to overthrow the government.

Film noir's tendency to link the gay male characters and the femme fatale iconographically is best explained in terms of the ideological pressure the discourses of national security brought to bear on even oppositional forms of mass culture. The unusual presence in film noir of characters who are explicitly identified as gay can be attributed to male homosexual panic. One of the ways in which the national-security state discouraged forms of male homosocial bonding that conflicted with the Fordist organization of production and consumption was by homosexualizing them. The intense male bonding promoted by the armed services became a source of anxiety once the war was over because it threatened to disrupt the transition to a Fordist regime of capital accumulation. As I indicated above, the economic restructuring of the postwar period required the production of new forms of male subjectivity. To achieve the levels of consumption necessary for sustaining economic growth, returning soldiers had to overcome their attachment to the all-male world of the armed services. They could not experience a conflict between their masculinity and their roles as breadwinners and homeowners, roles that increasingly revolved around the consumption of durable goods. The men who were most likely to become objects of suspicion in the intensely homophobic climate of the postwar period were not those who participated actively in the domestic sphere or who submitted passively to corporate structures—modes of behavior that in another context might have marked them as insufficiently masculine—but those who refused to settle down and raise a family. Thus one possible function of the clearly marked gay male characters in film noir was to reassure spectators that the independent, self-reliant hero was straight, despite his intense attachments to other men. Spectators were unlikely to confuse the gay male characters with the hero, because they were linked iconographically to the femme fatale. At the same time, however, film noir's strategic deployment of the traditional signifiers of male homosexuality provided a counter to the project undertaken by the national-security state to render gay men invisible. Its iconographic mode of representation returned gay men to national visibility, albeit in ways that were deeply homophobic. In this respect, it had more in common with the work of the writers examined in this study than with the discourses of national security.

Although film noir's project to expose the corruption of American society was typical of forms of classical Hollywood cinema inspired by the Popular Front, its cynicism about the American dream was not. The films Frank Capra made between 1936 and 1948, his so-called middle period, were more representative of the left-wing populism that inspired the cultural production of the Popular Front era, in that they made a sentimental appeal on behalf of the "common man."[34] Although they tended to advocate the moral regeneration of American society rather than a structural transformation of the economic system, these films, which included *Mr. Deeds Goes to Town* (1936) and *State of the Union* (1948), were admired by Hollywood's left-wing community because they exposed the extent to which the interests of corporate capitalism dominated American politics. The typical Capra hero is a plain-speaking man of the people who discovers that his meteoric rise to power has been engineered by a corrupt political machine that is beholden to corporate America. Recalling the nation to its founding democratic principles, the hero exposes the corruption and elitism of the political system. By contrast, film noir was deeply skeptical about the possibility of achieving meaningful political and economic reform. The alienation and despair pervading film noir (which has led many critics to see a connection between it and existentialism, the popularity of which also reached its peak in the period immediately following World War II) called into question the common man's ability to intervene in the political system. The form of corruption encountered by the noir hero is systemic, and he is unable to overcome it.

The emphasis in film noir on the dark side of the American dream is best explained in terms of the breakup of the Popular Front and the postwar retreat from the New Deal.[35] Although the Popular Front was revived briefly at the end of World War II, support for the New Deal had begun to erode as early as the mid-term elections of 1942. Following the reelection of President Truman in 1948, a coalition of conservative Republicans and southern Democrats, who were angered by Truman's civil rights policies, forced him to abandon key aspects of the New Deal. When Truman introduced the "Fair Deal" in 1949, a package of social programs designed to consolidate the New Deal, Congress deadlocked on his more radical proposals.[36] It passed a low-income housing bill (the Housing Act of 1949 discussed above), increased social security benefits and the minimum wage, and approved higher price-supports for farmers. But it rejected Truman's proposals for a national health-care plan and federal aid to education and refused to repeal the Taft-Hartley Act of 1947, which restricted the right of workers to strike, a right that had been guaranteed under the New Deal. Meanwhile, the 1947 hearings of HUAC devastated Hollywood's left-wing community, fragmenting and dispersing it.[37] Many of the directors and screenwriters who were called before the committee were imprisoned for contempt of Congress when they refused to name names, while others left the country to escape prosecution and the blacklist. It became increasingly difficult for Hollywood to treat potentially controversial issues even from a liberal perspective. Left-wing disillusionment with American society manifested itself not only in film noir's thematic content but also in its visual style. Film noir's emphatic use of shadows, expressionistic lighting, and marked camera angles translated into visual terms left-wing pessimism about the prospect of meaningful political and economic reform.

My goal in using film noir to clarify the limitations of popular forms of resistance to the reorganization of masculinity is to establish the importance of Williams's, Vidal's, and Baldwin's project to dismantle the regulatory fictions that governed the production of gender and sexual identity in the Cold War era. Although I follow the example of other scholars in claiming that film noir contested the Cold War consensus, I also argue that it did so in ways that undercut its emancipatory potential. In contesting the domestication of masculinity, film noir expressed nostalgia for a form of male identity that was no longer dominant but had become residual because it conflicted with the reorganization of the economy along Fordist lines. Underlying this nostalgia was a desire to return to an earlier stage of capitalism before the rise of mass culture, when male subjectivity had supposedly not yet been penetrated by the commodity form. Despite its oppositional content, film noir tended to manage and contain the fears and anxieties the reorganization of the economy provoked in many men. As I show in chapter 1, many men experienced the postwar shift from production to consumption as a threat to their masculinity. By encouraging them to identify with the hard-boiled detective, film noir allowed these men to recover temporarily their masculinity. A descendant of the gangster, the hard-boiled detective embodied the form of male identity many men sought to recover as an antidote to their disaffection. Film noir, in other words, acknowledged many men's anxiety and frustration with the reorganization of the economy only to defuse it by refracting it through the lens of gender. The male spectator's identification with the hard-boiled detective reinforced his tendency to express his antagonism toward the new economic order as a desire to return to an earlier stage of capitalism where the entrepreneurial spirit flourished.

Where film noir posed a more serious threat to the emergence and consolidation of the Cold War consensus was at the level of form. In emphasizing stylistic innovation at the expense of narrative coherence, film noir promoted a mode of spectatorship that inadvertently legitimated the practices and forms of identity gay men had created as strategies of survival. The inconsistency of the characters and the lack of a coherent plot hindered the spectator's perceptual placement within the film's narrative space. The spectator became fixated on elements of the diegesis that were peripheral to the linear unfolding of the film's plot. In chapter 2, I argue that this visual economy was subversive, for in reversing the hierarchical relation between spectacle and narrative that normally prevailed in classical Hollywood cinema, it encouraged a homosexualization of the spectator's gaze.

Despite its potential to disrupt the Cold War consensus by legitimating gay male forms of spectatorship, however, film noir tended to disavow its organization of the look and to accede to the dominance of the classical system and its subordination of spectacle to narrative. In chapter 2, I clarify this aspect of film noir by examining *Laura* (Otto Preminger, 1944) and its thematization of gay male spectatorship. Whereas on the level of form *Laura* legitimated gay male camp as an oppositional mode of spectatorship that undermined the role of classical Hollywood cinema in the production of heterosexual subjectivity, on the level of content it linked camp to the crisis of masculinity precipitated by the rise of the "organization man." Insofar as it encouraged the spectator to become distracted by the surface of the image, the film enacted the very threat it sought to dispel. Its lush visual style promoted a homosexualization of the spectator's gaze that made her/him more susceptible to the lure of the commodity. To contain the impact of its visual economy, the film linked gay male modes of consumption to the sort of looking on which postwar consumer culture depended. The hard-boiled detective Mark McPherson's (Dana Andrews) obsession with Laura (Gene Tierney), the beautiful and glamorous advertising executive whose death he has been assigned to investigate, reproduces the cult of the star and functions as a sign of the homosexualization of his gaze. His fetishistic relation to her portrait expresses symbolically the penetration of his subjectivity by the commodity form.

The other example of film noir I examine is *Crossfire* (1947). Produced by Adrian Scott and directed by Edward Dmytryk, both of whom were convicted of contempt of Congress for refusing to name names when they appeared before HUAC in 1947, *Crossfire* is more overtly political than most films noirs. Although it was based on a novel by Richard Brooks in which a soldier brutally rapes and murders a gay interior designer while on leave, the film concerns a soldier who murders a Jewish veteran he meets in a bar while waiting to be discharged from the army. Scott and Dmytryk were eager to make a film about anti-Semitism and cannot be accused of indifference to the problem of anti-gay violence. Yet in refusing to address the novel's sexual topic, they inadvertently legitimated the project undertaken by the national-security state to render gay men invisible. Their substitution of a Jewish veteran for the gay interior designer of the novel showed that they did not understand the importance of Brooks's treatment of homophobia, which was intended to position gay men as bearers of rights. My goal in examining the differences between the film and the novel is to identify more fully the liberatory possibilities opened up by film noir. I argue that film noir's subversive potential lay less in its critique of postwar consumer culture than in its inclusion of explicitly marked gay male characters. To be sure, such characters reinforced homophobic stereotypes, but their presence provided the basis for an alternative public sphere in which gay men retained visibility.

Having established the limitations of popular forms of resistance to the reorganization of masculinity, I turn in the second part of this study to the work of Williams, Vidal, and Baldwin, which I argue provided a potentially more productive knowledge of postwar structures of oppression than did film noir. Like film noir, the work of these writers sought to exploit the subversive potential of the form of male identity displaced by the rise of the "organization man," but it did not express a desire to return to an earlier stage of capitalism. Film noir's tendency to contest the Fordist organization of production and consumption in ways that were complicit with the discourses of national security can in part be attributed to its political genealogy. The cultural production of the Popular Front era was similarly hampered by a limited understanding of the politics of gender. Granted, writers and artists affiliated with the Communist party were committed to addressing the "woman question," but only insofar as it could be understood as a superstructural expression of the capitalist relations of production. The focus in film noir on the femme fatale and her refusal to restrict her sexuality to the domestic sphere is best understood as a product of this failure adequately to address the "woman question." In film noir, the femme fatale's transgressive sexuality eventually displaces the crime as the object of the hard-boiled detective's investigation. By contrast, the writers examined in this study treated gender as a constitutive category of identity and experience. Unencumbered by a history of involvement with the Communist party, they seem to have been better able to judge postwar developments.[38] They treated the discourses and institutions that governed the production of gender as crucial sites for political intervention and struggle. They understood that one of the ways in which the discourses of national security guaranteed that Americans internalized the dominant constructions of masculinity and femininity was by positioning those who did not conform to them as national-security risks.

Although postwar critics never specifically addressed the ways in which the writers examined in this study foregrounded the politics of gender and sexual identity in the Cold War era, they were clearly threatened by this aspect of their work. They were especially critical of Williams, whose plays centered on female experience. They denounced Williams's female characters as gay men in drag and implied that male characters such as Stanley Kowalski in A Streetcar Named Desire (1947) who embodied an especially phallic form of masculinity were a projection of Williams's own desire.[39]

Gay male critics writing in the early years of gay liberation were no less critical of Williams's focus on female experience, which they interpreted as a displacement of his gay identity. For them, Williams was a casualty of the closeted gay male subculture of the fifties, the stereotypical self-hating gay man who was unable to come to terms with his homosexuality. These criticisms seem particularly ironic, given that the closet is a recurrent trope in Williams's work. In chapter 4, I examine Williams's thematization of the closet and try to show that for all intents and purposes he was "out" in his plays. Although I follow the example of postwar critics in locating the gay element of his plays in their focus on female experience, I argue that that focus reflected an identification with women that was not Oedipal but political, which is why it was so threatening to postwar critics. To be sure, his plays eroticize subjugated forms of masculinity (working-class, ethnic, and so on) and thus are grounded in fantasies and desires similar to those that propel film noir. But, unlike film noir, they treat these forms of masculinity as symptomatic of patriarchal structures of oppression and foreground the sexual violence to which they invariably lead.

Vidal also tended to eroticize forms of masculinity that had become residual in the face of the rise of the "organization man." But whereas Williams was unwilling to glamorize such forms of masculinity as potential sites of resistance to the Cold War consensus, Vidal tried to show that they could be recuperated by gay men as part of their opposition to postwar structures of oppression. In chapter 5, I use Vidal's controversial novel *The City and the Pillar* (1946) to examine the emergence of the gay macho style. The masculinization of urban gay communities has usually been attributed to the influence of the gay liberation movement of the sixties. But I show that it began much earlier and that it is best understood as a response to the rise of the "organization man." Gay male appropriations of the signifiers of working-class and other forms of subjugated masculinity should be seen as part of a project to eroticize gay male identity. To clarify this aspect of the gay macho style, I examine Vidal's attempt to disarticulate masculinity from patriarchal structures of oppression.

In the chapter on Baldwin, I examine the way in which both white and black left-wing intellectuals romanticized black male identity, treating it as a privileged site of resistance to postwar structures of oppression. I argue that insofar as it reinforced racist stereotypes, this construction hindered Baldwin from identifying fully as an African American, for it was used to deprive him and other gay African Americans of their claims to blackness. Baldwin also resisted identifying fully as a gay man. In the postwar period, gay male identity was largely a white middle-class construction rooted in consumer culture. Focusing on his narrative strategies in *Another Country* (1962), I claim that Baldwin tried to resolve the conflict between blackness and gayness at the level of form. By combining Henry James's formal strategies with the thematic concerns of the naturalistic novel, the form of novelistic discourse postwar critics tended to think was most appropriate for capturing "the black experience," Baldwin creolized the Jamesian novel. In so doing, he contested the dominant theory and tradition of American literature in the Cold War era. This theory and tradition reproduced the homophobic categories of the discourses of national security, marginalizing writers such as Theodore Dreiser and Richard Wright because they used a naturalistic mode of narration and because their focus on the material conditions of existence supposedly indicated a lack of maturity of vision. Baldwin's use of a Jamesian mode of narration demonstrated his mastery of the novel form, as it was defined by this theory and tradition, and thus he could not be accused of lacking maturity of vision, despite the fact that he was both gay and left-wing.

Homosexuality in Cold War America, then, builds on my previous work on the political construction of gender and sexual identity in the Cold War era. But whereas *In the Name of National Security* focused on the way in which the homosexualization of left-wing political activity enabled Cold War liberals to achieve and retain hegemony over American society, in this project I examine gay male resistance to that homosexualization. I have wanted to contest a view of postwar urban gay communities that first gained currency in the early years of gay liberation and that has gone largely unchallenged in gay studies.[40] According to the received narrative of the postwar gay rights movement, in the fifties urban gay communities revolved around the closeted world of gay bars. The men who participated most actively in this world were supposedly unable to accept their homosexuality and saw the bars as places not where they could experience solidarity with other gay men but where they could solicit sex. This narrative has led to the misunderstanding that gay male resistance was limited to camp, an oppositional practice that destabilized the binarisms governing the production of gender.[41] By examining the work of Williams, Vidal, and Baldwin, I hope to show that there were other forms of gay male resistance that emerged in the postwar period and that have been marginalized by this narrative. As we will see in the chapters that follow, Williams's, Vidal's, and Baldwin's exposure of the regulatory fictions that governed the production of gender was part of a larger critique of postwar relations of power. These writers understood that one of the ways in which Cold War liberals maintained their hegemony was by linking questions of gender and sexual identity directly to issues of national security. Thus their work should be seen as having paved the way for the emergence of the gay liberation movement of the sixties.

Ultimately my aim in challenging the dominant construction of postwar gay male experience is to further recent attempts to rewrite the history of the postwar gay rights movement.[42] According to the dominant construction of that history, the Mattachine Society and the Daughters of Bilitis, the first gay and lesbian rights organizations founded in the postwar period, were politically ineffective because they did not adequately interrogate the normative status of heterosexuality but sought the assimilation of gay men and women into mainstream American society. The postwar gay rights movement, it is claimed, did not truly begin until the night of 27 June 1969, when a group of drag queens who frequented the Stonewall Inn on Christopher Street in New York City violently and courageously resisted arrest on charges of disorderly conduct.[43] The gay liberation movement, it is also claimed, is properly understood as an extension of the black power and women's liberation movements.[44] Gay rights activists merely applied the political claims of black nationalists and radical feminists to gay men and women. But as Elizabeth Kennedy and Madeline Davis have recently pointed out, this understanding of the postwar gay rights movement cannot explain how gay liberation quickly became a mass movement.[45] The role of the Stonewall rebellion in mobilizing gay men and women across the nation and inspiring them to come out of the closet has been greatly exaggerated. It seems unlikely that gay liberation would have emerged so quickly as a mass movement if Williams, Vidal, and Baldwin, in conjunction with other progressive cultural workers, had not already begun the task of challenging the discourses and institutions that naturalized the construction of gender and sexual identity. I hope that by examining the work of these writers in the context of the postwar crisis of masculinity, this study will show that the roots of the gay liberation movement lay in gay male opposition to the Cold War consensus.

PART 1

Film Noir and the Political Economy

of Cold War Masculinity

CHAPTER ONE

Masculinizing the American Dream: Discourses
of Resistance in the Cold War Era

The modern populace decides not by votes but by the tickets it buys
and the money it pays.—C. L. R. James, *American Civilization*

The only thing you got in this world is what you can sell.
—Charley in *Death of a Salesman*

In 1950, the Marxist critic C. L. R. James distributed to a small group of
trusted colleagues in the Trotskyist movement a lengthy description of a
proposed study of American culture that he hoped the average American
would be able to "read on a Sunday or on two evenings."[1] James eventually
broke with the Trotskyist movement in part because of its vanguardist
politics, which he thought underestimated the American people's capacity
for self-mobilization. But he detected in the popularity of gangster films
and other forms of mass culture that glamorized crime and violence the
potential for a progressive social movement, and he sought to intervene by
making available to the American people a Marxist critique of existing
social and economic arrangements written in accessible language. In the
proposal, eventually published posthumously as *American Civilization*
(1993), James claimed that "within the last dozen years, the always volatile,
restless, aggressive American individual, has now reached a pitch of exas-
peration, suppressed aggressiveness, anger and fear which irresistibly ex-
plode in private life but represent a profoundly social situation. The signs
of an accumulating social explosion are everywhere" (274). James realized
that this explosion could be easily defused by the American government,
but he predicted that the emerging crisis would eventually lead to the

formation of a mass movement in which politics would finally become an expression of "a totally integrated human existence" (275).

Many readers will no doubt interpret James's belief in the potential for a progressive social movement as a sign that he seriously misunderstood the postwar political climate. In light of the wave of anti-Communist hysteria unleashed by the McCarthy hearings, James does seem to have underestimated the forces of reaction in postwar American society. Yet his optimism about the American people's capacity for self-mobilization needs to be understood in the context of his belief in the distinctiveness of American civilization. The American people, he explained, had created a truly democratic nation in which "the absence of sharp social differentiation and conflict" (42) was the defining characteristic. Thus the struggle for popular democracy was more advanced in America than elsewhere. Although James conceded that America's artistic and literary achievements were inferior to those of Europe, he nevertheless maintained that its creation of a democratic political culture represented "a landmark in the history of civilization" (33). James believed that the ideals and aspirations embodied by America's democratic traditions continued to influence the people's expectations, despite the increasing routinization of everyday life and the loss of personal freedom to which it had led. Unlike Europeans, James asserted, Americans had been "soaked to the marrow in a tradition of individual freedom, individual security, free association, a tradition which is constantly held before them as the basis of their civilization" (116). He saw the contradiction between this tradition and the social and economic realities of the postwar period as the primary source of the people's anger and frustration with the dominant order. The people had inherited an image of America as a nation of unlimited economic opportunity that was more appropriate to the days of the frontier and that was contradicted by their experience. James claimed that "upon this people more than all others has been imposed a mechanized way of life at work, mechanized forms of living, a mechanized totality which from morning till night, week after week, day after day" (116) reminded them of the emptiness of America's traditional significance.

James's emphasis on the distinctiveness of American civilization suggests that he sought to identify his project with that of the American studies movement, which had begun to solidify its legitimacy as an academic discipline in the late forties.[2] According to Robert A. Hill, James's literary executor, James derived his understanding of American civilization largely from F. O. Matthiessen, whose study of classic nineteenth-century American writers, *American Renaissance* (1941), is generally considered the founding text of American studies.[3] James followed Matthiessen's example in locating the distinctiveness of American civilization in its democratic political culture, which had supposedly led to the production of an art that expressed the people's needs and aspirations. Moreover, like Matthiessen, James believed that the classics of nineteenth-century American literature were key to understanding American civilization. His study would include detailed discussions of Whitman and Melville, he explained, because "we cannot begin to grapple with the basic realities of modern America without as serious an analysis as possible of what they saw and wrote" (31). At the same time, however, James also sought to distinguish his project from that of the American studies movement. As Jonathan Arac has shown, American studies secured its hegemonic position in the university by appropriating Matthiessen's work nationalistically.[4] The consolidation of American studies as an academic discipline must be understood in the context of the Cold War and the cultural nationalism to which it gave rise. Scholars in American studies helped to solidify America's position as the leader of the so-called free world by increasing the symbolic capital of its literature and culture.[5]

In proposing to undertake a Marxist study of American civilization, James seems in part to have wanted to rectify the nationalistic appropriation of Matthiessen's work. He intended to elaborate aspects of Matthiessen's critical practice in *American Renaissance* that American studies had failed to incorporate because they reflected Matthiessen's desire to achieve a synthesis of the populist aesthetic of the Popular Front and the formalism of the New Criticism.[6] Whereas American studies scholars influenced by Matthiessen's work tended to seek the distinctiveness of American civilization in the classics of American literature, particularly those of the nineteenth century, James argued for the importance of mass culture.[7] He conceived of mass culture as "one of the most powerful social and psychological manifestations of the American life and character" (37). Thus its products could provide more insight into the character of the American people, their needs and desires, than could the classics of American literature. James held the view, highly unorthodox in the Cold War era, that a careful examination of mass culture would reveal why "to this day the distinctive literary talents, Hemingway, Wolfe, Faulkner, Wright, to the extent that they continue in the traditions of Hawthorne, Melville and Poe, remain, as does all American art from the beginning to the present day, divorced from any significant current in modern life" (37). Unlike American studies scholars who tended to see mass culture as a debased form of art that manipulated the American people, James stressed its emancipatory potential.[8]

In focusing on the heterogeneity of its products and their potentially contradictory effects, James's theory of mass culture was similar to that of Walter Benjamin, although it is unlikely that he was familiar with Benjamin's work. Like Benjamin, James believed that the mechanical reproduction of art enabled collective forms of reception that had the potential to mobilize the masses.[9] He argued that mass cultural products such as Hollywood film constituted a counter public sphere in which the American people could register their opposition to existing social and economic arrangements and express their desire for ones that were more responsive to their needs and aspirations: "The modern populace decides not by votes but by the tickets it buys and the money it pays" (36). He realized that mass cultural products often functioned as vehicles of ideology, but, unlike more orthodox Marxist critics, he refused to believe that the rise of mass culture marked the final triumph of capitalism and the reification of experience. For him, such a view was reminiscent of the economic determinism of vulgar forms of Marxist thought. The capitalists who financed the production of mass culture, he claimed, were "as dependent upon the mass audience for their success as were Euripides and Sophocles for their prizes" (36), and thus they had no alternative but to give expression to the American people's fantasies and aspirations, regardless of how much they conflicted with their own needs and interests. Given this understanding of mass culture, it is hardly surprising that James thought it was possible for critics to deduce from its products "the social and political needs, sufferings, aspirations and rejections of modern civilization" (37) to which the reorganization of the economy along Fordist lines had led.

For James, the mass cultural product that most accurately reflected the aspirations and fantasies of the American people was a type of film that was particularly popular in the postwar period. Inspired by the hard-boiled detective novels of Dashiell Hammett, Raymond Chandler, James M. Cain, and Cornell Woolrich, this type of film would eventually become known as film noir, for its pessimistic view of American society.[10] James saw the popularity of film noir as the most obvious sign that America was about to experience a "social explosion." According to him, film noir had replaced the gangster films of the thirties, which had legitimated popular resistance to Prohibition by glamorizing the gangster. He conceived of the hard-boiled detective of film noir as a direct descendant of the gangster, despite the fact that he was aligned with the law and often functioned as its instrument. Like the gangster, he asserted, the hard-boiled detective "lives in a world of his own according to ethics of his own. . . . He, Philip Marlowe, the detective creation of Raymond Chandler, Perry Mason, and others, are in constant warfare with the police, sometimes in danger of arrest, imprisonment and the chair" (125). For James, film noir's reincarnation of the gangster was a clear indication that the American people's disillusionment and resentment had the potential to lead to a social explosion. James described the gangster as "the persistent symbol of the national past which now has no meaning—the past in which energy, determination, bravery were certain to get a man somewhere in the line of opportunity" (127). The American people identified with the gangster, despite his violence and brutality, because he displayed "all the old heroic qualities in the only way he can display them" (127). They understood that the only avenue of upward mobility open to the gangster was through the criminal underworld.

Hollywood's reincarnation of the gangster as the hard-boiled detective of film noir showed that it understood the American people's needs and desires. It realized that because of their dissatisfaction with the dominant order, they would be unable to identify with a hero who was too closely aligned with the law: "He had to be an ordinary guy—*one who went out and did the job himself*" (121). Film noir brought into focus the conflict between the hopes and dreams inspired by America's democratic traditions and the social and economic realities of the postwar period. In film noir, the hard-boiled detective is unable to reconcile America's role as the leader of the free world with the bureaucratized society he encounters in his fight against crime. The American people identified with the hard-boiled detective, despite his involvement in the criminal underworld, because his defiant behavior expressed their own anger and frustration. In the hard-boiled detective, the American people saw reflected their own needs and aspirations. For them, he represented "the individual seeking individuality in a mechanized, socialized society, where his life is ordered and restricted at every turn, where there is no certainty of employment, far less of being able to rise by energy and ability or going West as in the old days" (127). In giving expression to the American people's hopes and dreams, film noir functioned therapeutically, enabling them to experience vicariously the freedom and independence that they had been taught was their birthright but that they had been denied. According to James, the American people derived from films noirs "a sense of active living, and in the bloodshed, the violence, the freedom from restraint to allow pent-up feelings free play, they have released the bitterness, hate, fear and sadism which simmer just below the surface" (127).

I have dwelt at such length on James's theory of mass culture because in this part of *Homosexuality in Cold War America* I want to follow his example and deduce from the contents of film noir the political needs and aspirations that the transition to a Fordist regime of capital accumulation inspired in the American people. Although James was overly optimistic about the potential for a social explosion in postwar America, he was right to detect in film noir an undercurrent of resentment and frustration with the dominant order. Film noir, we recall, differed from other forms of cinematic discourse in that it bore the marks of the influence of the Popular Front on Hollywood's left-wing community. Until the late 1940s, when the hearings of the House Un-American Activities Committee into alleged Communist infiltration of the film industry devastated Hollywood's left-wing community, film noir enabled left-wing directors and screenwriters to focus on a neglected stratum of postwar American society while escaping censorship. Despite its political genealogy, however, we should be careful not to exaggerate film noir's emancipatory potential. Film noir's reincarnation of the gangster is perhaps best understood as an example of what Fredric Jameson has called mass culture's fantasy bribe.[11] Despite the intentions of left-wing directors and screenwriters, film noir contained the American people's fantasies and desires even as it gave expression to them. Film noir tended to undercut its oppositional content by expressing a desire to recover a form of male identity that had become residual in the face of the rise of the "organization man." Many men experienced the postwar shift from production to consumption as a threat to their masculinity. In depicting a hero who embodied an entrepreneurial spirit that could no longer find expression in American society, film noir enabled these men to experience a temporary reassertion of that masculinity. In other words, film noir acknowledged many men's anxiety and frustration with the Fordist organization of production and consumption, only to diffuse it by refracting it through the lens of gender. The creation of a self-reliant, independent hero who did not hesitate to show contempt for the domestic sphere reinforced the male spectator's tendency to express his antagonism toward the dominant order as a desire to return to an earlier stage of capitalism in which the entrepreneurial spirit flourished.

I will return to this aspect of film noir in following chapters. For now I want to concentrate on reconstructing film noir's political preconscious. By political preconscious I mean the fantasies and desires that were not *explicitly* present in film noir but that it nevertheless sought to tap through its reincarnation of the gangster.[12] I will show that film noir's tendency to undercut its oppositional content by expressing a desire to return to an earlier stage of capitalism was typical of left-wing critiques of the Cold War consensus. In each of the texts examined below, chosen because of their influence on the New Left and the counterculture of the sixties, the critique of postwar structures of oppression is grounded in a masculinist understanding of the needs and desires inspired by the American dream. Like C. L. R. James, the authors of these texts foregrounded the contradiction between the ideals and values embodied by America's democratic traditions and the social and economic realities of the postwar period. But unlike James, they tended to equate the decline of the entrepreneurial spirit, of which the rise of the "organization man" was symptomatic, with a feminization of male subjectivity. Despite their oppositional content, these texts reduced the fantasies and aspirations inspired by the American dream to the exclusive property of white heterosexual men, thereby bequeathing to the New Left a masculinist understanding of America's symbolic significance. The masculinism of these texts explains in part why their critique of postwar structures of oppression failed to mobilize more Americans. Their focus on the needs and aspirations of white heterosexual men failed to address the concerns of women, African Americans, gays, and other groups disenfranchised by the postwar settlement. Having identified the limitations and omissions of left-wing critiques of the Cold War consensus, we will be better able in the chapters that follow to situate film noir in relation to the postwar crisis of masculinity.

Tracing the Decline of the Entrepreneurial Spirit:
C. Wright Mills and the Feminization of Male Subjectivity

I want to begin reconstructing film noir's political preconscious by examining C. Wright Mills's highly influential study, *White Collar* (1951). Mills was careful to state in his introduction that the "Marxian view, popular in the American 'thirties, is now often inadequate" and thus to distinguish his cultural politics from those of Popular Front artists and writers.[13] Yet his analysis of the shift from industrial to monopoly capitalism in the late nineteenth century and the new forms of subjectivity that emerged in its wake provides an important link between the Old and New Lefts.[14] Mills saw the routinization of everyday life as another example of the way in which America had failed to fulfill its utopian promise. But this is not to exaggerate Mills's ties to the Old Left. Mills owed his interest in issues of subjectivity more to the Frankfurt school than to the strain of left-wing populism he had inherited from the Popular Front.[15] Like the Frankfurt school, he stressed the derailment of the Enlightenment project. Rather than benefiting humanity by contributing to its full development, scientific reason had provided the capitalist state with the means to improve its techniques of social control. Mills complained that "rationality seems to have taken on a new form, to have its seat not in individual men, but in social institutions which by their bureaucratic planning and mathematical foresight usurp both freedom and rationality from the little individual men caught in them" (xvii). Thus the processes of rationalization and routinization he described in *White Collar* were not specific to America but were typical of capitalist social formations. What was disturbing about these processes, however, was that they threatened to undermine the values and ideals Mills thought defined the American character.

Mills also owed his understanding of mass culture to the Frankfurt school.[16] Unlike James, he refused to acknowledge mass culture's heterogeneity, its potential to elicit a critical or oppositional response and to provide insight into the social and political needs of the people. For him, the collective forms of reception that the mechanical reproduction of art made possible simply increased the state's ability to manage and contain the people's fantasies and aspirations. He followed the example of the Frankfurt school in conceiving of mass culture as a "culture industry" geared to the production of "false consciousness."[17] He was troubled by the forms of subjectivity to which mass culture had given rise: "The contents of the mass media seep into our images of self, becoming that which is taken for granted, so imperceptibly and so surely that to modify them drastically, over a generation or two, would be to change profoundly modern man's [sic] experience and characters" (334). Rather than contributing to the flow of information, mass culture encouraged a passive relation to knowledge, thus making the American people more susceptible to manipulation by the state. Mass culture was able to function so effectively as a mechanism of social control because it was seen not as propaganda but as entertainment: "People are often exposed to it when most relaxed of mind and tired of body; and its characters offer easy targets of identification, easy answers to stereotyped personal problems" (336). According to Mills, mass culture colonized the American people's unconscious, implanting in them hopes and desires that conformed to capitalism's needs and interests.

But Mills's study of the growth of bureaucratic structures is also of interest because of the influence it exerted on the New Left. Mills bequeathed to the New Left a critique of postwar American society whose categories and assumptions were deeply masculinist. As we will see, Mills bemoaned the reorganization of work because he thought that it inserted men into a feminine subject-position. Mills's influence on the New Left, however, was not limited to his masculinist understanding of postwar structures of oppression. Mills was widely regarded as the antithesis of the white-collar worker, whose supposedly passive relation to mass culture he examined in *White Collar*.[18] Mills was thought to embody the outmoded form of male identity that many men longed to recover as an antidote to the anger and frustration they experienced as a result of the domestication of masculinity.[19] His leather jacket and motorcycle (not a Harley Davidson but a BMW) were legendary in New Left circles and clearly underlay the appeal of his work. His image as an academic outlaw whose relation to his work was more entrepreneurial than scholarly seems to have legitimated the attempts of white male New Leftists to create an oppositional form of masculinity by fusing various aspects of rock 'n' roll and African American subcultures. Todd Gitlin, for example, in his controversial memoir of the New Left, *The Sixties: Years of Hope, Days of Rage,* recalled that Mills "was a hero in student radical circles for his books, of course, but it was no small part of the persona for which he was cherished that he was a motorcycle-riding, cabin-building Texan, cultivating the image of a gun-slinging homesteader of the old frontier."[20] Given the sort of image Mills projected, it is hardly surprising that in *White Collar* he should have focused on the way in which the rise of the white-collar worker threatened traditional forms of male identity.

Despite its nostalgia for an earlier stage of capitalism in which the entrepreneurial spirit flourished, Mills's analysis of the routinization of everyday life in postwar America bears a striking resemblance to James's. Like James, Mills stressed the contradiction between the fantasies and desires inspired by the American dream of upward mobility and postwar realities. According to Mills, the growth of bureaucratic structures and the increasing division of labor had transformed the American character. Whereas in the nineteenth century the qualities that distinguished the American worker were thrift, discipline, persistence, and initiative, in the twentieth they were caution, efficiency, and a desire to please others. By focusing on the rise of the white-collar worker, Mills hoped to show that these qualities had become "more typically 'American' than the frontier character probably ever was" (xv). This did not mean, however, that the entrepreneurial spirit had ceased to shape the American people's hopes and dreams. On the contrary, despite the constraints on their freedom and mobility, the American people continued to perceive America as a land of unlimited economic opportunity and to aspire to a level of independence and freedom precluded by the increasing division of labor. Mills explained that the small entrepreneur of the nineteenth century, who had embodied the myth of the frontier, persisted "as an ideological figment and a political force" (35) and thus continued to influence the way in which Americans thought and lived.

Like James, then, Mills saw the erosion of the ideals and values America traditionally symbolized as a major source of tension in postwar American society. But whereas James was optimistic that this tension would eventually mobilize the American people, leading to the formation of a new type of politics, Mills was skeptical about the American people's capacity for self-organization. He argued that because the shift from industrial to monopoly capitalism had been "a slow process rather than a sharp break inside the life span of one generation" (297), the American people did not fully grasp its significance. But even if the shift had occurred more rapidly, he doubted that it would have prompted the American people to form a political movement responsive to their needs and interests. Unlike James, he tended to totalize the ability of the capitalist mode of production to reproduce itself, and therefore he precluded the possibility of resistance. According to him, mass culture naturalized capitalist structures of oppression by manipulating and diffusing the fantasies and desires inspired by the American dream. Having internalized the myth of the self-made man, the American people were more likely to blame themselves than the "system" for their lack of freedom and mobility. Mills claimed that the "principle of the self-made man, and the justification of his superior position by the competitive fire through which he has come, require and in turn support the ideology of free competition" (36). For the mass of Americans, it was not that the shift from industrial to monopoly capitalism had eroded the basis of the American dream but that American workers lacked the skills necessary for succeeding in an increasingly competitive labor market.

But as I have already indicated, the greatest difference between James and Mills lay in Mills's desire to recover an outmoded form of male identity. Mills's anxieties about his masculinity, no doubt exacerbated by his entanglement in the bureaucratic structure of the modern university, prevented him from adequately theorizing postwar developments. For him, the entrepreneurial spirit represented the fullest expression of American manhood, and thus its decline marked a feminization of male subjectivity. This is not to say that Mills ignored the impact of the growth of bureaucratic structures on female workers. Several sections of *White Collar* highlight the way in which the increasing division of labor limited female workers' personal freedom. But Mills tended to perceive the white-collar worker as male. His use of the third-person masculine pronoun throughout *White Collar* cannot be explained away as a convention of the times. He clearly believed that the processes of rationalization and routinization had more fully transformed the identities of male workers than those of female workers. He saw the white-collar worker's passive relation to authority as her/his defining characteristic. The white-collar worker, he explained, was "pushed by forces beyond his [*sic*] control, pulled into movements he does not understand; he gets into situations in which his is the most helpless position" (xii). The passivity of this position did not have the same impact on female workers as it did on male workers because their relation to authority had traditionally been a passive one. Male workers, on the other hand, were used to asserting their freedom and independence. Thus, whereas the rise of monopoly capitalism had reaffirmed the identities of female workers by placing them in a position of dependence that corresponded to their femininity, it had undermined those of the male workers by placing them in a position in which they were unable to exercise the prerogatives that had traditionally defined American manhood.

Mills clearly intended his emphasis on the uneven way in which the bureaucratization of work affected male and female workers to underscore the erosion of male heterosexual privilege. With the shift from industrial to monopoly capitalism, Mills complained, men had lost the ability to "realize [themselves] in [their] work" (14). The increasing division of labor had reduced them to "cogs in a business machinery" (109), and thus they were forced to define themselves through their identities as consumers rather than as producers. Moreover, the corporation's bureaucratic structure feminized their relation to the world by instilling in them a sense of powerlessness. Intimidated by the impersonal way in which they were treated by the corporation, male workers became passive and indecisive. The corporation was a highly centralized organization in which the delegation of responsibility insured that those in power remained inaccessible. Consequently, they were unable "to locate the enemy and declare war upon him. Targets for aggression are unavailable, and certainty is taken from men" (119). Thus what was most disturbing to Mills about the emergence of a Fordist regime of capital accumulation was its potential to insert men into a feminine subject-position. According to him, the corporation's impersonal, bureaucratic structure left men feeling "dwarfed and helpless before the managerial cadres and their manipulated and manipulative minions" (111). In such a world, it was not possible to express the entrepreneurial spirit; indeed, corporate structures seemed designed to prevent the expression of the entrepreneurial spirit.

According to Mills, the feminization of male subjectivity was most apparent in the rise of what he called the "personality market." With the shift from industrial to monopoly capitalism the qualities considered necessary for success had undergone a transformation. Whereas in the era of industrial capitalism success had depended on initiative, drive, and ambition, it now depended on whether one had "personality" and an attractive personal appearance.[21] In the corporate world where the "personality market" dominated, Mills explained, "personal or even intimate traits of the employee are drawn into the sphere of exchange and become of commercial relevance, become commodities in the labor market" (182). In the corporate world, men occupied a traditionally feminine position in relation to others. Postwar success literature and advice manuals urged men to develop qualities that would attract, please, and impress their superiors in the corporate hierarchy. Moreover, they were encouraged to pay careful attention to how they dressed, perhaps the most obvious sign of their feminization. For Mills, the rise of the personality market signaled the penetration of male subjectivity by the commodity form. The reorganization of work reduced men to instrumentalizing their own appearance in order to increase its exchange-value. The image they projected would ultimately determine whether they succeeded in obtaining a secure place in the corporate hierarchy. In this way, the personality market further eroded the differences between men and women. Men now resembled women in that their ability to successfully negotiate the labor market was dependent on the exchange-value of their personal appearance.

For Mills, this development was the most disturbing aspect of the shift from industrial to monopoly capitalism. He associated commodity culture in general with a feminization of male subjectivity.[22] Unlike James, he refused to entertain the possibility that commodity culture afforded the American people a freedom and power to express themselves which was denied them in the sphere of work. On the contrary, he saw the rise of commodity culture as another indication of the way in which the shift from industrial to monopoly capitalism had undermined American manhood. The rise of commodity culture marked the erosion of the work ethic, which had been "central to the historic tradition of America, to its image of itself, and to the images the rest of the world has of America" (219). The qualities the work ethic fostered, such as "will power and thrift, habits of order, neatness, and the constitutional inability to say Yes to the easy road" (260), might disrupt the Fordist organization of production and consumption, and so they were discouraged. For Mills, what was most troubling about the decline of the American gospel of work was that it marked the erosion of the qualities that had hitherto defined American manhood. He complained that "a bureaucracy is no testing field for heroes" (263) and expressed concern that men's ambition had become "lost in consumer dreams" (283). The lure of the commodity had drawn men into the traditionally female spheres of consumption and domesticity. In commodity culture, men were no longer governed by the reality principle but succumbed to the pleasure principle. Paraphrasing conservative social critic R. H. Tawney, Mills complained that in a society dominated by the commodity form "leisure contains all good things and all goals dreamed of and actively pursued. The dreariest part of life . . . is where and when you work, the gayest where and when you consume" (237). Moreover, men's immersion in commodity culture encouraged them to submit to mass-produced fantasies, to lose themselves in "consumer dreams." The white-collar worker relied increasingly on the culture industries for "his standard of reality, his standard of experience" (334), and thus was no longer inspired by the myth of the self-made man.

Arthur Miller and the Tragedy of the Rise of the White-Collar Worker

Having examined the masculinist assumptions underlying Mills's understanding of the ideals and values America traditionally symbolized, I want now to turn to Arthur Miller's highly successful Broadway play, *Death of a Salesman* (1949). Miller provides another important link between the Old and New Lefts.[23] When Miller was subpoenaed to testify before the House Un-American Activities Committee in 1956, he refused to name names and denounced the hearings as a form of censorship that threatened the quality of literary production in the United States. Without freedom of expression, he asserted, "I can't operate and neither can literature in this country."[24] Moreover, Miller's indictment of the McCarthy hearings in *The Crucible* (1953), a play ostensibly about the Salem witchcraft trials but which clearly referred to the McCarthy hearings, and his belief that cultural production in general was a form of political practice made him a frequent target of Cold War liberals, who saw him as a threat to their hegemony.[25] Such liberals sought to counteract Miller's popularity by depicting him as an unreconstructed Stalinist who owed his pessimistic view of American society to the Popular Front. They were particularly critical of *Death of a Salesman,* which they saw as evidence that the nation's cultural institutions were thoroughly Stalinized. Robert Warshow, for example, in an essay that first appeared in *Commentary* in 1952, compared Miller to Clifford Odets, the left-wing playwright who had helped found the Group Theater. Warshow saw in the "mechanical realism" that characterized the work of both playwrights a Stalinist adherence to the Communist party line, and he dismissed Willy Loman, the hero of *Death of a Salesman,* as "Andy Hardy broken on the wheel of social criticism."[26]

Cold War liberals were perhaps right to attribute Miller's skepticism about the American dream in *Death of a Salesman* to the influence of the Popular Front. The play's critique of postwar American society is remarkably similar to that of Mills in *White Collar*. Indeed, given the similarities between the two texts, it would not be an overstatement to say that Mills's analysis of the rise of the white-collar worker achieved dramatic form in Miller's play, although, as we will see, Miller's conception of tragedy did not always accommodate his materialist perspective. This is not to say that Miller's understanding of postwar structures of oppression was influenced by Mills. *White Collar,* after all, was published in 1951, two years after *Death of a Salesman* first opened on Broadway. I simply mean to underscore the similarities between the two texts. Like Mills, Miller focuses on the construction of male subjectivity in relation to the rise of consumer capitalism. Willy Loman adheres to a set of values and ideals more appropriate to the industrial stage of capitalism, and so he has been unable to adjust to the rise of the white-collar worker. He longs to recover the form of male identity displaced by the growth of bureaucratic structures. His tired physical appearance in the play's opening scene can be attributed to the increasing routinization of everyday life. He seems defeated, worn out by his life as a white-collar worker. According to the stage directions, when he enters, "his exhaustion is apparent."[27] And when his wife, Linda, asks why he has returned from his sales trip so soon, he replies: "I'm tired to the death" (13). The play's setting expresses the causes for his exhaustion symbolically. Surrounded by a "solid vault" (11) of new apartment buildings, Willy's house appears "fragile" (11), as if it were unable to withstand the economic forces represented by the new buildings and were about to be displaced by them.

Moreover, like the white-collar worker of Mills's analysis, Willy emerges as a pawn of impersonal forces that are beyond his control and comprehension. His complaints about his lack of freedom and mobility are impotent and misdirected. He realizes that his way of life is quickly becoming outmoded, but he is powerless to do anything about it and is forced to accept it: "The way they boxed us in here. Bricks and windows, windows and bricks" (17). Like Mills's white-collar worker, he is unable to locate an enemy against whom he can vent his frustration. The reasons for the transformation of his neighborhood elude him, and he is reduced to complaining about a seemingly omnipotent "system" that victimizes "little guys" like him. He complains to Linda that "they massacred the neighborhood" (17), but he is unable to identify who "they" are and becomes increasingly bitter and resentful. Nor does he fully understand the economic forces that are behind the increasing division of labor. Again like Mills's white-collar worker, he has internalized the myth of the self-made man, and he blames his anger and frustration with his job on increasing competition: "There's more people! That's what's ruining this country! Population is getting out of control. The competition is maddening!" (17). Despite his alienation and disaffection, he retains his belief in the American dream of upward mobility.

In linking Willy's physical and spiritual depletion to the decline of the entrepreneurial spirit, Miller anticipated Mills's discussion of the impact of the rise of monopoly capitalism on the salesman. Mills was particularly disturbed by the salesman's transformation into a white-collar worker. According to Mills, the increasing division of labor had stripped the salesman of his freedom and independence. Before the rise of the corporation the salesman was "on his own in manner and even in territory" (180) and embodied the entrepreneurial spirit. With the shift to monopoly capitalism, however, he became subject to the same forces as the white-collar worker. He was no longer an independent agent but "one unit in an elaborate marketing organization" (180). Like the white-collar worker, he was expected to have "personality" and to pay careful attention to his personal appearance. Moreover, he was discouraged from showing initiative or relying on his own judgment and was forced to occupy a passive position in relation to authority. The qualities he had mastered had been expropriated "by a machinery that codifies [them] and controls their acquisition and display by individual salesmen" (179). Thus the salesman's personality had become part of the means of production. The rise of the personality market prevented him from realizing himself through his work. Like the white-collar worker, he had become a cog in an impersonal, bureaucratic organization. With the rise of advertising, Mills maintained, selling had become "a pervasive process, of which the personal salesman, crucial though he may be, is only one link" (181).

The salesman's transformation into a white-collar worker provides the basis for Miller's tragedy. Willy is unable to withstand the pressures placed on him to conform to the domestic model of masculinity. Despite the rise of commodity culture, he continues to try to realize himself through his work.

He does not want to become a mere cog in an impersonal, bureaucratic corporation but longs to express the initiative and daring that are characteristic of the entrepreneurial spirit. Willy's physical and spiritual depletion can in part be attributed to the rise of the personality market. Like the white-collar worker, he is forced to instrumentalize his personality. He knows that "the man who makes an appearance in the business world, the man who creates personal interest, is the man who gets ahead" (33). Thus he is convinced that Biff will be a successful salesman, despite his poor performance in school. He thinks that Bernard's academic achievements are more of a liability than an asset, and he tells Biff that they are not worth emulating. Unlike Biff, Bernard lacks "personality," and so he will be unable to make an appearance in the business world: "Bernard can get the best marks in school, y'understand, but when he gets out in the business world, y'understand, you are going to be fives times ahead of him" (33). Willy's awareness that one's personality often determines whether one gets ahead reflects his experience as a salesman. Although he knows that he must try to create "personal interest," he talks too much and so "people don't seem to take to me. . . . I don't know the reason for it, but they just pass me by. I'm not noticed" (36).

But Willy's physical and spiritual depletion is primarily related to the emergence of a domestic model of masculinity. His failure to impress others with his personality is compounded by his adherence to an outmoded definition of masculinity. He is disgusted by Charley's inability to repair his house and tells him that "a man who can't handle tools is not a man" (44). Moreover, he resents the pressure placed on him to participate in the traditionally female spheres of consumption and domesticity and thinks that men should assert their freedom and independence. Thus, when Linda complains that Biff is "too rough with the girls" (40) and that he needs to work harder in school, Willy explodes: "There's nothing the matter with him! You want him to be a worm like Bernard? He's got spirit, personality" (40). Willy sees Biff's irresponsibility and lack of respect for his teachers as an assertion of his masculinity. Unlike Bernard, who tries to impress his teachers, Biff refuses to occupy a passive position in relation to authority. But Willy also knows that one of the consequences of resisting the domestication of masculinity is downward mobility. For this reason, he is largely to blame for Biff's inability to get ahead in the business world. He gives Biff mixed messages. On the other hand, he expects Biff to show that he is a "real" man by asserting his independence; on the other hand, he constantly tells him that he must learn how to exploit his personality.

In making Willy's inability to adjust to the rise of the white-collar worker the basis of a tragedy, Miller expresses a desire to return to an earlier stage of capitalism. Willy's adherence to an outmoded definition of masculinity is perhaps most apparent in his admiration for his brother, Ben. Unlike Willy, Ben expresses the independence and daring that are the hallmarks of the entrepreneurial spirit, and Willy encourages Biff and Happy to model themselves after him: "The man knew what he wanted and went out and got it! Walked into a jungle, and comes out, the age of twenty-one, and he's rich!" (41). Willy's failure to accompany Ben to Alaska leads him to question his masculinity. He thinks that in remaining behind with Linda, he showed a lack of initiative and independence: "Why didn't I go to Alaska with my brother Ben that time! Ben! That man was a genius, that man was success incarnate! What a mistake! He begged me to go" (41). But Willy's self-reproach here seems misdirected. The form of male identity that Ben embodies was available to few men in twentieth-century America. As we have seen, following the shift to monopoly capitalism in the late nineteenth century, success was measured increasingly in terms of consumption. Men were encouraged to pursue economic security and to define themselves through their identities as breadwinners and homeowners. The character in the play who most fully endorses this model of masculinity is Linda. She does not understand Willy's frustration with his job and encourages him to realize himself through domesticity and consumption. When he complains that he would like to "own something outright before it's broken" (73), she replies that weathering a twenty-five-year mortgage is "an accomplishment" (73).[28] Nor does she understand his desire to test his manhood by accompanying Ben to Alaska. Her fantasies and desires have been shaped by commodity culture, and so she convinces him to remain behind with her: "Why must everybody conquer the world?" (85).

Miller's politics of nostalgia surface most fully in the play's final scene. Because Willy was about to make the final payment on the house, Linda does not understand why he killed himself. After Willy's funeral, when the others have returned to the car, she approaches his grave and says: "I made the last payment on the house today" (139). For her, Willy's death is particularly tragic because it prevented him from achieving the economic security that previously eluded him. She continues to measure success in terms of homeownership and does not understand that Willy would not have seen paying off the mortgage as an "accomplishment." Unaware of the economic forces that led to Willy's death, she repeats ruefully: "We're free and clear . . . We're free . . . We're free . . . We're free . . ." (130). Here Miller's critique of the rise of the white-collar worker surfaces most fully. For him, the Fordist organization of production and consumption had reduced the utopian promise of America to paying off a mortgage. The shift from industrial to monopoly capitalism had made a mockery of the values and ideals America traditionally symbolized. Although America continued to inspire dreams of personal freedom and unlimited social mobility, those dreams revolved increasingly around homeownership and the achievement of economic security.

The masculinism underlying Miller's understanding of America's symbolic significance is perhaps most apparent in his treatment of Biff and Happy, whose desire to recover an outmoded form of male identity he romanticizes. Biff's and Happy's struggles to resist the pressures to conform to the dominant construction of masculinity are more poignant than Willy's. On the one hand, Biff and Happy embody the traditional form of American manhood. They are accomplished athletes, have muscular builds, and are sexually virile. On the other hand, they are unable to succeed in a world in which it is more important to have "personality" than to show initiative or ambition. Thus they not only experience downward mobility but also increasingly question their manhood. Biff, for example, wonders whether his refusal to get married and buy a house is a sign of immaturity rather than an assertion of his masculinity. Although in working on a ranch he displays the fortitude and daring that defined the frontier spirit, he is unable to escape the domestication of masculinity, which influences the way he perceives himself. Shortly after returning home, he says to Happy: "Maybe I oughta get married. Maybe I oughta get stuck into something. Maybe that's my trouble. I'm like a boy. I'm not married, I'm not in business, I just—I'm like a boy" (23). Happy is similarly unable to resist the pressure to conform to the domestic model of masculinity. Although he can "outbox, outrun and outlift" (24) all of the executives in his store, he is forced to occupy a subordinate position in relation to them that conflicts with his masculine self-image. To recover his masculinity, he resorts to fantasy. He tells Biff that he sometimes becomes so frustrated that "I just want to rip my clothes off in the middle of the store and outbox that goddam merchandise manager" (24), as though beating him up would show that he was superior to him.

In stressing Biff's and Happy's inability to assert their freedom and independence, Miller clearly meant to highlight the erosion of the American dream. Like both James and Mills, Miller foregrounded the tension between the hopes and dreams America inspired and the lack of mobility and personal freedom to which bureaucratization had led. But insofar as it was grounded in a masculinist understanding of the American people's needs and aspirations, Miller's critique of the rise of the white-collar worker had more in common with Mills's than with James's. For Miller, what was most disturbing about the increasing division of labor was that it prevented men from freely expressing their masculinity. Like Mills, he equated the decline of the entrepreneurial spirit with an erosion of male heterosexual privilege. Biff sums up Miller's criticisms of monopoly capitalism when he explains to Happy his reasons for moving out west. Biff could no longer bear to be in a job in which he was expected "to suffer fifty weeks of the year for the sake of a two-week vacation, when all you really desire is to be outdoors, with your shirt off" (22). This statement highlights Miller's debt to the populist aesthetic embraced by Popular Front writers and artists. Biff's desire to work outdoors with his shirt off recalls the image of the American worker circulated by the Popular Front. As Paula Rabinowitz has shown, Popular Front writers and artists tended to fetishize the male proletarian body.[29] In cultural production inspired by the Popular Front, the proletariat was invariably represented by a muscle-bound male worker who embodied phallic power.

Like Mills, then, Miller tended to masculinize America's symbolic significance. He was not interested in the fantasies and desires the American dream may have inspired in women, African Americans, gays, and other groups disenfranchised by the postwar settlement or in the different meaning such groups may have attached to America. After all, such groups did not have the opportunity to become white-collar workers, and thus they could not afford the luxury of longing to return to an earlier stage of capitalism.[30] Despite the similarities of their texts, however, Miller's critique of the growth of bureaucratic structures was not as coherent as Mills's.

Miller's adherence to a classical definition of tragedy prevented him from maintaining a materialist perspective. Although he wanted to call attention to the material forces that conditioned the construction of male subjectivity in the Cold War era, he increasingly psychologizes Willy's frustration.[31] As we saw above, he makes Linda the chief advocate in the play for the domestic model of masculinity. She does not understand Willy's desire to "conquer" the world and encourages him to see the domestic sphere as a more appropriate field of endeavor and accomplishment. In this way, Miller blames women for the alienation and disaffection many men experienced in the postwar period. The decline of the entrepreneurial spirit is a result not of government policies designed to consolidate the Fordist organization of production and consumption but of women's influence over the domestic sphere.

Insofar as it led him to stress Willy's uncertainty and confusion as a man, Miller's conception of tragedy further undermined the coherence of his critique of postwar American society. Willy has never fully recovered from the traumatic loss of his father when he was a small boy. He begs Ben to prolong his visit so that he can seek fatherly advice from him: "Can't you stay a few days? You're just what I need, Ben, because I—I have a fine position here, but I—well, Dad left when I was such a baby and I never had a chance to talk to him and I still feel—kind of temporary about myself" (51). In accordance with the conventions of classical tragedy, Miller clearly wants to build toward a single climactic peripety, or sudden reversal of circumstances, in which we learn information about Willy that helps to explain his "fall."[32] But Miller's emphasis on Willy's loss as a small boy conflicts with his desire to expose the material forces that condition the construction of Willy's subjectivity. Willy's uncertainty and frustration can be traced simultaneously to a tragic flaw in his character and to the rise of consumer capitalism. Unlike Mills, then, Miller psychologized postwar structures of oppression rather than dramatizing their internalization. Willy's difficulty adjusting to the growth of bureaucratic structures is a personal rather than a social problem. His need for fatherly advice is a sign of his inadequacy as a man. He refuses to accompany Ben to Alaska not because he knows that resisting the reorganization of masculinity would lead to downward mobility but because he lacks Ben's initiative and daring and therefore is insufficiently masculine.

The Erotics of Black Male Identity:
Left-Wing Intellectuals and the Search for an Authentic Masculinity

The degree to which a masculinist construction of America prevented left-wing intellectuals from providing a coherent critique of postwar structures of oppression becomes even more apparent when we turn to a group of texts published later in the decade. These texts had an even greater influence on the social movements of the sixties than did *White Collar* and *Death of a Salesman*. In these texts, the masculinist fantasies that inform Mills's and Miller's critique of the rise of the white-collar worker are compounded by a racist construction of black male identity. These texts treat black male identity as an important site of resistance to the domestication of masculinity. In these texts, African American men embody an oppositional form of masculinity that has the potential to disrupt the reorganization of the economy. To paraphrase James, they emerge as "persistent symbols" of America's utopian promise and therefore resemble the gangster and the hard-boiled detective of his analysis of the culture industries. Unlike white men, they refuse to occupy a passive position in relation to authority and are social and sexual outlaws. In ascribing an oppositional form of masculinity to African American men, these texts sought to exploit the anxiety the myth of black male sexual prowess aroused in white men. The contrast between the sexually virile black men exalted by these texts and the popular image of the white-collar worker as a domesticated consumer helped to mobilize opposition to the reorganization of masculinity. At the same time, however, in depicting African American men as social and sexual outlaws, these texts legitimated the criminalization of black male identity and thus undercut their oppositional content.

The *locus classicus* of left-wing racist constructions of black male identity is Norman Mailer's controversial essay "The White Negro: Superficial Reflections on the Hipster," which first appeared in *Dissent* in 1957. As Andrew Ross has pointed out, Mailer was primarily interested in giving political form to the fantasies and desires expressed in the hipster's alienation and disaffection from mainstream American society.[33] In many respects, the hipster was a product of the disillusionment and estrangement the African American community experienced following the defeat of its aspirations after World War II. But the hipster's anger and frustration were only vaguely political, and in "The White Negro" Mailer sought to harness them for concrete change. Mailer's celebration of the hipster reflected in part his disillusionment with the Communist party and its expectation that members would strictly adhere to the party line, even when it conflicted with their own knowledge and experience. Implicit in his analysis is a contrast between the hipster and the working class, which had failed to constitute itself as an agent of historical change. Mailer did not believe that historical agency was located uniquely in the relations of production, and so he sought to replace the working class with the hipster as the privileged subject of history. According to him, the greatest difference between the hipster and the Communist party was that the hipster operated according to a political knowledge that was necessarily fragmentary and provisional. The hipster, he explained, had "no interest in viewing human nature, or better, in judging human nature from a set of standards conceived a priori to the experience, standards inherited from the past."[34] Rather, the hipster understood that experience constantly gave rise to new knowledge and that one could not always rationally anticipate one's political needs and interests, which were not fixed but historically contingent. Having learned from experience that "the results of our actions are unforeseeable, and so we cannot know if we do good and bad" (326), the hipster did not interpret his experience according to a party line but realized that his understanding of the world had to remain provisional.

Moreover, unlike the working class, the hipster could not be co-opted by the promise of homeownership, and thus his anger and disaffection had the potential to become a flash point for all those groups disenfranchised by the postwar settlement. Mailer stressed the hipster's capacity for self-mobilization. According to Mailer, unlike the working class, the hipster did not have to depend on an intellectual elite or party vanguard to raise levels of consciousness; rather, he had an automatic constituency in America's youth. The hipster, he claimed, spoke "a language most adolescents understand instinctively" (317) because it was a language that corresponded to their fantasies and desires. Like James, then, Mailer stressed the potential for a social explosion in postwar America.[35] He was particularly optimistic because he saw the hipster as the antithesis of the white-collar worker. For him, the hipster's criminal behavior represented a form of oppositional consciousness. The hipster refused to confine his sexuality to the domestic sphere. By redounding against "the anti-sexual foundation of every organized power in America" (329), such a refusal promised to disrupt the Cold

War consensus, which operated according to the principle that American society could accommodate and absorb every oppositional tendency without collapsing. The hipster's refusal to conform to the dominant construction of masculinity would eventually "bring into the air such animosities, antipathies and new conflicts of interest that the mean empty hypocrisies of mass conformity will no longer work" (329). Thus the emergence of the hipster inspired Mailer to look forward to a time "when every political guide post will be gone, and millions of liberals will be faced with political dilemmas they have so far succeeded in evading, and with a view of human nature they do not wish to accept" (329–30).

Mailer's implicit criticisms of the working class suggests that his controversial essay should in part be read as a response to the postwar decline of working-class militancy. For Mailer, although the hipster's needs and aspirations were only vaguely political, they could not be manipulated and defused by the promise of enfranchisement through consumption. But this does not excuse the racist assumptions underlying Mailer's critique of postwar American society. His attempt to substitute the hipster for the working class was based on a racist construction of black male identity that conflicted with his stated objectives. Black men functioned as the repository of his political fantasies and desires. He ascribed to them a form of male identity that in the wake of the postwar reorganization of the economy was no longer available to white men. As we have seen, this form of identity continued to shape white men's needs and aspirations. Mailer described the hipster as a "frontiersman in the Wild West of American night life" who refused to allow himself to become "trapped in the totalitarian tissues of American society" (313). Glamorizing the violence and brutality of ghetto life, Mailer claimed that the struggle to survive in which African American men were constantly engaged made conforming to the domestic model of masculinity a luxury they could not afford. The ghetto had replaced the frontier as a "testing field" for heroes: "Any Negro who wishes to live must live with danger from his [sic] first day, and no experience can ever be casual to him, no Negro can saunter down a street with any real certainty that violence will not visit him on his walk" (314). Thus it seemed doubtful that African American men would lose themselves in consumer dreams or be seduced by mass-produced fantasies.

Nor was it likely that they would be persuaded to restrict their sexuality to the domestic sphere. Prevented from achieving the American dream because of their race, they had nothing to lose by becoming social and sexual outlaws. According to Mailer, the black man "could rarely afford the sophisticated inhibitions of civilization, and so he kept for his survival the art of the primitive" (314). In short, African American men could not be domesticated. The brutality of their experience forced them to relinquish "the pleasures of the mind for the more obligatory pleasures of the body" (314). In the violent world of the ghetto, African American men had no choice but to explore "all those moral wildernesses of civilized life which the Square automatically condemns as delinquent or evil or immature or morbid or self-destructive or corrupt" (321). Thus the real target of Mailer's critique was not the Fordist organization of the economy but the domestication of masculinity. In his essay, African American men emerge as the only remaining representatives of the frontier spirit. The oppositional form of masculinity they embody is a product of the "frontier" of ghetto life. Thus in "The White Negro" the masculinist assumptions underlying Mills and Miller's critique of consumer capitalism are compounded by a racist fantasy of black masculinity. In depicting black men as outlaws whose anger and resentment toward white America had the potential to disrupt the reorganization of masculinity, Mailer legitimated the criminalization of black male identity. His desire to identify an agent of historical change that could not be co-opted by commodity culture led him to embrace the myth of the threatening black phallus.

To clarify the political liabilities of Mailer's racist construction of black male identity, I want to examine briefly Eldridge Cleaver's *Soul on Ice* (1968), one of the founding texts of the Black Panther movement, which used Mailer's essay to justify excluding James Baldwin from the African American community because he was gay. Cleaver's homophobic attack on Baldwin indicates that Mailer's construction of black masculinity expressed fantasies and aspirations that were not limited to white male left-wing intellectuals. Cleaver claimed that he could no longer accept Baldwin as a spokesman for the African American community because in "The Black Boy Looks at the White Boy," an essay that first appeared in *Esquire* in 1961, Baldwin had criticized Mailer for exploiting the anxieties the myth of the threatening black phallus aroused in white men. I examine Baldwin's objections to Mailer's racist construction of black male identity in detail in chapter 6. Suffice it to say here that Baldwin worried that Mailer's legitimation of racist stereotypes would be used to deny gay African American men their claims to blackness. Cleaver's attack on Baldwin showed that his fears were not unfounded. For Cleaver, homosexuality was culturally white.[36] He equated it with a reactionary Uncle Tomism in which gay black men supposedly colluded with white America to emasculate straight black men.[37] Cleaver conceived of homosexuality as an extreme form of the ethnic self-hatred he thought plagued the black community: "Many Negro homosexuals, acquiescing in this racial death-wish, are outraged and frustrated because in their sickness they are unable to have a baby by a white man."[38] Cleaver, then, did not consider Baldwin truly black. As a gay man who was allegedly consumed by the desire to have a white man's baby, Baldwin necessarily occupied a passive position in relation to white America. Cleaver detected in Baldwin's work "the most grueling, agonizing, total hatred of the blacks, particularly of himself, and the most shameful, fanatical, fawning, sycophantic love of the whites that one can find in the writings of any black American writer of note in our time" (97). In short, Baldwin's homosexuality was a sign that he was incapable of representing the black man's needs and interests.

Cleaver was perhaps right to conceive of homosexuality and blackness as mutually exclusive categories of identity. After all, in the postwar period gay male identity was largely a white middle-class construction. As Tomas Almaguer has pointed out, the gay men who were responsible for creating the newly emergent urban gay communities, as well as those who participated most actively in them, were predominantly white and middle class.[39] Because of their racial and class privilege, such men had the skills and resources necessary for creating the practices, institutions, and forms of identity that provided the foundation for the postwar gay male subculture. Such men were also better able to endure the ostracism to which identifying as gay inevitably led. Unlike African Americans and Latinos, such men did not identify themselves primarily in terms of their class and ethnic background. As we saw in the introduction, in the Cold War era race increasingly displaced class and ethnicity as the most important markers of identity. Even working-class ethnics tended to identify with the white middle class. Insofar as class and ethnicity played an increasingly unimportant role in determining the identities of white Americans, it was easier for them to identify primarily as gay and to risk marginalization by participating in the gay male subculture. Unlike men of color for whom ethnicity necessarily remained the basis of group identity and survival, white Americans did not have to depend on their families and ethnic group for protection and support.

But the racial and class politics of postwar gay male identity does not wholly explain Cleaver's homophobia. He questioned Baldwin's claims to blackness primarily because in Rufus Scott, the black male protagonist of his novel *Another Country* (1962), Baldwin had created a black male character "who lets a white bisexual homosexual [*sic*] fuck him in the ass" (104). In trying to challenge racist constructions of black male identity, Baldwin had supposedly legitimated white America's attempts to police and contain black masculinity. Since the days of slavery, Cleaver explained, the white man had refused to allow the black man to fulfill his traditional role as a man, that is, to serve as his family's sole provider and protector. Rather, it had delegated that responsibility to the black woman. In thus robbing the black man of his traditional role, the white man had deprived him "of his masculinity, castrated him in the center of his burning skull" (101). Baldwin's criticisms of Mailer's essay led Cleaver to compare him unfavorably to Richard Wright, the bestselling author of *Native Son* (1940). Unlike Baldwin, Cleaver claimed, Wright "understood and lived the truth of what Norman Mailer meant" (106) when he described the ghetto as a kind of "testing field" for black masculinity. Baldwin failed to realize that rather than reinforcing racist stereotypes, Mailer had heroically recuperated the black man's masculinity. According to Cleaver, in criticizing Mailer for embracing the myth of the threatening black phallus, Baldwin had "resorted to a despicable underground guerilla war, waged on paper, against black masculinity" (106). Granted, Cleaver's repudiation and disavowal of African American homosexuality can in part be explained by the fact that black men were prevented from exercising the prerogatives that defined masculinity in the Cold War era. But his emphasis on the "guerilla war" against black masculinity came perilously close to asserting that black men would not achieve political and economic equality until they had obtained access to patriarchal privilege.[40]

Jack Kerouac and the Racist Construction of "America"

Despite the fact that it seems to have authorized Cleaver's attack on Baldwin, who became known in black nationalist circles as Martin Luther

Queen for his allegedly assimilationist views, Mailer's essay was highly controversial, and its influence on postwar left-wing intellectuals was limited.[41] Indeed, the intellectuals one might have thought would have been most inspired by the essay, namely the Beats, were either puzzled or amused by its macho posturing. Jack Kerouac, for example, was disturbed by the implications of its celebration of psychopathic violence, and Allen Ginsberg later recalled that Mailer's depiction of the hipster "as being cool and psychopathic and cutting his way through society was a kind of macho folly that we [the Beats] giggled at."[42] Despite Kerouac's and Ginsberg's criticisms of the essay, however, their rebellion against the reorganization of masculinity was informed by many of the same fantasies and desires that underlay Mailer's racist construction of black masculinity. In the writings of the Beats, African American men function as the repositories of the needs and aspirations many white men experienced in the face of the emergence of a domestic model of masculinity. The Beats' tendency to project onto African American men their own fantasies and desires is particularly ironic, given that their rebellion against the conformity of postwar American society was seen by many men as a heroic refusal to submit to the domestication of masculinity. That is to say, they themselves functioned as a repository for the hopes and dreams of the many men who had become disillusioned by the emergence of a new corporate order. Such men tended to ascribe to the Beats an oppositional form of masculinity that had the potential to reverse the postwar shift from production to consumption.

The similarities between Mailer and the Beats are perhaps most apparent in Jack Kerouac's novel *On the Road*, which was written in the early 1950s but not published until 1957. Kerouac's novel deeply influenced the sixties counterculture and was widely seen at the time of its publication as the manifesto of a generation in revolt against the rise of the white-collar worker.[43] Kerouac conceived of the novel as an epic "whose background is the recurrence of the pioneering instinct in American life and its expression in the migration of the present generation."[44] But a more accurate description of the novel's background might be the loss of the pioneering instinct and the desire to recover it that obsessed so many white men in the Cold War era. One way of reading Sal Paradise's travels on the road is as his search for a masculinity that is commensurate with his fantasies and desires. By taking to the road, he hopes to recover the form of male identity displaced by the rise of the white-collar worker. Although he has rejected the domesticated model of masculinity, like Biff and Happy in *Death of a Salesman,* Sal is unable to escape its influence and constantly questions whether he is sufficiently masculine. When he encounters a cowboy on his first road trip, he imagines that "it was the spirit of the West sitting right next to me. I wished I knew his whole raw life and what the hell he'd been doing all these years besides laughing and yelling like that. Whooee, I told my soul, and the cowboy came back and off we went to Grand Island."[45] Although the difference between desire and identification is not always easy to locate, it seems to me that Sal's excitement in this passage ("whooee") is more identificatory than homoerotic.[46] Sal does not want to possess the cowboy sexually so much as to inhabit his body, to experience his masculinity as though it were his own. Sal clearly thinks that the cowboy is more of a man than he is. Despite his working-class background, Sal has been pampered by comparison to the cowboy, whose life has been "raw" and austere.

Sal's desire to recover a form of male identity that was no longer available to white middle-class men surfaces most fully in relation to the working-class men of color he encounters on the road. In perhaps the novel's most famous passage, he describes the combination of envy and desire Denver's ghettos arouse in him: "At lilac evening I walked with every muscle aching among the lights of 27th and Welton in the Denver colored section, wishing I were a Negro, feeling that the best the white world had offered was not enough ecstasy for me, not enough life, joy, kicks, darkness, music, not enough night. . . . I wished I were a Denver Mexican, or even a poor overworked Jap, anything but what I was so drearily, a 'white man' disillusioned" (180). Sal's insecurity about his masculinity makes him wish he were one of the men of color described in this passage. Unlike them, he is not "poor" but "overworked," so his disillusionment with the dominant order seems childish and unwarranted, and he feels less manly than they. Like Mailer's essay, then, *On the Road* tended to reinforce racist stereotypes by romanticizing the practices and forms of identity that men of color had invented as strategies of survival. Sal's lyrical description conveniently overlooks the poverty and violence of ghetto life. Moreover, the men of color he describes in the passage recall the sexually uninhibited hipster of Mailer's essay. Like the hipster, they are the antithesis of the white-collar worker. If they are more manly than Sal, that is because they are more "primitive" and thus less likely than he to lose themselves in consumer dreams. Granted, unlike Mailer, Kerouac did not glamorize ghetto violence by encouraging readers to express the "psychopath" in themselves; nor did he exalt black male rage as a form of oppositional consciousness. But the qualities he attributed to the men in this passage nevertheless reinforced the popular image of the white-collar worker as a feminized man.

Despite its similarity to Mailer's essay, however, *On the Road* provided readers with a potentially more useful knowledge of postwar structures of oppression. Kerouac's needs and desires did not wholly blind him to the fantasies and aspirations of women, African Americans, and other groups disenfranchised by the postwar settlement. The political liabilities of his tendency to ascribe to men of color an oppositional form of masculinity surface most fully in his treatment of Terry, the young Chicana with whom Sal becomes briefly involved during one of his trips to California. He realizes through her, albeit briefly, the hopes and dreams that motivate his travels on the road. Their life together as migrant farmworkers enables him to imagine that he is "a man of the earth, precisely as I had dreamed I would be, in Paterson" (97), the small town in New Jersey where he lives with his aunt. Moreover, he recalls proudly that because of his relationship with Terry, the "Okies" in the camp where they stay while picking cotton "thought I was Mexican . . . and in a way I am" (97). But whereas Terry has no avenue of escape and is tied to the land by poverty and lack of education, he has the material resources to return to Paterson whenever he chooses. When he grows tired of working in the fields and begins to "feel the pull of my own life calling me back" (98), he does not hesitate to leave Terry and simply writes to his aunt asking for bus fare home.

The exploitative element of Sal's relationship with Terry should not, however, be interpreted to mean that, like Mailer, Kerouac lacked insight into the racist and sexist structures of postwar American society. Sal's willingness to use his relationship with Terry to secure his masculinity does not blind him to the racial and class differences between them. He realizes that despite his working-class background, he is relatively privileged in comparison to her because of his race and gender. When he receives a money order from his aunt, he is disgusted by how easy it is for him to return home. Unlike Terry, he does have an avenue of escape: "My aunt had saved my lazy butt again" (101). Moreover, he realizes that Terry's oppression as a woman is compounded by her race and class. He becomes angry when her family calls her a whore "because she'd left her no-good husband

and gone to LA and left [her son] with them" (98). And when he takes his friend Stan to a hospital in Mexico City so that he can be treated for an infected insect bite, the Chicanas who are waiting in the emergency room remind him of Terry's vulnerability as a working-class woman of color: "The hall of the hospital was full of poor Mexican women, some of them pregnant, some of them sick or bringing their little sick kiddies. It was sad. I thought of poor Terry" (272). Unlike Mailer's essay, then, *On the Road* provided insight into the way in which racial, class, and gender differences intersected in the postwar period. This is not to exaggerate the importance of the novel's treatment of postwar structures of oppression, nor is it to minimize the racism and sexism underlying Sal's needs and aspirations in the face of the reorganization of masculinity. It is simply to highlight the differences between the two texts and to suggest that Kerouac was able to imagine possibilities and alternatives that Mailer was not.

Film Noir and the Politics of Homophobia

I have stressed the masculinist fantasy of American national identity that informed left-wing critiques of the rise of the white-collar worker in order to elucidate film noir's political imaginary. In the chapters that follow, we will see that although film noir did nor explicitly address the resistance to the domestication of masculinity, it nevertheless tried to tap the needs and aspirations expressed in that resistance. Like the texts we have examined in this chapter, film noir expressed a desire to recover the form of male identity displaced by the rise of commodity culture. Its critique of postwar American society was similarly shaped by a desire to return to an earlier stage of capital accumulation, when male subjectivity supposedly had not yet been penetrated by the commodity form. This desire is perhaps most apparent in the iconographic mode of representation deployed by film noir to distinguish the hard-boiled detective from the gay male characters. We will see that the hard-boiled detective's refusal to participate in the traditionally female spheres of domesticity and consumption is expressed visually by his association with unkempt offices and seedy boardinghouses. His disheveled appearance makes clear that he has been able to resist the lure of the commodity. By contrast, the gay male characters' association with luxurious surroundings suggests that they occupy the same position in relation to the commodity form as the femme fatale. Wholly immersed in commodity culture, they are the antithesis of the hardworking, self-denying entrepreneur.

My goal in examining the differences between the hard-boiled detective and the gay male characters in film noir is to clarify the relation between homophobia and Fordism. As I noted in the introduction, the transition to a Fordist regime of capital accumulation required the creation of new forms of male subjectivity. To sustain the economic growth of the postwar period, men had to learn to define themselves through their roles as breadwinners and homeowners. As the texts examined in this chapter indicate, however, many men experienced the shift from production to consumption as a threat to their masculinity. One of the ways in which the discourses of national security defused this threat was by homosexualizing the form of male identity embodied by the entrepreneurial spirit. In the following chapters, I use two examples of film noir, Otto Preminger's *Laura* (1944) and Edward Dmytryk's *Crossfire* (1947), to clarify this aspect of postwar American culture. Film noir's insistence on the differences between the hard-boiled detective and the gay male characters indicates that it was uncertain about how spectators would interpret the hard-boiled detective's resistance to the domestication of masculinity. Film noir, then, can be used to show how, in promoting male homosexual panic, the discourses of national security were able to contain opposition to the reorganization of the economy. Film noir raises doubts about the fantasies and aspirations informing the desire to return to an earlier stage of capitalism even as it gives expression to them. In film noir, the distinction between homoeroticism and the desire to recover the form of male identity embodied by the entrepreneurial spirit is not as secure as it is in the texts we have been examining. Thus film noir provides a particularly useful example of the way in which even the most progressive products of mass culture tended to tap the opposition to the domestication of masculinity only to recode it in ways that were thoroughly compatible with the new economic order.

CHAPTER TWO

Resisting the Lure of the Commodity:
Laura *and the Spectacle of the Gay Male Body*

Laura, you have one tragic weakness. With you, a lean, strong body is
the measure of a man, and you always get hurt.
—Lydecker in *Laura*

Otto Preminger's *Laura* (1944) has achieved status as a classic film noir
primarily for two reasons. First, it was one of five films the French critic
Nino Frank identified as films noirs when he coined the term in 1946 to
designate the resemblance between a group of recently released Hollywood
films and the hard-boiled detective fiction then being published by Gallimard as part of its *Serie noire*.[1] Second, Preminger had to fight with Twentieth Century–Fox, which did not want Clifton Webb to play the part of
Waldo Lydecker because he supposedly "flaunted" his homosexuality. The
story of the studio's opposition to Webb, who received an Academy Award
nomination for Best Supporting Actor for his performance as the witty,
urbane Lydecker, has become part of Hollywood lore, thanks in part to
Preminger's account in his autobiography.[2] According to Preminger, when
he first suggested Webb for the part, Darryl Zanuck, the head of Twentieth
Century–Fox, strenuously objected, claiming that he was too effeminate.
Rufus LeMaire, the head of the casting department, who was also at the
meeting, agreed. LeMaire claimed to have seen a screen test that Webb had
made for Metro-Goldwyn-Mayer: "[LeMaire] said the man was impossible.
'He doesn't walk, he flies,' implying that [Webb] was effeminate."[3] Preminger was probably right to assume that the studio's objections to Webb
centered on his effeminacy, which would have marked him as gay. After all,
the Production Code, which was established by the film industry in 1934 to

forestall government censorship by demonstrating its capacity to regulate itself, prohibited the explicit treatment of homosexuality.[4] The studio was undoubtedly concerned that Webb's tendency to "fly" would violate the code by rendering Lydecker's homosexuality explicit.

Although I have no desire to question the accuracy of Preminger's account, it seems to me that there may have been more at stake in the studio's objections to Webb than he realized. In this chapter, I want to use Preminger's controversial decision to cast Webb to shed light on an aspect of film noir that has been overlooked by film scholars. I will argue that Webb's tendency to flaunt his homosexuality promoted a mode of spectatorship to which the hard-boiled detective film did not usually lend itself and which the classical system had in part been designed to suppress. This mode of spectatorship was rooted in the tension between spectacle and narrative in classical Hollywood cinema. Webb's willingness to make a spectacle of his homosexuality hindered the spectator's absorption in the diegesis, which was one of the primary goals of the classical system. It encouraged a mobile and ambulatory gaze that was easily distracted by the surface of the image. The spectator became fixated on elements of the diegesis, such as Webb's performance, that are peripheral to the linear unfolding of the film's plot. Insofar as it disrupted the hierarchical relationship between spectacle and narrative that normally prevailed in classical cinema, Webb's refusal to mask his homosexuality was subversive. When not wholly contained or suppressed, the element of spectacle in Hollywood film had the potential to function as a site for the production of a gay male subject. I will show that this aspect of classical cinema was especially pronounced in film noir, in which stylistic innovation dominated at the expense of narrative coherence. Webb's tendency to "fly" merely reinforced the transgressive form of visual pleasure film noir offered spectators.

*Subordinating Spectacle to Narrative: Hollywood and
Gay Male Spectatorship*

To clarify the potentially subversive mode of spectatorship that Webb's willingness to flaunt his homosexuality promoted, I want to review briefly the relationship between spectacle and narrative in classical Hollywood cinema. Film scholars have identified a tension in Hollywood film between spectacle and narrative that can be traced to its roots in nineteenth-century melodrama and other forms of popular entertainment.[5] According to these scholars, before the emergence and consolidation of the classical paradigm in the second decade of the twentieth century, the cinematic apparatus had more in common with the variety show and the fairground attraction than with the nineteenth-century realistic novel.[6] So-called primitive cinema directly solicited the spectator's gaze by engaging in the sort of bold visual display one encountered in shopping arcades and department stores. Like the display window, early cinema encouraged a mobile and ambulatory gaze that combined leisurely contemplation and self-gratification.[7] The type of shot most characteristic of the "primitive" system was the theatrical tableau.[8] Whereas in the classical system the shot is conceived of as part of a sequence, in the "primitive" system it is conceived of as an autonomous unit. Like the display window, early cinema presented the spectator with a framed and inaccessible tableau whose static and uniform composition encouraged a mobility of vision. Distracted by an excess of visual meaning, the spectator of early cinema wavered between multiple points of view. Unlike the classical system, the "primitive" system did not rely on compositional unity to center the spectator's subjectivity, to insert her/him into a unified, coherent subject-position.

The thrill of display characteristic of early cinema did not totally disappear with the emergence of the classical paradigm but remained a constitutive element of Hollywood cinema.[9] Where the classical system differed from its predecessor was in its subordination of spectacle to narrative. Classical cinema avoided engaging in forms of spectacle that might hinder or prevent it from accomplishing its primary goal, the telling of a story.[10] The use of lavish costumes, stage sets, and/or color had to be justified by the narrative and was limited to genres such as the musical or the historical period piece in which spectacle was an integral part of the story. In reversing the hierarchical relation between spectacle and narrative in early cinema, the classical system promoted the spectator's absorption in the diegesis. In order to accomplish its goal of storytelling, the classical text could not allow the spectator to become distracted by an excess of visual meaning. The forms of desire most fully exploited by the classical system were voyeurism and fetishism. By allowing the spectator to transgress the prohibitions against voyeurism and fetishism in an "official" setting, Hollywood film virtually guaranteed her/his perceptual placement within the film's narrative space.[11]

But despite its indirect mode of address, the ability of the classical system to subordinate the element of spectacle to the telling of a story remained limited. Indeed, there were aspects of the classical system that actually hindered the spectator's immersion in the linear movement of the film's narrative. Marketing strategies such as fan magazines and clubs that were originally designed to promote the consumption of films encouraged a fetishistic relation to the star that hindered the ability of the cinematic apparatus to bind the spectator into the film's fictional world.[12] On the one hand, the star's presence facilitated the spectator's identification with the character s/he played by mobilizing her/his psychic investment in a particular ego ideal and object attachment. On the other hand, the cult of the star took on a momentum of its own, functioning as a kind of centrifugal force that counteracted the spectator's willingness to become part of the film's fictional world. The spectator was in constant danger of paying more attention to the star's glamorous image than to the part s/he played in the film. The cult of the star fostered a gaze that wandered in and out of the narrative and that became fixated on aspects of the film, such as the star's costumes, that were peripheral to the plot. Distracted by the surface of the image, the spectator threatened to become indifferent to the temporal dimension of the cinematic experience.[13] A desire to possess the objects displayed on the screen and associated with the star competed with a desire to enter into the film's story as it unfolded. In this respect, the cult of the star marked the persistence of the "primitive" system and its direct mode of address.

Recent work on subcultural modes of spectatorship has shown that historically disenfranchised groups such as working-class immigrant women and gay men were especially susceptible to the element of spectacle in classical cinema. For these groups, the film frame functioned as a display window, and the cinematic experience resembled a form of window-shopping.[14] In the shopping arcade or department store, working-class immigrant women often fell prey to what Rachel Bowlby, borrowing from Theodore Dreiser, has called "the drag of desire," or the lure of commodities they could not afford.[15] Moreover, if their ethnic and class backgrounds were legible, they were often treated indifferently by salesclerks or rudely shoved aside by more "respectable" shoppers. Whereas for middle-class women the department store provided an escape from domestic drudgery and a home away from home where they were made to feel pampered, for working-class immigrant women it functioned primarily as a site for the reproduction and consolidation of racial and class hierarchies.[16] This may explain why working-class immigrant women were especially drawn to Hollywood cinema: It permitted them to experience unharassed forms of visual pleasure that resembled those of the shopping arcade and department store. For the price of admission, they could indulge their fantasies of consumption uninterrupted. In the privacy and darkness of the movie theater, there were no salesclerks to remind them of their ethnic and class backgrounds.

Hollywood similarly affirmed the fantasies and desires the commodity form inspired in gay men. When it was insufficiently contained, the element of spectacle in classical Hollywood cinema encouraged gay men to engage in oppositional forms of spectatorship that were rooted in their exclusion from mainstream American society. Despite its subordination of spectacle to narrative, the classical system could not wholly prevent gay men from focusing on the film's purely visual aspects. For many gay male spectators, the source of cinematic pleasure lay in the opportunity to experience the thrill of display and not in the temporal dimension of the cinematic experience. As we saw above, many of the marketing strategies developed by the film industry for promoting the consumption of its products fostered a gaze that was easily distracted and that hovered over the surface of the image. The musical and the melodrama, in which the use of lavish costumes, stage sets, and color was often justified by the narrative, were especially susceptible to what we might call "camp" forms of reception.[17] The privileging of style over content in the production and consumption of aesthetic objects is usually understood as one of the defining characteristics of camp and describes the form of spectatorship I am attributing to gay men.[18] This understanding of camp may explain the place Vincente Minnelli's musicals and Douglas Sirk's melodramas occupied in the gay male imaginary throughout the Cold War era.[19]

Film Noir and the Homosexualization of Visual Pleasure

I have dwelt on the tension in classical Hollywood cinema between spectacle and narrative and the subcultural forms of spectatorship it enabled in order to deepen our understanding of film noir as a type of cinematic discourse that promoted potentially subversive forms of visual pleasure. The role of homophobia in the elaboration and refinement of the classical system was not incidental but structural. In subordinating spectacle to narrative, the classical system sought to discourage gay male as well as other subcultural modes of spectatorship. To be sure, the classical system was designed primarily to anticipate and standardize the reception of Hollywood films. Recent work in film studies has emphasized the diversity and heterogeneity of early film audiences, which were deeply divided along racial, class, and gender lines.[20] The use of an indirect mode of address, which all but guaranteed the spectator's absorption in the diegesis, helped to contain the divisions in these audiences and promoted their homogenization. The spectator's perceptual placement within the film's narrative space minimized the unpredictability characteristic of "primitive" forms of reception. The suppression or containment of the element of spectacle prevented the spectator from becoming distracted by the purely visual aspects of the filmic text. With the emergence of the classical system, the reception of the filmic text became less dependent on the spectator's racial, class, and sexual identity.[21] Thus the subordination of spectacle to narrative in the classical system was in part designed to discourage gay men from engaging in oppositional modes of spectatorship and to promote a heterosexualization of their subjectivity. The spectator constructed by the classical system is purportedly generic and disembodied, but, as feminist film critics have shown, he is actually white, middle class, and heterosexual.[22] Continuity editing, invisible narration, and other textual practices designed to bind the spectator into the film's fictional world prevented the gay male spectator's gaze from hovering over the surface of the image and from becoming fixated on elements of the diegesis whose contribution to the unfolding of the film's plot was marginal. This is why gay male forms of spectatorship that focused on the element of spectacle should be understood as oppositional. The gay male spectator's tendency to allow his gaze to become distracted by the purely visual aspects of the cinematic experience may have reflected his desire to avoid occupying the heterosexual subject-position it made available to him.

Thus, to return to the topic with which we began, Twentieth Century–Fox's opposition to Webb may have reflected a concern that Webb's refusal to mask his homosexuality would make the film susceptible to gay male forms of spectatorship. Such forms were more often associated with the musical and the melodrama, genres to which gay male audiences were particularly drawn, than with the hard-boiled detective film. Reviews of *Laura* shortly after its release suggest that the studio's concerns were not wholly unfounded. The film clearly fostered a mobile and ambulatory gaze that was easily distracted by the surface of the image. Although the film lacks narrative coherence, reviewers were distracted by its lush visual style and do not seem to have noticed. The review in *Time* was typical. It described the film as a "highly polished and debonair whodunit with only one inelegant smudge on its gleaming surface. In swank settings that cry out for a pinch of poison or at least a dainty derringer, the victim is obliged for purposes of plot to have her pretty face blown off by a double-barreled shotgun fired at close range."[23] Webb, aptly described by Vito Russo as a "deadly sissy," clearly contributed to the fascination the film's "gleaming" surface inspired in spectators.[24] Despite the studio's concern that Webb's tendency to "fly" would scandalize audiences, his highly polished performance seems to have diverted attention from the potentially controversial issue of his homosexuality.[25] Indeed, many reviewers treated his homosexuality as an asset, implying that it lent his performance an authenticity it would otherwise have lacked. Bosley Crowther, for example, in a review that appeared in the *New York Times*, praised Webb as "an actor who fits like a fine suede glove."[26]

The potential for the element of spectacle in Hollywood film to become uncontained and to hinder the spectator's absorption in the diegesis was particularly pronounced in film noir and may indicate why reviewers were so easily distracted by *Laura*'s lush visual style. Film scholars usually identify film noir by its distinctive visual style and strategies of narration.[27] The innovative use of lighting, marked camera angles, voice-over narration, and multiple flashbacks dominates at the expense of narrative coherence. The multiple use of flashbacks interrupts the linearity of the narrative and contributes to its lack of coherence. The inconsistency of the characters and the lack of a coherent plot are subsumed by stylistic innovation and formal excess. Because its tendency to privilege form over content hindered the spectator's absorption in the diegesis, some film scholars have seen film noir as a subversive genre that had the potential to disrupt the classical system.[28] To be sure, its emphasis on visual style distinguished it from the classical detective film.[29] Whereas in the classical detective film the investigation of the crime is governed by the assumption that a solution can be found through the tracing of a logical process of cause and effect, in film noir the detective is forced to rely on intuition rather than deductive reasoning and is unable to impose a coherent pattern on the seemingly unrelated events leading up to the crime. Film noir also differs from the classical detective film in that the unfolding of the plot is determined less by the processes of detection than by the ups and downs of the detective's relationship with the femme fatale.[30] The detective becomes increasingly obsessed with the femme fatale, whose transgressive sexuality eventually displaces the crime as the object of his investigation.

This understanding of the differences between film noir and the classical detective film may explain why spectators were fascinated with rather than scandalized by Webb's refusal to mask his homosexuality. Despite the studio's concern that it would distract spectators, Webb's willingness to make a spectacle of his homosexuality contributed to the transgressive form of visual pleasure spectators expected from film noir. But this does not wholly explain why spectators were so fascinated by Webb's performance and were willing to disregard the way in which it flaunted his homosexuality. Perhaps the film's most innovative aspect was not its expressionistic use of lighting, which was limited to the final scene, in which Lydecker returns to Laura's apartment and tries to kill her. Nor was it the film's use of multiple flashbacks, which following the release of Orson Welles's *Citizen Kane* in 1941 had become a standard narrative device in Hollywood cinema. Rather, it was the way in which the film assigned to Webb the role usually reserved in film noir for the femme fatale. Although the film concerns the detective Mark McPherson's (Dana Andrews) obsession with Laura (Gene Tierney), a beautiful and glamorous advertising executive whose murder he has been assigned to investigate, the character who manipulates him sexually and eventually becomes the object of his investigation is not Laura but Lydecker. As we will see, Lydecker's flashback in which he recalls how he met Laura and engineered her rise in the advertising world functions as a kind of seduction scenario. The glamorous and sexually desirable woman Lydecker describes in the flashback is largely a projection of his desire and bears only a vague resemblance to the woman who later returns to discover that she is the object of a murder investigation. The film further positions Lydecker as a femme fatale by counterposing him to Laura. In film noir, the femme fatale is frequently contrasted with a marginal female character who is more worthy of the hero's love and devotion.[31] Although Laura is more glamorous and sexually desirable than this marginal female character, she occupies the position usually assigned to her. Unlike Lydecker, she does not try to deceive Mark but shows that she is worthy of becoming his wife by helping him to solve Diane Redfern's murder.

Lee Edelman has recently claimed that Lydecker's association with visual excess—his lavishly decorated apartment, which is filled with priceless antiques; his dandified appearance, which advertises his homosexuality—is deeply homophobic.[32] According to him, the association of homosexuality with theatricality, masquerade, and other forms of spectacle can be explained in terms of the threat the gay male body poses to the system of representation that naturalizes sexual difference by locating it on the body. Homosexuality constitutes a form of sexual difference that cannot be located on the body, and thus it threatens to expose as a patriarchal fiction the belief that the differences between the sexes are biologically determined. But the association of homosexuality with spectacle, he argues, counteracts this threat to patriarchal power by making the gay male body legible. The construction of gay male identity as a form of gender inversion encourages the belief that homosexuality *can* be read on the body. Given his understanding of the privileged position the gay male body occupies in relation to the visual, it is not surprising that Edelman sees Lydecker's excess visibility in *Laura* as part of a project to make the gay male body legible by bringing it into the realm of representation. According to his reading of the film, the primary function of Lydecker's excess visibility is to provide homosexuality with a recognizable face.

Although Edelman's analysis of the gay male body's susceptibility to containment through representation is compelling, its applicability to the Cold War era seems limited. It would be more accurate to say that the Cold War era was marked by a project to make the gay male body *ilegible*. As I have shown elsewhere, the discourses of national security exploited fears that there was no way to tell homosexuals apart from heterosexuals.[33] These fears can in part be traced to the publication in 1948 of the first Kinsey report, which challenged the stereotype of the effeminate homosexual with statistical evidence that gay men did not differ significantly from straight men.[34] By distorting the Kinsey report's findings, the discourses of national security not only contained their potentially liberatory impact but also reinforced the link between homosexuality and Communism in the nation's political imaginary. For if, as the Kinsey report claimed, gay men could not be easily identified and were present in all walks of American life, then they resembled the Communists, who had allegedly infiltrated the nation's political and cultural institutions and threatened to subvert them from within. In promoting fears about the potential illegibility of the gay male body, the discourses of national security sought to contain the increasing visibility of gay men. Inspired by the civil rights movement, gay men began to mobilize politically and to challenge the medicalization of homosexuality.[35] Gay rights organizations such as the Mattachine Society sought to extend the discourse of minority rights to gay men, claiming that they constituted an oppressed minority. Moreover, gay male writers such as the ones examined in the second part of this study increasingly dominated the nation's cultural life. Edelman's claims about the link between homosexuality and spectacle overlook the project undertaken by the national-security state to counteract gay men's attempts to achieve visibility in the public sphere.

But there is a more serious problem with Edelman's reading, for it overlooks the possibility that the film's representation of Lydecker may not have been monolithically and totalizingly homophobic. By returning the gay male body to national visibility, the film's tendency to make a spectacle of Lydecker's homosexuality counteracted the project undertaken by the national-security state to expel gay men from the realm of representation. The position Lydecker occupies in the film's visual economy insists on the legibility of his body. Like Laura, he is constantly framed as an icon, or object to be looked at, and thus is aligned with the surface of the image. The film's determination to establish the legibility of the gay male body is perhaps most obvious in the opening sequence. In a shot clearly designed to transfix the spectator's gaze, Lydecker is shown sitting naked in his bathtub composing at his typewriter. In framing him as an icon that interrupts the film's narrative flow, the shot serves the same function as Laura's portrait. The spectacle of Lydecker's naked body establishes a fetishistic relation between him and the spectator that positions him as an object of display.

In claiming that the film's emphasis on the legibility of the gay male body was potentially subversive, I do not mean to minimize the homophobia pervading its representation of Lydecker. The spectacularization of Lydecker's body not only feminizes him but also prevents him from functioning as a point of identification for the spectator. My point is simply that in an era in which gay men threatened to become invisible, the impact of the film's representation of Lydecker may have been more progressive than regressive, despite the way in which it reinforced homophobic stereotypes. For many gay male spectators, the film's representation of Lydecker may have amounted to official recognition of a practice—gay male camp—in which they engaged as a strategy of survival. Edelman does not adequately acknowledge that the stereotype of the effeminate homosexual was not simply imposed on gay men by a hostile society but was also produced by them as a means of making themselves visible both to each other and to the dominant culture.[36] Nor does he consider the possibility that Webb may have actually sought to align himself with the surface of the image. In making a spectacle of his homosexuality, Webb may have tried to exploit the potential for the element of spectacle in Hollywood film to insert the spectator into a gay male subject-position. His "campy" performance helped to reverse the hierarchical relation in the film between spectacle and narrative and thus contributed significantly to the homosexualization of its visual economy.

Just as the film may have been unable to contain the effects of its spectacularization of the gay male body, so too may it have been unable to anticipate the impact of its construction of Lydecker as a femme fatale. Feminist film critics have shown that film noir differed from other forms of cinematic discourse in that it afforded women roles that were active and driven by sexual desire.[37] The femme fatale is a powerful figure who, in refusing to occupy a passive position in relation to desire, threatens to disrupt the organization of the look in classical cinema. Rather than submitting passively to the male gaze, she dares to return it; thus the male spectator is unable to elude the threat of castration signified by her image. Moreover, her punishment at the end of the film cannot counteract the spectator's fascination with her image. As one feminist film critic has said about the sexually destructive women who inhabit film noir, "it is not their inevitable demise we remember but rather their strong, dangerous, and above all, exciting sexuality."[38] Thus Lydecker's position as a femme fatale may have offset the effects of his association with visual excess. Neither his feminine position in the film's visual economy nor his exposure as Diane Redfern's murderer can detract from the power of his image. As a femme fatale, he emerges as a fascinating, if destructive, character who because he threatens to gain control of the narrative must be forcibly expelled from the diegesis. It is not surprising, then, that reviewers were more fascinated by Webb than by Tierney, even though the film was supposed to make her a star. It bears repeating that in stressing the liberatory possibilities opened up by the film's representation of Lydecker, I do not mean to minimize the homophobia which the image of homosexuality in the film put into circulation. I simply mean to point out that the effects of that image may have been more heterogeneous and contradictory than Edelman's argument about the association of the gay male body with visual excess allows for.

I have emphasized the lack of historical specificity of Edelman's reading of *Laura* in order to clarify the potentially subversive form of visual pleasure mobilized by film noir. Discussions of film noir often focus on the way in which it contested the postwar American dream of owning a home in the suburbs.[39] As I noted in the introduction, as a cinematic practice film noir appealed primarily to left-wing directors and screenwriters who were interested in calling attention to a stratum of postwar American society whose existence was not officially acknowledged until the publication in 1962 of Michael Harrington's *The Other America*. In many films noirs, the recovery of the economy has been uneven, and mass unemployment and widespread food shortages threaten to return. The stability and prosperity of the suburbs remain tantalizingly out of reach for the characters. Film noir further contested the postwar American dream by foregrounding the impact of the growth of the suburbs on the city.[40] Films noirs were often shot on location, and although it may not have been intentional, they captured the abandonment and decline of the city partially caused by the set of government policies we examined in the introduction. The city emerges as a desolate and menacing place filled with empty lots and abandoned buildings. But this does not capture the full extent to which film noir contested the emergence and consolidation of the Cold War consensus. As we have seen, the emphasis in film noir on stylistic innovation fostered a gaze that hovered over the surface of the image. For this reason, it inadvertently affirmed the practices and modes of identity gay men had created in response to their oppression. In privileging surface over depth, film noir encouraged what I have called "camp" modes of spectatorship. It is no coincidence that Susan Sontag in her famous essay "Notes on Camp" identified one of the earliest and most influential examples of film noir, *The Maltese Falcon* (John Huston, 1941), as the greatest camp movie ever made.[41] The gay male spectator's tendency to allow himself to become distracted by elements of the diegesis that were peripheral to the film's plot short-circuited Hollywood's role in the consolidation and perpetuation of the dominant modes of heterosexual subjectivity.

Laura *and the Heterosexualization of Consumer Desire*

In claiming that film noir encouraged a mode of spectatorship that indirectly affirmed gay male identity, I do not mean to exaggerate its emancipatory potential. As I suggested in chapter 1, film noir tended to undercut its oppositional content by promoting a politics of nostalgia. In contesting the postwar shift from production to consumption, it expressed a desire to recover the form of male identity embodied by the entrepreneurial spirit. This aspect of film noir is particularly pronounced in *Laura*. Where *Laura* is undeniably homophobic is in its identification of Lydecker with the lure of the commodity. Lydecker embodies the feminization of male subjectivity that many postwar writers worried the reorganization of the economy would bring about. In an obvious reference to his homosexuality, the original script described Lydecker's apartment as "too exquisite for a man."[42] Although the description was later cut from the script at the request of the Breen office because it violated the Production Code's prohibition of the explicit treatment of homosexuality, we are clearly meant to think that Lydecker's apartment *is* too exquisite for a man. In the opening sequence, the camera pans the apartment, lingering over the exquisite furnishings and priceless objets d'art Lydecker has accumulated. In this way, it links Lydecker visually to the commodity form. He emerges as an example of the way in which the penetration of male subjectivity by the commodity form supposedly threatened to feminize it. His lavishly furnished apartment serves as evidence of the feminine position he occupies in relation to commodity culture.

The film further emphasizes the threat the postwar shift from production to consumption allegedly posed to male heterosexual subjectivity by establishing a contrast between Lydecker and the hard-boiled detective Mark McPherson that is rooted in their different ways of relating to the world of commodities. Unlike Lydecker, Mark occupies a masculine position in relation to commodity culture. He has not yet succumbed to the lure of the commodity and thus has retained his masculinity. Until he becomes obsessed with Laura's portrait, the only commodity on which we see him fix his gaze is a pocket baseball game. Unlike Lydecker, Mark is not easily distracted by appearances. Whereas Lydecker accumulates commodities primarily on the basis of their symbolic capital, Mark does so on the basis of their ability to satisfy more basic needs. At one point in the film, when Lydecker asks him to stop "dawdling" with the baseball game because "it's getting on my nerves," Mark replies, "Yes, I know, but it keeps me calm." Mark also differs from Lydecker in that he does not enjoy engaging in the sort of looking promoted by consumer capitalism. For Mark, shopping is a specifically feminine activity centered on the domestic sphere. When Lydecker asks him if he has ever fallen in love with a woman "who wasn't a doll or a dame," Mark explains that he once almost got married to a woman in Queens but "she kept walking me past furniture stores to look at parlor suites." Mark is immune, in other words, to the sort of domestic reverie the commodity form was supposed to induce in postwar consumers, male and female alike. He does not allow himself to become distracted by the thrill of display. Indeed, the solicitation of his gaze by the display of commodities suppresses rather than incites his desire to settle down and get married.

The film establishes Mark's ability to resist the lure of the commodity in the opening sequence of shots. We see Lydecker looking at himself in the mirror as he finishes arranging his tie. As he admires himself, he says, "McPherson, if you know anything about faces look at mine. How singularly innocent I look this morning. Have you ever seen such candid eyes?" The camera then cuts to a close-up of the pocket baseball game, emphatically registering Mark's refusal to look at Lydecker's face: His gaze remains steadfastly fixed on the baseball game. The shot is clearly meant to reassure spectators that Mark is heterosexual, despite his potentially incriminating presence in a gay man's bathroom. Mark does not allow his gaze to become distracted by the exhibitionistic display of Lydecker's body. Indeed, when Lydecker emerges from the bathtub, the camera cuts to a shot of Mark in which he is shown smiling contemptuously at Lydecker's underdeveloped body. Lydecker's exhibitionistic display cannot compensate for his bodily insufficiency, or lack, in relation to masculinity. Although in directly soliciting Mark's gaze, Lydecker tries to divert attention from his guilt and focus it on his homosexuality, Mark does not succumb to the ploy but remains fixated on the baseball game, a reassuringly masculine activity. Despite the effect it is obviously meant to have, however, the shot of the baseball game raises more questions than it answers. We know from what he tells Lydecker that Mark plays with the game only when he needs to calm his nerves. Thus the shot indicates that he has not been wholly able to resist Lydecker's exhibitionistic display. He avoids looking at the gay man's face because he is afraid that he might succumb to its lure.

This is not to suggest, however, that Mark's susceptibility to the exhibitionistic display of Lydecker's body is an indication that he is "really" homosexual. Mark's struggle to resist Lydecker's solicitation of his gaze serves to emphasize the threat posed by the commodity form. Lydecker embodies the dangers of consumer desire, as many men experienced them in the Cold War era. Even a hard-boiled detective like Mark must struggle to resist the lure of the commodity, which threatens to divert his attention from traditional masculine activities such as baseball. As I mentioned earlier, exhibitionistic display was an integral part of the merchandising and advertising of commodities. Department stores relied on bold visual display to solicit the consumer's gaze and to promote desire for their merchandise.[43] Commodities were arranged in such a way as to seduce the shopper into making a purchase. The primary purpose of merchandising was to deliver a minimum of use-value, disguised and staged by a maximum of seductive illusion. Looking and buying became increasingly linked through the exhibitionistic display of commodities. This linkage helps to clarify the function of Lydecker's association with visual excess in the film. Lydecker embodies the seductive power of the commodity form. His lavishly furnished apartment and elegant wardrobe function as a form of merchandising. They solicit the gaze and promote desire for his body by diverting attention from its semiotic deficiency in relation to the conventional signs of masculinity. Thus the exhibitionistic display of his body and his possessions threatens to transform Mark not into a homosexual but into a consumer by inducing in him what Walter Benjamin called the "dream-sleep" of consumer capitalism.[44] Mark increasingly engages in the sort of looking on which the postwar reorganization of the economy depended.

The consumerization of Mark's gaze is perhaps most obvious in his fetishistic relation to Laura's portrait. Following the flashback in which Lydecker describes Laura's rise in the advertising world, Mark becomes increasingly obsessed with Laura and places a bid on her portrait, indicating that he has finally succumbed to consumer desire. Lydecker's construction of Laura as a beautiful, sexually desirable woman is clearly designed to seduce Mark. His reconstruction of her transformation into a glamorous advertising executive positions Laura as a sort of trademark that, like his lavishly furnished apartment, is meant to transfix Mark's gaze. Lydecker takes full credit for Laura's rise in the advertising world. He tells Mark that he secured clients for her and that he even taught her what clothes to wear. His descriptions, in other words, are intended to focus attention on himself rather than on her; they provide evidence of *his* sophistication and taste and not hers. He tells Mark, "Wherever we went she stood out. Men admired her, women envied her. She became as well-known as Waldo Lydecker's walking stick and his white carnation," objects the film identifies as his trademarks. W. F. Haug defines the trademark as a "second skin" that triangulates the relationship between the consumer and the commodity.[45] The trademark is designed to increase the consumer's identification with a particular product by appearing to address her/him personally. It casts "amorous glances" at the consumer, seducing her/him with the promise of satisfying her/his needs and desires.[46] We can use Haug's analysis to clarify the function of Lydecker's flashback. The sexually promiscuous Laura of the flashback is meant to triangulate the relationship between Lydecker and Mark. Like a trademark, she solicits Mark's gaze, casting "amorous glances" at him that promise to satisfy his needs and desires. In this way, she compensates for Lydecker's insufficiently masculine body, underwriting his authority as an arbiter of taste and fashion.

The penetration of Mark's subjectivity by the commodity form manifests itself primarily in his fetishistic relation to Laura's portrait. As I noted above, before the flashback he is relatively immune to the thrill of display. In the scene in which he visits the apartment with Lydecker and Shelby (Vincent Price), when Lydecker directs his gaze to Laura's portrait, he barely glances at it, simply remarking in typical hard-boiled fashion, "Not bad." Following the flashback, however, he occupies an increasingly feminine position in relation to the commodity form. Laura's portrait threatens to displace the pocket baseball game as the primary object of his gaze. The consumerization of Mark's gaze first becomes apparent in the sequence of shots immediately preceding Laura's return. His desire for Laura becomes displaced onto her personal belongings. We see him enter her bedroom and remove one of her handkerchiefs from her dresser drawer. He then picks up a bottle of her perfume and sniffs it. Finally, he examines some of the clothes in her closet before returning to her portrait, which he stares at longingly before falling into a deep sleep.

This sequence has usually been interpreted as evidence of the fetishistic structure of Mark's desire for Laura. To be sure, Mark's examination of Laura's personal belongings recalls the sort of fetishistic scopophilia that feminist film critics, following Laura Mulvey, have claimed underlies the organization of the look in classical Hollywood cinema. The fragmentation and dispersal of Laura's body in objects that are intimately associated with her reassures Mark of the totality and coherence of his own body, and thus he can return her look without fear of castration. It seems to me, however, that Mark's examination of Laura's personal belongings can also be seen as a form of commodity fetishism. The sort of looking he engages in has more in common with window-shopping than with cinematic spectatorship, as it has been defined by Lacanian film theory. His actions seem motivated less by a drive to achieve a fetishistic distance from Laura's image—after all, he places a bid on her portrait, indicating a desire to bridge the distance between him and her image—than by a desire to possess her personal belongings. They are tokens of her rise in the advertising world and thus promise to provide him with access to the world of commodities.

Mark's seduction by the commodity form threatens to transform him from a hard-boiled detective into an "organization man." As I indicated in the introduction, the rise of the "organization man" facilitated the transition to a Fordist regime of capital accumulation by promoting the consumption of durable goods such as refrigerators, televisions, and automobiles. Although in accordance with the postwar shift from production to consumption men were encouraged to define themselves as consumers rather than as producers, their fantasies of consumption were supposed to remain contained within the domestic sphere and to revolve around their roles as breadwinners and homeowners. For this reason, many spectators would have seen the sort of consumption Lydecker engages in as transgressive and as another indication that he is homosexual. As we have seen, Lydecker does not accumulate durable goods but luxury items that function purely as objects of visual pleasure. By contrast, the sort of consumption Mark increasingly fantasizes about centers on the domestic sphere and thus conforms to the Fordist organization of production and consumption. When Lydecker finds him in Laura's apartment reading her diary, he asks him sarcastically, "Have you ever dreamed of Laura as your wife by your side at the policeman's ball, or in the bleachers, or listening to the heroic story of how you got a silver shinbone from a gun battle with a gangster?" It is clear from Mark's reaction—he plays with the baseball game, indicating that he needs to calm his nerves—that he has indeed dreamed of such things. Foreshadowing Mark's transformation into an "organization man," this scene shows how, in expressing a desire to recover an outmoded form of male identity, the film tended to undercut its critique of commodity culture. The film tapped the male spectator's anger and frustration in ways that diverted them from the new economic order and redirected them toward women. For many male spectators, Mark's fantasies about settling down with Laura would have been a sign of his co-optation. After all, the more he desires Laura, the more he fantasizes about becoming a bread-winner and a homeowner. Although in tracing the gradual penetration of Mark's subjectivity by the commodity form the film gave expression to the male spectator's disaffection from the dominant order, it managed and contained that disaffection by tracing it to women's increasing influence over the domestic sphere.

The link in the film between the lure of the commodity and homosexual seduction was clearly intended to discourage gay male forms of spectator-ship. Mark's fetishistic relation to Laura's portrait reproduces the cult of the star and functions as a sign of the homosexualization of his gaze. As I mentioned earlier, the star's presence was supposed to reinforce the specta-tor's absorption in the diegesis by mobilizing her/his investment in a par-ticular ego ideal. But it actually hindered the spectator's perceptual place-ment within the film's narrative space by focusing attention on the star's personality rather than on the characters s/he played. Gay men were par-ticularly susceptible to the mode of spectatorship fostered by the cult of the star because of its association with camp. Mark's increasing obsession with Laura's portrait follows a pattern similar to the one I have been describing. As we have seen, he allows the portrait to divert his attention from the case. Although, as a detective, it is his responsibility to construct a coherent narrative from the events leading up to the murder, he becomes increas-ingly distracted by his obsession with Laura. In this way, the film sought to limit the impact of its lush visual style. Such a style fostered the sort of looking in which Mark increasingly engages. By encouraging the spectator to become distracted by elements of the diegesis that were peripheral to the plot, the film inadvertently promoted a homosexualization of her/his gaze that made her/him more susceptible to the lure of the commodity. That is, the film enacted the very threat to male subjectivity it was intended to dispel.

The film's attempt to discourage gay male forms of spectatorship undermined what was arguably the most progressive aspect of its critique of postwar consumer culture. Although the film affirmed gay male practices of consumption at the level of form, it disavowed them at the level of content. The film's anxiety about the mode of spectatorship its textual practices promoted surfaces most fully in its emphasis on Lydecker's voyeuristic relation to Laura, a relation that is meant to exemplify the "unnatural" gaze promoted by the Fordist organization of production and consumption. A number of critics have noted how the film divides the two different ways of looking mobilized by the cinematic apparatus (fetishistic scopophilia and voyeurism) between Mark and Lydecker.[47] Whereas Mark's way of looking at Laura is fetishistic, Lydecker's is voyeuristic. During the flashback, Lydecker recalls how he stood outside Laura's apartment and watched her and the painter Jacoby while they had drinks. He also recalls how he followed Laura and Shelby to a restaurant, where he eavesdropped on their conversation as they danced and flirted. Lydecker's voyeuristic relation to Laura enables him to satisfy his desire for her lovers indirectly. He constantly projects his own desire onto Laura. In one scene, he accuses her: "Laura, you have one tragic weakness. With you, a lean, strong body is the measure of a man." In another, he admonishes her: "If McPherson weren't muscular and handsome in a cheap sort of way, you'd see through him in a minute." In emphasizing Lydecker's inability to achieve a fetishistic distance from Laura, a distance that would heterosexualize his gaze by preventing him from identifying with her, the film seeks to immobilize the ambulatory gaze fostered by its lush visual style. The voyeuristic structure of Lydecker's gaze implies that the sort of looking on which postwar consumer culture depended threatens to result in a homosexualization of spectatorial pleasure. Lydecker's mode of spectatorship reverses the relations of looking that traditionally governed the production of sexual difference. His voyeuristic relation to Laura reduces the straight male body to an object of visual pleasure, thereby feminizing it. In seeking to repudiate its textual practices in this way, the film acceded to the dominance of the classical system and its subordination of spectacle to narrative.

But the film undercuts its emancipatory potential primarily by having Laura return. In an influential reading of the film, Kristin Thompson suggests that Laura's return may be only a dream.[48] She examines a number of films made in the forties in which a series of apparently real events turns out to be a dream and concludes that the sequence of shots preceding Laura's return conforms to the set of conventions developed by the film industry for signaling that a character is dreaming. Thompson is primarily interested in clarifying the way in which the film deviates from the classical paradigm. According to her, the film's use of these conventions prevents it from achieving narrative closure. Although Mark's dream creates a gap in our knowledge and thus is consistent with the conventions of the detective genre, it is not sufficiently motivated by the plot and undermines the film's narrative coherence: We never know for certain if Laura has returned or if Mark has merely dreamed that she has. To be sure, the sequence of shots immediately preceding Laura's return conforms to the set of conventions Thompson meticulously reconstructs. As Mark begins to fall asleep in a chair facing Laura's portrait, the camera tracks in, pauses briefly, then tracks away again. We hear a door close offscreen, and the camera cuts to a shot in which we see Laura standing in front of the door about to put her suitcase down.

Despite the way in which it carefully marshals the evidence, however, Thompson's reading is not wholly convincing. It does not adequately consider the film's desire to contain the potentially subversive effects of its visual economy, a desire that in many respects requires Laura's return. The unmotivated movement of the camera can also be interpreted as an indication that Mark has abandoned himself to the sort of reverie, or dream-sleep, that the commodity typically induces in the consumer. He dreams not that Laura has returned but that he has become a part of her world, a world wholly penetrated by the commodity form. The scene is preceded by the sequence of shots discussed above in which we see Mark wistfully examine Laura's personal belongings. From this perspective, Laura's return seems wholly consistent with the film's narrative trajectory. It breaks the spell the commodity form has cast on Mark, thereby paving the way for the re-heterosexualization of his gaze. The Laura who returns appears more desirable than the glamorous advertising executive Lydecker describes in the flashback. She turns out to be the type of woman Mark has fantasized about settling down with. Despite her glamorous image, she would not hesitate to accompany him to the policeman's ball or to sit beside him in the bleachers at a baseball game. The plain blouse and skirt she wears in this scene serve to underscore the discrepancy between her and her image: They contrast markedly with the elegant wardrobe of the flashback and portrait. Thus her return promises to counteract the consumerization of Mark's gaze by making it less susceptible to distraction by the thrill of display. The differences between her and her image expose Lydecker's flashback as a seductive illusion designed to transfix Mark's gaze. Her return guarantees that Mark will no longer become diverted by her image but will remain fixated on her.

Contrary to Thompson's claim, then, Laura's return does seem sufficiently motivated by the plot. Insofar as it paves the way for Mark's rehabilitation as a consumer, it is wholly consistent with the film's narrative trajectory. Where Laura's return does not seem wholly consistent with the film's narrative trajectory is in the way in which it tacitly endorses the modes of consumption the Fordist organization of production and consumption not only promoted but depended upon. As I suggested above, Lydecker engages in a subversive mode of consumption that conflicts with the reorganization of the economy along Fordist lines. His fantasies of consumption do not revolve around the sort of commodities (washing machines, refrigerators, and so on) whose production and consumption spurred the economic recovery of the postwar period. Rather, he is easily distracted by the thrill of display and buys commodities solely on the basis of their appeal to the eye. Despite its potential to disrupt the reorganization of the economy, however, the film disavows this potentially subversive mode of consumption by having Laura's return reheterosexualize Mark's gaze. The implication is that as Laura's husband Mark will no longer resist engaging in the sort of looking in store windows he disparaged earlier in the film. In this way, the film sought to manage and contain the spectator's relation to the newly emergent consumer culture. Laura's return insures that Mark's gaze will remain fixated on the domestic sphere.

The film further endorses the mode of consumption promoted by the reorganization of the economy by using Laura's return to reclaim her from the world of advertising. As an advertising executive, Laura occupies a privileged position in relation to the commodity form. Her advertising campaigns are designed to promote the consumer's desire for specific products by eroticizing her/his relation to them. In all of the examples of her work we are shown in the film, glamorous female models display their bodies seductively. She engages for a living, in other words, in the sort of seductive illusion that is the object of the film's critique of consumer capitalism. As an advertising executive, she contributes to the commodity's seductive power, which is why the film eventually seeks to return her to the domestic sphere. Still, her experience as an advertising executive has taught her how to negotiate the duplicitous world of the commodity. Her lavishly furnished apartment and glamorous wardrobe are evidence of her discriminating taste. She has clearly learned how to increase her exchange-value through the exhibitionistic display of her body. For this reason, the film does not wholly disavow her mode of consumption, despite its similarity to Lydecker's. After all, as a woman, she is supposed to occupy a feminine position in relation to commodity culture. Although her glamorous wardrobe functions as a form of merchandising that is meant to transfix the male gaze, it helps to promote the circulation of her body and thus is fully consistent with her status as a commodity.

Despite the way in which it increases her exchange-value, however, Laura's mode of consumption is a sign that she is overly susceptible to consumer desire, and thus the film does not wholly endorse it. Because she does not adequately control the circulation of her body, Laura threatens to disrupt the postwar reorganization of masculinity. Her exhibitionistic display is a sign of her refusal to restrict her sexuality to the domestic sphere. This helps to explain the link in the film between her and Diane Redfern, the model who is mistakenly identified as Laura when she is found dead in Laura's apartment wearing Laura's robe. The mutilation of Diane's face serves as a warning about the commodification of the female body promoted by the advertising industry. Although we are never shown the police photograph of Diane's mutilated body, the film implicitly contrasts it with the advertisement that Laura shows Mark when she discovers one of Diane's dresses in her closet and realizes that it must have been Diane who was murdered. In the advertisement, Diane solicits the consumer's gaze by displaying her body seductively. By contrast, the police photograph supposedly shows her as she really was, a sexually promiscuous woman who was engaged in an assignation with Shelby, Laura's fiancé, when Lydecker mistook her for Laura and killed her. When Lydecker asks Mark why the police had to photograph her in "that horrible condition," Mark replies, "When a dame gets killed, she doesn't worry about how she looks." The police photograph, in other words, "corrects" the image of Diane circulated by the advertising industry, reversing the commodification of her body. Diane was not a "lady" but a "dame" whose glamorous image was nothing but a seductive illusion that diverted attention from her sexual promiscuity. In this way, the film discouraged modes of female consumption that were not centered on the domestic sphere. Laura's susceptibility to the lure of the commodity undermines her ability to control the circulation of her body, and thus she threatens to end up like Diane.

Laura's susceptibility to the lure of the commodity manifests itself primarily in the type of man to whom she is attracted. Her knowledge of consumer culture does not sufficiently protect her from the commodity's empty promise to satisfy her needs and desires. She becomes involved with men whose lean, strong bodies function as a form of merchandising. Their muscular builds are meant to conceal a deficiency in relation to masculinity by distracting her gaze and focusing it on their bodies. Shelby, for example, who is described by Lydecker as a "male beauty in distress," occupies an insufficiently masculine position in the film's gender hierarchy. He willingly functions as an object of visual pleasure, boldly exposing his body to the female gaze. He has never worked for a living and constantly borrows money from Anne Treadwell (Judith Anderson), who has been seduced by his lean, strong body and is willing to support his lavish lifestyle. Despite his tendency to perform masculinity to excess, or perhaps even because of it, Laura allows her gaze to become transfixed by him. Shelby resembles Lydecker in that he tries to divert attention from his deficient relation to masculinity by engaging in the exhibitionistic display of his body. His muscular build is designed to signify masculinity, but like a trademark, or "second skin," it promises more use-value than it can deliver. Deceived by his body's semiotic excess, Laura gives him a job in her advertising firm, thereby consolidating his feminine position in relation to her. Thus in having Laura return, the film not only reclaims Mark by reversing the consumerization of his gaze but contains Laura's sexuality within the domestic sphere, where she will no longer threaten to disrupt the postwar reorganization of masculinity. Unlike Shelby's, Mark's muscular body does not promise more use-value than it can deliver, and thus it can fully satisfy her needs and desires.

In order to clarify the relationship between Fordism and homophobia, I have tried to show that the film undercut its emancipatory potential by tacitly endorsing a mode of consumption that was compatible with rather than disruptive of the reorganization of the economy. We have seen that the film's textual practices legitimated gay male camp as a form of spectatorship. We have also seen that its desire to tap the frustration and resentment that the rise of the "organization man" provoked in many men led it to disavow its textual practices. To prevent its visual economy from homosexualizing the spectator's gaze, the film ultimately acceded to the dominance of the classical system, reinstating the hierarchical relation between narrative and spectacle. For this reason, the film can be used to elucidate the way in which mass consumption functioned throughout the Cold War era as a disciplinary technology, insuring that men consented to the reorganization of masculinity, despite their anger and resentment. The association in the film between the lure of the commodity and the gay male body inadvertently underwrote the emergence of Fordism by encouraging a mode of consumption that was centered on the domestic sphere. In depicting his lavishly furnished apartment and elegant wardrobe as a sign that he has forfeited his claims to masculinity, the film repudiated Lydecker's mode of consumption, despite the liberatory possibilities it opened up. Thus the film exposes the extent to which the consolidation of Fordism depended upon homophobia as a mechanism for regulating consumer desire. The identification of various modes of consumption not only with masculinity and femininity but also with heterosexuality and homosexuality worked to bring the desire of male and female consumers alike into alignment with Fordism's needs and aims. The film's disavowal of its own visual economy, a visual economy that legitimated gay male forms of identity, helped to make certain that the male spectator's gaze remained fixated on the sort of commodities whose production and consumption underlay the emergence of Fordism.

CHAPTER THREE

"Real American History": Crossfire and the Increasing Invisibility of Gay Men in the Cold War Era

Monty was strongly American. Frenchmen were Frogs; Negroes, niggers;
Poles, Polacks; Italians, wops; Chinese, Chinks; Jews, Christ-killers.
—*The Brick Foxhole*

That's history, Leroy. They don't teach it in schools,
but it's real American history just the same.
—Finlay in *Crossfire*

When she was interviewed by Rudy Behlmer in the early 1980s for his
"behind-the-scenes-look" at the making of *Laura,* Vera Caspary, the author
of the bestselling novel on which the film was based, recalled her disappointment with its treatment of Lydecker. According to her, the film did not
adequately convey Lydecker's "impotence and destructiveness," which she
considered one of the novel's major themes; rather, it allowed his wit and
sophistication partially to redeem him.[1] In light of our examination of the
film in the previous chapter, Caspary's criticisms of the film will hardly
seem surprising. As we saw there, the film's treatment of Lydecker was
deeply ambivalent, simultaneously affirming and contesting the stereotype
of the effeminate homosexual. By contrast, Caspary's treatment of Lydecker
strictly adhered to the conventions governing the representation of homosexuality. Not only are his "impotence and destructiveness" directly related
to his homosexuality, but his charm cannot counteract them. Nowhere are

the differences between the novel and the film more apparent than in the novel's association of Lydecker's homosexuality with bodily corruption. Lydecker's corpulent body functions as a sign of his sexual perversity. We first become aware that he is homosexual when Mark interviews him about the murder and pointedly asks him: "You like a man better if he's not hundred per cent, don't you, Mr. Lydecker?"[2] Lydecker's elegant wardrobe and acerbic wit are unable to divert Mark's attention from his homosexuality, which is inscribed on his body. After Mark interviews him, Lydecker provides the most accurate description of himself in the novel. Mark's athletic build and hard-boiled manner make him feel insufficiently masculine, and he reluctantly admits that his sophistication and charm are an illusion intended to deceive others: "Upon that Sunday noon I saw myself a fat, fussy, and useless male of middle age and doubtful charm" (21). Unlike the Lydecker of the film, in other words, the Lydecker of the novel is beyond redemption.

In her interview with Behlmer, Caspary limited her criticisms of the film to its treatment of Lydecker, but it is difficult to believe that she was not also disappointed by the way in which the film emptied her novel of its feminist content, marginalizing Laura's struggles as a professional woman and focusing instead on Mark's relationship with Lydecker. Despite the fact that Caspary did not hesitate to legitimate the dominant construction of homosexuality, she was known in Hollywood as a progressive writer with strong ties to the Left. A member of the Communist party and the League of American Writers, she was afraid that she might be subpoenaed to appear before the House Un-American Activities Committee when it began investigating Communist infiltration of the film industry, and so she emigrated to Europe in the early 1950s.[3] Her involvement in the Communist party manifested itself primarily in her tendency to focus in her work on the "woman question." But whereas the Communist party sought primarily to show that women constituted a reserve labor army and that they faced exploitation at home as well as at work, Caspary focused on misogynistic practices that were irreducible to the capitalist relations of production.[4] Her version of *Laura* examines the sexual policing to which even the upperclass female body was subject. Although Laura's wealth and glamor shelter her from the most exploitative forms of labor, she is unwilling to restrict her sexuality to the domestic sphere, and thus becomes the target of misogynistic constructions of female sexuality.

Caspary's desire to broaden the "woman question" to include structures of oppression that did not fit the base/superstructure model that dominated Marxist thought in the thirties and forties is perhaps most apparent in her emphasis on the lack of categories available for describing Laura. Laura is a sexually desirable woman who does not conform to the stereotype of the career woman, usually understood derogatorily as either a lesbian or an old maid, and thus she is thought to pose a threat to the dominant order. She has achieved the American dream of upward mobility through a combination of hard work, perseverance, and talent. But rather than a source of admiration or inspiration for other women, her success as an advertising executive renders her an object of suspicion, exposing her to the disciplinary machinery of public scandal. The public does not understand why a woman of her beauty and glamor would prefer a career over marriage and assumes that it is because she is unwilling to restrict her sexuality to the domestic sphere. When a woman is found dead in her apartment clad in nothing but a silk robe, the newspapers are quick to exploit the sensationalistic aspects of the case: "By the necromancy of modern journalism, a gracious young woman had been transformed into a dangerous siren who practiced her wiles in the fascinating neighborhood where Park Avenue meets Bohemia. Her generous way of life had become an uninterrupted orgy of drunkeness, lust, and deceit, as titivating [sic] to the masses as it was profitable to the publishers" (34). The difficulty of understanding Laura in terms of the available categories surfaces most fully in Mark's tendency to call her a "doll" and a "dame," even though he has seen her apartment, read her diary, and knows that she does not remotely resemble the stereotype of the sexually promiscuous woman. Laura's defiance of middle-class conventions links her to the gangster molls he has encountered as a detective, and thus he is unable to think of her in any other terms. When Lydecker insists that "she was not the sort of woman you call a dame" (37), Mark replies: "She had a lot of men in love with her, didn't she?" (41). Lydecker provides perhaps the most accurate description of Laura when he calls her a "complicated, cultivated modern woman" (17), but even this description does not wholly capture her complexity.

Caspary's interest in forms of alienation and exploitation not ordinarily addressed by the Communist party did not preclude her from examining the "woman question" from a more orthodox Marxist perspective.[5] Whereas in the film Laura and Diane Redfern are linked through their sexual promiscuity, which threatens male heterosexual privilege, in the novel they are linked through their vulnerability to patriarchal oppression. Although Laura's accumulation of cultural capital protects her from economic exploitation, her position in society does not differ significantly from Diane's. Diane longs to overcome her working-class immigrant background, even if doing so requires cutting her ties to her family. Born Jennie Swobodo, she has left her family behind in Paterson, New Jersey, an industrial city famous for the militancy of its labor unions, to seek a more exciting and glamorous life in New York City. In searching her apartment for clues to her murder, Mark finds stacks of movie magazines in which she has marked various passages: "You could tell that Diane had dreamed of Hollywood. Less beautiful girls had become stars, married stars, and owned swimming pools" (140–41). Diane pursues a career as a model in order to experience vicariously the glamorous lifestyle she aspires to but cannot afford. She covers the walls of her dingy apartment with "proofs and glossy prints of [herself] at work; Diane Redfern in Fifth Avenue furs; Diane at the opera; Diane pouring coffee from a silver pot; Diane in a satin nightgown with a satin quilt falling off the chaise-lounge in a way that showed a pretty leg" (141). In light of her dreams of Hollywood stardom, the categories *doll* and *dame* seem more applicable to her than to Laura, whose fantasies of consumption conform to her status as a middle-class professional. Diane's appearance in advertisements designed to promote the products of consumer capitalism functions as a sign of the alienation of her labor. Her career as a model cannot compensate for her lack of cultural capital. The shabbiness of her apartment leads Mark to conclude that she must have been "hurt by the contrast between those sleek studio interiors and the second-hand furniture of the boarding-house; between the silky models who posed with her and the poor slobs she met on the mouldy staircase" (141).

In emphasizing Diane's working-class immigrant background, Caspary indirectly challenged the tendency of writers and artists affiliated with the Communist party to treat class and ethnicity as the most important markers of identity. Despite the differences in their backgrounds and aspirations, Laura readily identifies with Diane. When Diane applies for a job with her advertising agency, Laura is immediately drawn to her because she can tell that she wants "something better than she'd had at home. Her life had been terribly sordid. Even her name, silly as it sounded, showed that she wanted a better sort of life" (130). Although Diane's desires and aspirations have been shaped by mass culture, Laura realizes that as women they have certain interests in common. When Mark asks her why she continued to allow Diane to work for her after it became clear that she was having an affair with her fiancé, Shelby, Laura explains: "I'm not so different. I came to New York, too, a poor kid without friends and money. People were kind to me . . . and I felt almost an obligation toward kids like Diane" (130). But Laura has more in common with Diane than a desire to achieve upward mobility. Despite her accumulated cultural capital, she proves just as susceptible to the seductions of mass culture as Diane. Like Diane, she succumbs to Shelby's glamorous image, even though it is an illusion designed to deceive her. When Mark first meets Shelby, he thinks that he has seen him before, but he soon realizes that it is simply that Shelby conforms to the image of masculinity circulated by commodity culture: "the young men who drove Packards and wore Arrow shirts, smoked Chesterfields, and paid their insurance premiums and clipped coupons were Shelby" (142). Shelby's adherence to a mass-mediated image of masculinity explains why he can so easily manipulate Laura and Diane sexually. For them, he is "a dream walking" (142); they see him as "God's gift to women" (142). In this way, the novel tries to show that gender is a more important determinant of women's identity and experience than class or ethnicity. That both Laura and Diane can see in Shelby "a dream walking" only serves to underscore the potential of mass culture to undermine women's professional ambitions by instilling in them fantasies and desires that accord with the needs and aims of consumer capitalism.

The film version of *Laura,* then, not only suppressed the feminist content of Caspary's novel, shifting attention away from Laura's struggles as a professional woman; it also recuperated the novel's critique of commodity culture for a masculinist agenda. As I was at pains to show in the previous chapter, the film version of *Laura* tapped the male spectator's anger and frustration with the new corporate order in ways that rechanneled them toward women and gay men. By contrast, Caspary's novel provided a more nuanced critique of consumer capitalism, one that stressed the complexity of its impact on women. In focusing on misogynistic structures that could not be understood in terms of orthodox Marxist categories, Caspary's novel broadened the "woman question" to include the construction of female subjectivity in relation to historically specific discourses, institutions, and practices. Its examination of women's fraught relation to commodity culture, a relation that was at once liberatory and oppressive, provided a potentially more progressive critique of consumer capitalism than did the film. Laura's susceptibility to mass-produced fantasies of masculinity underscored the potential of commodity culture to instill in women fantasies and desires that virtually guaranteed the reproduction of the dominant constructions of masculinity and femininity at the level of their subjectivity. At the same time, commodity culture provides Laura with a vehicle for realizing the American dream. Caspary's critique of consumer capitalism did not prevent her from acknowledging that advertising was one of the few industries in which women could pursue potentially rewarding careers.

I have been focusing on the differences between Caspary's novel and the film version of *Laura* because in this chapter I want to clarify a tendency overlooked by scholars interested in the relation between film noir and the hard-boiled detective fiction that inspired it.[6] In suppressing the most progressive aspects of the novel, the film version of *Laura* was not unique but exemplary of film noir. As I have already noted, left-wing directors and screenwriters approached film noir as a cinematic practice that was especially conducive to their political aims in that it enabled them to circumvent the Production Code. But it was not unusual for them to suppress the most progressive aspects of the hard-boiled detective fiction from which they adapted their films. I want to clarify this aspect of film noir by examining the relation between *Crossfire* (1947) and the novel on which it was based, Richard Brooks's *The Brick Foxhole* (1945). Despite its potentially controversial topic (anti-Semitism), low production values, and relatively unknown cast at the time of its release, *Crossfire* was one of the most popular films of the 1940s. It is particularly useful for the purposes of my argument because it was more explicitly political than most films noirs. Produced by Adrian Scott and directed by Edward Dmytryk, both of whom were part of the Hollywood Ten, the group of directors and screenwriters convicted of contempt of Congress for refusing to name names when they testified before the House Un-American Activities Committee in 1947, *Crossfire* is best understood as part social-problem film, part film noir.[7] Both Scott and Dmytryk, who had worked together on *Murder, My Sweet* (1944), one of the earliest examples of film noir, were eager to make a film about anti-Semitism.[8] They realized that support for the New Deal was eroding, and they worried that a fascist movement might emerge. According to John Paxton, who wrote the script for the film, they decided to follow the same formula they had used in *Murder, My Sweet* because they thought that "the tension and menace [it] created would provide the most interesting and acceptable mode of treatment for the theme."[9] They assumed, in other words, that adhering to the conventions of film noir would allow them to examine the anti-Semitic structures of American society without appearing to engage in propaganda.

But *Crossfire* is also useful for the purposes of my argument because it provides a concrete example of the way in which gay men were expelled from the realm of representation in the Cold War era. *The Brick Foxhole* concerns a soldier who brutally rapes and murders a gay interior decorator while on leave. Although the novel addresses the issue of anti-Semitism (the soldier's contempt for gay men is matched only by his contempt for Jews and other minoritized groups), it is not its primary focus. Rather, the novel explored the way in which the military simultaneously encouraged and prohibited homoerotic male bonding. I will argue that, in suppressing the theme of homophobia, the film became complicitous with the project undertaken by the national-security state to render gay men invisible. Scott and Dmytryk's refusal to address the issue of homophobia can be traced to the film's partial status as a social-problem film. In the Cold War era, virtually the only way in which homosexuality could become a topic of debate in the political public sphere was as a form of psychopathology that threatened national security. My goal in focusing on the relation between the film and the novel is to elaborate further my argument in the previous chapter concerning the potential of film noir to reverse the increasing invisibility of gay men. I will try to show that, at least with respect to the representation of gay men, film noir should be understood as more progressive than the self-consciously liberal social-problem film of the postwar period, for the desire of the social-problem film to influence national politics set limits not only on what issues it could address but on how it could address them. To be sure, in linking homosexuality to a mode of consumption that threatened to disrupt the reorganization of the economy, films such as *Laura* reinforced homophobic stereotypes. But such films also functioned as an alternative public sphere, compensating gay men for their exclusion from the realm of political representation.

Redefining the "Common Man":
Richard Brooks and the Discourse of Minority Rights

In changing the focus to anti-Semitism, Scott and Dmytryk were not wholly indifferent to the problem of anti-gay violence. Rather, they seem to have misunderstood the novel's political project.[10] Outlining the novel in a memo to William Dozier and Charles Kormer, the heads of RKO, Scott asserted that he and Dmytryk would have little difficulty turning the novel into a story about anti-Semitism: "In the book [the soldier] murders a fairy. He could have murdered a negro, a foreigner or a jew. It would have been the same thing."[11] But in assuming that the homosexuality of Edwards, the interior decorator who is raped and murdered, was less important than his status as a victim, Scott seems to have misunderstood the point of the novel's examination of homophobic violence—which may explain why he did not hesitate to use the term *fairies* but avoided calling Negroes "niggers" or Jews "kikes." Although he was right that the novel tried to show that, like African Americans and Jews, gays were persecuted *as a group,* this does not mean that it treated minoritized groups as interchangeable. The links among them were meant to clarify rather than obscure the incommensurability of their oppression. But, more important, they were also meant to position gay men as bearers of rights. Because they are stigmatized, gay men emerge as an oppressed minority entitled to the same legal protections as other oppressed minorities. Thus, in substituting a Jewish veteran for the gay interior decorator, Scott and Dmytryk overlooked what was arguably the most important aspect of the novel's treatment of minorities. Despite Scott's belief to the contrary, such a substitution profoundly distorted the novel's intentions.

Brooks was not a member of the Communist party or the League of American Writers, but his novel, like Caspary's version of *Laura,* is best understood as a product of the Popular Front, which as I noted in the introduction was briefly revived in Hollywood at the end of World War II.[12] His treatment of minoritized groups was clearly in dialogue with the categories and assumptions that informed the Popular Front agenda. After the formation of the Popular Front in 1935, the category of the "common man" replaced that of the worker as the primary focus of the Communist party's political and rhetorical strategies.[13] As Brooks seems to have realized, however, there were several problems with the new category. To begin with, like the category of "the people," it was highly volatile. Although it had an advantage over the category of the worker in that it had no fixed class content, it was particularly susceptible to recuperation by the Right. McCarthy, for example, through a similar rhetorical strategy, located himself on political terrain occupied by the Left since the thirties. Granted, he never explicitly invoked the category of the "common man," but he reclaimed the authority to speak on her/his behalf—an authority exercised almost exclusively by left-wing writers and artists since the Popular Front era—when he attacked the State Department as made up of an intellectual elite that had not been elected to public office but that nevertheless determined foreign policy.[14]

But there was a more serious problem with the category of the "common man" than its recuperability. For although it was supposedly more generic and universal than the category of the worker, it tended to exclude Americans who were not white, male, and heterosexual. In its lack of specificity, it reproduced the abstract, universalizing logic of American citizenship. Feminist scholars have shown that the framers of the Constitution defined citizenship in such a way as to establish whiteness and maleness as its prerequisites.[15] Considered universal forms of identity, whiteness and maleness were particularly conducive to the bodily abstraction that participation in the political public sphere was thought to require.[16] Women and racial minorities, on the other hand, were burdened with a surplus embodiment that supposedly prevented them from bracketing their interests while debating the common good. Thus they were denied access to the political public sphere. Brooks seems to have understood that the same logic of exclusion governed the category of the "common man," for, by examining the violence directed against the nation's racial and sexual minorities, he exposed the way in which the political and rhetorical strategies of the Popular Front rendered invisible groups that were particularly vulnerable in American society.

Brooks's desire to interrogate Popular Front categories and assumptions is perhaps most apparent in his tendency to position Monty Crawford, the soldier who rapes and murders Edwards, as a representative American, or "common man." Although as with most soldiers in the novel, "liberty, humanity, freedom were merely words" to him, Monty is deeply patriotic and cries maudlinly when the military band plays "God Bless America."[17] Moreover, he is a model soldier who strictly enforces military discipline. He constantly chides the soldiers in his battalion for refusing to follow military rules and regulations. In the mornings when he inspects the barracks, he invariably threatens to report them to Lieutenant Moore: "You didn't learn anything. You're nothing but civilians, the whole damned bunch of you, and you'll never be anything else. You don't even try to act like real soldiers" (77). Indeed, Monty's commitment to the military is so deeply engrained that he "was the kind of soldier . . . who in peacetime would still be a soldier" (30). At first Monty's intolerance of racial and sexual minorities is difficult to reconcile with his patriotism, but as the novel progresses it becomes increasingly apparent that they are mutually reinforcing. The majority of soldiers in the novel are motivated by a desire not to defeat fascism or to make the world safe for democracy but to preserve America's racial purity: "Many of the men who had fought on Eniwetok and Kwajalein and Guadalcanal had peculiar ideas about liberty and freedom which sounded like white supremacy and Protestant justice" (23). Thus their beliefs and attitudes do not differ significantly from those of the Nazis.

This is not to suggest that the novel wholly abandoned the category of the "common man." Rather, it tried to redefine the category by providing in Jeff Mitchell, the protagonist, an alternative example of the national character. Although Jeff does not share Monty's sentimental attachment to America, unlike him, he has internalized its official meaning. He is increasingly alienated by the racial intolerance he encounters in the military. For him, the principles enshrined in the Constitution are not mere abstractions but concrete guides to everyday life. His belief in racial equality alienates the other soldiers in his battalion, who make fun of him because he refuses to call African Americans "niggers." When he tries to explain his position, Floyd Bowers, a soldier from the South, calls him a "nigger lover" (12). The more Jeff defends his beliefs, the more abusive Floyd becomes: "Je-suss, you don't even like to call them niggers. You love niggers. An'you know same as I do that there ain't a good nigger in the world 'less he's dead" (12). Jeff, then, differs from the other soldiers in that he is unwilling to die for the sake of preserving the nation's racial purity. Although when he first enlists he is eager to do his part to help win the war, he becomes increasingly disaffected by the attitudes and beliefs the military fosters: "A long time ago he had felt his job a necessary one. He had felt that his work was contributing to the winning of the war. But not any more. Now he felt the only contribution was killing Japs. That was the work by which you were judged" (20). With the defeat of the Nazis, the war had become a struggle to subdue a racialized Other.

Peter Keely provides a less typical example of the American national character. He functions as the novel's moral center and embodies the nation's utopian promise. Whereas Jeff becomes increasingly cynical, Keely retains his faith in American democracy and is willing to die preserving it. The racial intolerance he encounters in the military convinces him that the greatest threat to American democracy is not Nazi Germany or Japan but bigots like Monty who confuse the nation's founding principles with white supremacy. Determined to expose Monty as Edwards's murderer, he sets a trap for him, luring him to the base's museum where he forces him to admit that he raped and murdered Edwards. In Keely's mind, Monty's beliefs and attitudes are no different from those of the Nazis, and he must die if the nation is to uphold its democratic traditions. Before killing Monty, Keely tells him that "this is the same war people are fighting all over the world, you poor sack. The same war" (224). When Monty tries to reason with him, reminding him that "we're on the same side" (224), Keely responds: "You're the enemy, too. And you've got to die" (225). Keely's willingness at the end of the novel to take the law into his own hands points to a serious inconsistency in the novel's analysis of racial and sexual intolerance. On the one hand, the novel mounts a powerful critique of the racism and homophobia of American society, equating Monty's hatred of racial and sexual minorities with fascism. Brooks appears to have foreseen the rise of McCarthyism. For him, the enemy within was composed not of Communists and homosexuals, who became the target of the McCarthy witch hunts, but of Americans who persecuted the nation's racial and sexual minorities. On the other hand, the novel embraces vigilantism as a solution to the problem of racial and sexual intolerance, thereby betraying the very principles it seeks to defend against the threat of fascism.

Where the novel was more successful in upholding democratic values and ideals was in its examination of the homophobia of the military. Monty and Floyd are simultaneously attracted to and repulsed by Edwards. Although it is clear when they accept a ride from him that they intend to beat him up, it is less clear whether their intentions are rooted in disgust or desire. When Edwards invites Floyd and Monty up to his apartment for drinks, Floyd can barely contain his excitement, which borders on sexual. He nudges Jeff and whispers: "We're set, buddy. Set. I ain't beaten up a queer in I don't know how long" (89). Monty in particular seems attracted to Edwards. His conversation seems designed partly to mimic him, partly to seduce him. Monty is too familiar with the practices of the gay male subculture simply to be leading Edwards on. He fills his conversation with the sort of innuendoes and equivocations gay men were forced to rely on when cruising for sex. When Edwards says that he has a place in the city where they can go for drinks, Monty repeats his words in a sexually suggestive way: "A little place . . . all your own?" (88). Moreover, his comments about women are ambiguous and could easily be interpreted as a sign that he prefers to have sex with men. He complains that women "are a lot of bother. There's always the worry that maybe you're knocking 'em up, too" (87). If he has sex with men, in other words, that is because it is less risky than having sex with women and not because he is homosexual. When the group finally arrives at Edwards's apartment, Monty becomes bolder and forces Edwards to dance with him: "Monty held Eddie too tightly. He made obscene motions with his body and made Eddie giggle" (93). But perhaps the strongest evidence that Monty's contempt for Edwards is rooted in desire is that Edwards's body is found naked, indicating that he was raped.

In suggesting that Monty simultaneously desires and abhors Edwards, the novel sought to provide an explanation for the homophobia of the military. In the military, homoerotic male bonding functions as a disciplinary technology that insures the reproduction of patriarchal values and attitudes at the level of the soldiers' subjectivity. Although Jeff can tell that Edwards is a "fairy" when he first meets him, he thinks that he is a "swell guy" (93) and cannot decide whether to intervene in Monty and Floyd's plan to beat him up. On the one hand, Monty's flirtatious behavior frightens him, and he wonders if he should warn Edwards not to let Monty into his apartment: "There was something about the way Monty was talking that frightened Jeff. Jeff had heard about the pastime of some soldiers. Their treatment of sexual perverts. The way they regarded them" (88). On the other hand, he worries about what Monty and Floyd will think if he does not go along with their plan. He knows how gay men are treated in the military. If he is to prove himself to the other soldiers, he must show that he too reviles gay men. When Edwards asks him to come with them to his apartment, he sets aside his misgivings, telling himself: "You wanted to be a soldier, didn't you? Well, now you're being a soldier" (89). Floyd has already called Jeff a "nigger lover," and Jeff does not want him and Monty to think that he is a "fairy," too.

Monty's attempts to implicate Jeff in the murder render more explicit the disciplinary function of homoerotic male bonding. Monty is unable to accept his desire for Edwards and projects it onto Jeff. When he is questioned by Finlay, the detective who investigates the murder, he tells him that Jeff is "an artist fella" who is "very sensitive and all that kind of stuff" (161), thereby implying that he is a "fairy." But Finlay is troubled by the inconsistencies in Monty's version of the events. When Finlay asks him to repeat his story, Monty answers by exploding: "I don't blame Jeff. It serves Edwards right. They oughta kill every one of them fairies. There ain't a court martial in the world would do anything to Jeff for that" (163). But Monty's attempt to divert attention from himself as a suspect does not work, and Finlay becomes still more suspicious. When Finlay asks him what motive Jeff would have had for killing Edwards, Monty replies: "Well, sometimes a guy is in the barracks for a long time and then he goes out and gets tight . . . and then . . . well . . . along comes a troublemaker like this Edwards and . . . well . . . a sensitive guy like Jeff . . . well . . . I don't know" (164). Here Monty inadvertently provides an explanation for why he raped and murdered Edwards. He has convinced himself that it was not he who violated Edwards, but Edwards who violated him. Not only had he been drinking when Edwards made a pass at him, but he had been confined to the barracks deprived of female companionship. In this way, the novel implies that the military is ultimately responsible for Edwards's death. The only way in which Monty can express his desire for Edwards is through violence. As a model soldier, he does not want to be identified as a "fairy," and so he cannot acknowledge his desire for other men.

It would be difficult to overstate the importance of the novel's exploration of the homophobia of American society, for in extending the discourse of minority rights to gay men, it anticipated by several years *The Homosexual in America* (1951), Donald Webster Corey's pioneering study of the similarities between gay men and other minoritized groups. Inspired by Gunnar Myrdal's influential analysis of race relations, *An American Dilemma* (1944), Corey argued that gay men constituted an oppressed minority and that as such they deserved the same legal protections as African Americans and other historically disenfranchised groups: "Our minority status is similar, in a variety of respects, to that of national, religious and other ethnic groups: in the denial of civil liberties; in the legal, extra-legal and quasi-legal discrimination; in the assignment of an inferior social position; in the exclusion from the mainstream of life and culture."[18] Corey's reliance on Myrdal's book as a model may explain some of the limitations of his approach to gay rights.[19] Although Myrdal acknowledged that racism was deeply engrained in American society, he criticized African Americans for failing to follow the example of immigrant groups and assimilating.[20] According to him, insofar as it discouraged African Americans from overcoming their bonds with the community, African American culture was "pathological." Corey was similarly committed to mainstream American values and ideals. Despite his belief that homosexuals were marginalized by the dominant culture, he refused to interrogate the normative status of heterosexuality. Instead, he asserted that homosexuals did not differ significantly from heterosexuals and could be easily assimilated into American society. Despite the limitations of his argument, however, Corey pioneered the minoritarian model of homosexuality that provided the basis for the postwar gay rights movement.[21]

Foreshadowing Corey's strategy for positioning homosexuals as bearers of rights, the novel tried to show that gay men's position in American society did not differ from that of racial and ethnic minorities, in that they too faced persecution as a group. Monty's single claim to fame is that, before the war when he was a police officer in Chicago, he was imprisoned three times, once for killing a Jewish "petty thief" (29) and twice for killing black suspects. Although each time the circumstances were highly suspicious, the killings "were thoroughly appreciated by the people of Chicago. On each occasion [he] had been released and exonerated as having killed the culprits in the line of duty" (29). This story, which is circulated in the military as an example of Monty's heroism, establishes a connection between gay men and other minoritized groups. Edwards resembles the suspects Monty unjustly killed in Chicago, insofar as his murder is motivated by bigotry. Finlay makes the resemblance explicit when he insists on treating Edwards's murder as a civil rights matter. Monty's attempts to minimize the murder by claiming that Edwards was a "fairy" appall him, and he explodes angrily: "You soldiers get some peculiar ideas. A man has strange sexual habits, so you take it upon yourselves to straighten him out—by murder" (166). Moreover, he is determined that the murderer will be unable to claim that he justifiably killed Edwards. Finlay is well aware of how soldiers treat gay men, and he intends to show that the murderer knew that Edwards was homosexual and thus cannot claim that he was outraged when Edwards made a pass at him: "Edwards takes three soldiers into his home and entertains them. Then when they've had his liquor and messed up his apartment, they kill him and rob him. . . . No uniform gives a man the right to do that" (166). Thus the novel tried to redefine the way in which readers thought of violence against gay men. If treated as a civil rights matter, gay bashing could not be dismissed as a "pastime" in which soldiers engaged while on leave. Rather, it was comparable to the lynching of blacks in the South.

Preserving the New Deal: Crossfire and the Psychologizing of Racial Intolerance

Perhaps the best place to begin examining the relationship between the novel and the film is with Scott's memo outlining *The Brick Foxhole* for the heads of RKO. Scott felt that the novel's treatment of racial intolerance was particularly relevant to postwar conditions. He thought that the novel explored "personal fascism as opposed to organized fascism" and thus showed "how it is possible for us to have a gestapo, if this country should go fascist. A character like Monty would qualify brilliantly for the leadership of the Belsen concentration camp."[22] Scott's mistaken belief that the novel focused on "personal" rather than "organized" forms of racial intolerance helps to explain one of the major differences between the novel and the film. In the film, Monty (Robert Ryan) is not a representative American whose attitudes and beliefs express the national character, but a psychopathic killer whose hatred of Jews is aberrational. In a scene in which the Capitol appears in the background, translating into visual terms Finlay's role as the guardian of the nation's democratic heritage, Finlay (Robert Young) distinguishes between the different kinds of anti-Semitism in American society: "This business of hating Jews comes in a lot of different sizes. There's the you-can't-join-our-country club kind and you-can't-live-in-our-neighborhood kind. And, yes, you-can't-work-here-kind. And because we stand for these, we get Monty's kind. He's just one guy. We don't get him very often, but he grows out of all the rest." Although Finlay here links Monty's anti-Semitism to larger forces in American society ("he grows out of all the rest"), the overall effect of his speech is to minimize anti-Semitism as a practice. Monty's hatred of Jews does not express in extreme form a deeply engrained attitude in American society, nor is it inextricably tied to his identity as an American. Rather, it is a personal aberration that can be explained away by his violent tendencies. In this respect, the film undercut its oppositional content. Its insistence on investigating "personal" forms of anti-Semitism shifted attention away from its institutional embodiments (what Finlay calls the "you-can't-join-our-country club" kind) and focused it instead on an individual whose attitudes and beliefs could be dismissed as peculiar to him.

One of the factors that contributed to the film's tendency to personalize the problem of anti-Semitism was the intensity of Robert Ryan's performance as Monty. As Forster Hirsch has pointed out, anti-Semitism alone cannot explain Monty's sudden bursts of anger.[23] Although Ryan's ability to shift moods suddenly and without warning serves to underscore Monty's violent tendencies, the overall effect of his performance is to divert attention from Monty's hatred of Jews. Ryan was best known for playing characters prone to psychopathic violence, which undoubtedly influenced how audiences interpreted his character in *Crossfire*. In addition to Monty, he also played an abnormally possessive husband in *Caught* (Max Ophüls, 1949), a violent policeman who uses excessive force in *On Dangerous Ground* (Nicholas Ray, 1951), a psychotic intruder in *Beware, My Lovely* (Harry Horner, 1952), and a crazed lover who stalks a former girlfriend in *Clash by Night* (Fritz Lang, 1952).[24] Because of Ryan's talent for portraying such characters, Monty's hatred of Jews seems at times merely to provide him with an excuse to commit murder. Whereas in the novel Monty methodically plans Edwards's murder, in the film he kills Samuels in an uncontrollable outburst of anger that defies explanation. One moment he is drunkenly thanking Samuels for his hospitality; the next he is grabbing Samuels by the lapels of his jacket and muttering anti-Semitic epithets. The film's tendency to divert attention from Monty's anti-Semitism is particularly apparent in the scene in which he kills Floyd. Unlike Samuels, Floyd is not Jewish, and thus his murder cannot be attributed to Monty's anti-Semitism. In a reenactment of the film's opening scene, in which he murders Samuels, Monty brutally beats Floyd before killing him. The scene is shot in such a way as to register Monty's sadistic pleasure. When Monty grabs Floyd around the neck, the camera cuts to a close-up of his face, in which he breaks into a sinister smile.

Thus the film did not just refuse to address the theme of homophobia; it also refused to treat anti-Semitism as a problem embedded in the nation's political and social institutions. A number of critics have attributed the limitations of the film's treatment of anti-Semitism to its use of low-key lighting and multiple flashbacks, which tended to highlight the characters' psychological motives.[25] Although such conventions undoubtedly contributed to the film's personalizing of anti-Semitism, they do not wholly account for it. Scott and Dmytryk seem to have conceived of anti-Semitism in purely psychological terms. Their refusal to engage the political aspects of anti-Semitism surfaces most fully in the scene in which Samuels tries to soothe Mitchell's (George Cooper) fears about returning to civilian life. Samuels explains that it is only natural for Mitchell to feel apprehensive: "We don't know what we're supposed to do. We don't know what's supposed to happen. We're too used to fightin'. But we just don't know what to fight. You can feel the tension in the air. A whole lot of fight and hate that doesn't know where to go." Samuels functions here as a diegetic substitute for Scott and Dmytryk, stating their understanding of the origin of racial and ethnic intolerance. According to Samuels, hatred of Jews and other minoritized groups is a product not of attitudes and beliefs endemic to American society, but of postwar anxiety and fear. Returning soldiers no longer have a legitimate outlet for their anger and resentment, and so they turn it against vulnerable racial and ethnic minorities. Thus the film's use of lighting techniques and narrative devices that were commonly associated with film noir should be seen as reinforcing rather than undercutting its central message, namely that anti-Semitism was psychological in origin. The potential for America to develop a gestapo supposedly lay not in deeply engrained beliefs and practices but in the difficulty many soldiers had readjusting to civilian life.

The film's tendency to personalize Monty's anti-Semitism is perhaps best explained in terms of Scott's and Dmytryk's ties to the Popular Front, ties that cost them dearly when HUAC began to investigate Hollywood's left-wing community. Whereas the novel indirectly challenged the political and rhetorical strategies of the Popular Front, the film closely adhered to the Popular Front agenda, expressing support for the New Deal. Dana Polan has shown how in many films of the forties Franklin Roosevelt functioned as the enunciative agent, or source and guarantor of the narration.[26] Roosevelt not only provided the voice-over narration that began or ended many films in that decade, but his actions as president often initiated their major narrative moves. Moreover, because of the length of his presidency, Roosevelt became a figure of stability and endurance. He embodied the nation's ability to overcome the forces that threatened it internally as well as externally. He not only led the nation to victory but also conquered a crippling disease. Although it was made two years after his death, Roosevelt serves a similar narrative function in *Crossfire*. His portrait is prominently displayed in Finlay's office. We first become aware of the portrait in the scene in which Finlay interviews Keely (Robert Mitchum) about the murder. As Keely enters Finlay's office, the camera cuts to a long shot of Finlay, who is shown sitting at his desk with his back to the spectator. He is talking to another detective whose hat blocks the portrait from view. As Keely enters the office, the detective moves offscreen, exposing the portrait. When Keely sits down across from Finlay, the composition of the shot shifts dramatically, directing the spectator's look straight to the portrait. The two men and the portrait form a triangle, with the portrait occupying the apex.

In this way, the film installs Roosevelt as the source and guarantor of the narration. He presides over the investigation into Samuels's murder, guiding Finlay's interpretation of the evidence and confirming his explanation of the anti-Semitism of American society. But the function of Roosevelt's portrait was not limited to authorizing an investigation that extended beyond Samuels's murder to racial and ethnic intolerance. It was also meant to dissuade spectators from abandoning the New Deal. In 1947 when the film was released, the postwar backlash against the New Deal that I described in the introduction was in full swing. Although the display of Roosevelt's portrait was clearly intended to establish when the film takes place—in 1945 in the final days of the war—it was also clearly intended to remind spectators of the values and ideals embodied in the New Deal, values and ideals that were increasingly under assault.

The film's desire to renew the spectator's commitment to the New Deal is perhaps most apparent in its use of its setting, the nation's capital. In conformity with the conventions of film noir, much of the film takes place at night and is shot in low-key lighting, creating a tense, foreboding mood. Finlay's office seems particularly portentous. Stark and bureaucratic, it is filled with ominous shadows, as if to confirm the spectator's loss of faith in big government. Finlay could not be more different from the self-assured, hard-boiled detective who usually appears in film noir. Rather than aggressively pursuing the case, he remains seated behind his desk throughout most of the film, interviewing suspects. As Siegfried Kracauer put it in a review that appeared in the *Nation* shortly after the film's release, Finlay seems "overwhelmed by a mood of resignation, as though he had discovered that the struggle for enlightenment is a Sisyphean task."[27] Finlay openly acknowledges that his methods are inefficient and unreliable. When Keely refuses to answer some questions, he does not interrogate him more aggressively but expresses frustration with the case: "Nothing interests me anymore. Used to, but not anymore. I've been at this job too long. I go about it the only way I know how. I collect all the facts possible. Most of them are useless." Finlay's skepticism about his own methods would seem to justify the backlash against the expanding bureaucracy of the welfare state. Yet Finlay eventually vindicates himself by exposing Monty as the murderer. Despite his apparent lack of enthusiasm for the case, he is deeply committed to obtaining justice, especially after he realizes that Samuels was killed because he was Jewish.

Finlay's exposure of Monty helps to vindicate the activist state inaugurated by the New Deal. When Finlay realizes why Samuels was killed, the film adopts more conventional lighting, expressing visually his victory in the struggle for enlightenment, to use Kracauer's terms. In the scene in which Finlay tells Keely that he suspects Samuels may have been murdered because he was Jewish, dawn gradually breaks and his office becomes flooded with sunlight. We also discover that the Capitol can be seen from his office window. The presence of the Capitol in the background was clearly intended to restore the spectator's faith in liberal government. When the Capitol is shrouded in darkness and cannot be seen from his office window, Finlay is unable to solve the murder. But when it is again visible, he is no longer baffled by the murderer's motive and undertakes to entrap Monty. In this way, the film suggested that retreating from the New Deal was tantamount to abandoning the nation's founding principles. Although the goals of the New Deal were increasingly attacked as socialist and therefore un-American, the film's use of its monumental setting made them appear firmly grounded in the nation's political traditions. In identifying

Monty as Samuels's murderer and bringing him to justice, Finlay upholds the beliefs enshrined in the Constitution, a copy of which, appropriately enough, hangs on the wall behind his desk.

A comparison between the film and the novel will help to clarify the film's use of its setting. Whereas in the film the setting is intended to express visually the link between the New Deal and the nation's founding principles, in the novel it is intended to symbolize the emptiness of the nation's utopian promise. Far from "hailing" the characters as citizens of a liberal democracy, the monumental landscape of the nation's capital functions as a playground where they can escape from the monotony of military life. As Jeff approaches the city in Edwards's car, he can barely contain his excitement: "A few miles away was D.C. All week-end liberties led to Washington, city of carnival. Go to D.C. and scoop yourself a hatful of fun" (89). Thus in the novel the nation's capital functions as a site not of democratic renewal and affirmation but of unbridled pleasure. When the novel refers to its monumental setting, it does so to underscore its lack of political referentiality. For the cab driver who shows Jeff the city's "sites," the monumental buildings that line Constitution Avenue merely provide evidence of the nation's economic might: "He liked Constitution Avenue. It was broad and pretty, and the buildings reminded him that America was an important place. It was all well and good to talk about America and make speeches, thought Herman, but you got to have something to show for it. Buildings like these were proof. They were something substantial" (112). Thus, whereas the film uses the monumental landscape of the nation's capital to position the spectator as the heir of a liberal democratic tradition that culminated in the New Deal, the novel uses it to reinforce its central message, namely that until the nation has overcome racial and sexual intolerance, its utopian promise will remain unfulfilled.

In addition to exploiting the capacity of its setting to invoke the nation's democratic heritage, the film also tried to counter the belief that the New Deal was un-American by having Finlay embody the American dream of upward mobility. Finlay is the descendant of Irish Catholics who immigrated to the United States in the mid–nineteenth century. He uses the story of his family's struggle to overcome anti-Irish prejudice and assimilate to persuade Leroy (William Phipps) to help him entrap Monty. In a skillfully edited sequence of shots, Finlay recalls how his grandfather's belief in the American dream eventually cost him his life. When his grandfather first arrived in the United States, he thought of himself as "just another man living in America," but hatred of Irish Catholics soon taught him that rather than an American citizen he was "a dirty Irish Mick, a priest lover, a spy from Rome, a foreigner trying to rob men of jobs." This sequence is edited in such a way as virtually to guarantee the spectator's perceptual placement within the film's narrative space. The spectator is made uncomfortable but not so uncomfortable that s/he resists Finlay's construction of American history as propaganda. As Finlay utters the phrase "dirty Irish Mick," he leans forward into the camera, shattering the distance between him and the spectator, whose gaze becomes riveted on his face. The harsh lighting of the shot—Finlay's face glows unnaturally—and the sudden amplification of Finlay's voice seem designed to insert the spectator into the subject-position occupied by Finlay's grandfather. When Finlay resumes his narrative, the camera cuts to a medium shot, thereby partially restoring the distance between him and the spectator. Having secured the spectator's attention, Finlay continues:

One day when a bunch of men attacked [my grandfather's] parish priest on the street, he waded in to help the priest. He managed to get him inside a store. That night on the way home from work, he stopped off for a beer. When he left the bar, two men followed him carrying empty whiskey bottles. They didn't mean to kill him. They were just going to rough him up a little. They didn't start out to kill. They just started out hating the way Monty started out, but twenty minutes later my grandfather was dead. That's history, Leroy. They don't teach it in schools, but it's real American history just the same.

In having Finlay narrate this episode from his family's past, the film constructs a counter history of the United States, one in which violence against racial and ethnic minorities is central. But it does so to affirm rather than to challenge the official meaning of America. America emerges as a melting pot in which the nation's racial and ethnic minorities partake equally of its opportunities and resources. Despite his Irish Catholic background, Finlay has assimilated into American society and even occupies the position of the law. Thus his grandfather's belief in the American dream is ultimately vindicated.

Finlay's narration of his family's past was also meant to show that the nation's capacity to absorb difference extended to the minority group whose history and experience most challenged the myth of the melting pot, namely African Americans. When Siegfried Kracauer reviewed the film for the *Nation,* he praised its courageous examination of anti-Semitism, but criticized it for refusing to address the problem of racism: "The film-makers have congratulated themselves for their courage in discussing the problem of the Jew, but they have not shown any greater interest in the problem of the Negro."[28] Although it is true that Scott and Dmytryk exaggerated their courage in making a film about anti-Semitism, it is not the case that they ignored the "problem" of race.[29] Kracauer's criticism overlooked Leroy's function as a representative of white southern values and attitudes. Although he is not openly racist, he refuses to believe that Monty would have killed Samuels simply because he was Jewish. At first, he is not persuaded by Finlay's claims about the anti-Semitism of American society and asks him: "How do I know you're not a Jewish person yourself?" But when Finlay recounts his family's past, he relents and agrees to help him entrap Monty. Here the film sought to reassure spectators that even African Americans could be assimilated into American society. Although Leroy is not particularly bright and resembles the stereotype of the redneck, he is well meaning and malleable. If he can be moved by Finlay's version of American history, a version not taught in schools, then he can also be persuaded to abandon Jim Crow and accept the integration of African Americans. But in trying to show that the nation would eventually absorb African Americans, just as it had the Irish and other immigrant groups, the film overlooked the specificity of black history and culture, which included the experience of slavery, the effects of which continued to limit black mobility.

Returning Gay Men to National Visibility:
Camp and the Emancipatory Potential of Film Noir

I have been focusing on the differences between the novel and the film in order to identify more fully the utopian aspect of film noir. In the previous chapter, I contended that the emancipatory potential of *Laura* lay not in its critique of the postwar shift from production to consumption, but in its visual economy, which indirectly affirmed gay male practices and forms of identity. In promoting a homosexualization of the spectator's gaze, the film partially counteracted the homophobic image of gay men it put into circulation. I want to conclude this chapter by elaborating this argument in relation to my discussion of the differences between *The Brick Foxhole* and *Crossfire*. *Crossfire* certainly deserves praise for its courage in treating the problem of anti-Semitism and in defending the New Deal at a time when it was under attack. But it was ultimately a less progressive film than *Laura*. Granted, the film version of *Laura* exemplifies the tendency I have tried to clarify in this chapter, insofar as it suppressed the feminist content of Caspary's novel. But its treatment of Lydecker provided gay men with an alternative form of publicity that compensated them for their exclusion from the political public sphere.

As I stated at the outset, *Crossfire*'s refusal to address the theme of homophobia can be attributed to its partial status as a social-problem film. The social-problem film evolved from the gangster film of the early 1930s and sought to intervene in the political public sphere.[30] It was particularly popular in the late 1940s, when it was dominated by a liberal perspective. In addition to anti-Semitism, the social problems most commonly addressed by the genre included racism (*Pinky* [Elia Kazan, 1949]), political corruption (*All the King's Men* [Robert Rosen, 1949]), alcoholism (*The Lost Weekend* [Billy Wilder, 1945]), drug addiction (*The Man with the Golden Arm* [Otto Preminger, 1956]), and juvenile delinquency (*The Blackboard Jungle* [Richard Brooks, 1955]). The popularity of the genre peaked in 1947, the year of *Crossfire*'s release, when it comprised 28 percent of the films produced by Hollywood.[31] With the rise of McCarthyism, the production of such films dropped precipitously, dwindling to a postwar low in 1954, when they comprised only 9.2 percent of the total output of Hollywood films. As the example of *Crossfire* attests, the desire of the social-problem film to intervene in the political public sphere limited the social problems it could address. Given the linkage between homosexuality and Communism in the Cold War political imaginary, it is hardly surprising that homosexuality did not become one of the "social problems" treated by the genre.[32] Still, the fact that it did not provides yet another example of the way in which gay men were expelled from the realm of representation.

Film noir provided a more effective vehicle for countering the dominant construction of gay male identity and experience. Unlike the social-problem film, it did not consciously seek to influence debates in the political public sphere and thus was in many respects more able to address potentially controversial topics from a progressive perspective. Nowhere was this ability more apparent than in its treatment of gay men. Insofar as it affirmed camp as an oppositional mode of identity, film noir functioned as an alternative public sphere in which the gay male subculture not only retained its visibility but was acknowledged as an integral part of American society. Camp is perhaps best understood as a way of inhabiting the body that provided gay men with access to the public sphere. Through camp, gay men were able to recuperate the stereotype of the effeminate homosexual. As Clifton Webb's widely praised performance in *Laura* attests, camp enabled gay men to stage their homosexuality for the public in ways that were at least potentially a source of admiration and inspiration. As a mode of publicity, camp linked homosexuality to wit, sophistication, and urbanity, partially counteracting its association with sexual deviance.[33] Moreover, camp positioned gay men as standard-bearers of taste and style, thereby enabling them to contest the middle-class suburban values that increasingly dominated American culture.[34] In its treatment of Lydecker, the film version of *Laura* acknowledged these aspects of camp. Its Lydecker is a media star who not only writes a newspaper column but also has his own radio show. Thus he not only has access to the public sphere, which enables him to function as a critic of middle-class tastes and attitudes, but ample opportunity to display his homosexuality in public. Indeed, it is through the public display of his homosexuality that he becomes a celebrity.

This is not to overstate the liberatory possibilities opened up by camp as a specifically public form of gay male identity. I will return to the question of camp and its effectiveness as a strategy for gaining access to the public sphere in chapter 5. Let me say here that one of the drawbacks of camp was that it tended to desexualize the gay male body. As the example of Lydecker indicates, camp was able to provide gay men with access to the public sphere primarily by desexualizing homosexuality and transforming it into an aesthetic identity. It diverted the public's attention from gay men's allegedly deviant sexuality and focused it instead on their wit and sophistication.[35] It was not until the sixties and seventies when the gay macho style emerged as the dominant practice of the gay male subculture that gay men invented an erotic way of inhabiting their bodies that, at least until the AIDS crisis, partially circumvented the public's homophobic gaze.[36] Nor do I want to exaggerate the degree to which, in affirming camp, film noir functioned as an alternative public sphere. As we have seen, in film noir the gay male characters are invariably exposed as psychopathic killers, and thus such films provided gay men with a tenuous foundation on which to construct their identities. Still, by making a spectacle of their homosexuality, many actors were able to counteract the homophobic stereotypes film noir endorsed.[37]

If in this and the previous chapter I have risked overstating the potential of film noir to reverse the increasing invisibility of gay men, that is because I have wanted to clarify its relation to the gay male writers we will be examining in the second part of this study. In an era in which gay men threatened to become invisible, the work of Williams, Vidal, and Baldwin was even more effective than film noir in putting into circulation a counter narrative of gay male identity and experience, one that deeply influenced the gay liberation movement of the sixties and seventies. How do we explain the ability of these writers to accomplish what neither film noir nor the social-problem film could, namely, approach the "problem" of homosexuality from a progressive perspective, especially in light of the hostile reviews their work received from critics disturbed both by its popularity and by its homoeroticism? I think the answer lies in the modes of production that governed the distribution and reception of their work. In an era in which the public sphere was rapidly becoming postliterary, in the sense that it was dominated by the mass media, and was facing competition from a growing number of subcultural formations that had their own distinct modes of publicity, the work of these writers was less likely to encounter censorship or to become the target of conservative religious and political groups than were Hollywood films. Marginalized by film, television, and other forms of mass communication, the nation's literary and theatrical institutions were valued primarily as forms of symbolic capital.[38] This may explain why films noirs avoided the most controversial issues addressed by the novels on which they were based. Still, as the influence of Williams's, Vidal's, and Baldwin's work on the social movements of the sixties amply demonstrates, this did not mean that literature and drama could not intervene in the political public sphere in decisive ways.

Where the work of Williams, Vidal, and Baldwin differed from film noir was in its tendency to masculinize gay male identity. These writers did not sufficiently appreciate the way in which camp enabled gay men to gain access to the public sphere. Thus they treated effeminate gay men in ways that were deeply homophobic. This blindness is best explained in terms of their desire to exploit the emancipatory potential of the form of male identity displaced by the rise of the "organization man," which is to say that their work was a product of the same discursive formation as film noir. But, unlike film noir, these writers were not motivated by a desire to recover the entrepreneurial spirit or to return to an earlier stage of capitalism. Rather, they wanted to promote a form of gay male identity that had the potential to disrupt the postwar settlement. As I noted in the introduction, one of the ways in which the discourses of national security marginalized forms of male identity that were not conducive to Fordism's needs and aims was by representing them as deviant, if not potentially homosexual. If Williams, Vidal, and Baldwin tried to recuperate these forms of male identity for gay men, that is because for the mass of Americans they signified a rejection of white, middle-class, suburban values.[39] This may explain why their work was able to intervene in the political public sphere in such decisive ways, despite its obsolescence as a mode of cultural production. These writers did not seek to reverse the postwar shift from production to consumption; rather, their goal was to dismantle the binary oppositions that organized everyday life in Cold War America (white vs. black, straight vs. gay, male vs. female). For this reason, their work helped women, gay men, and other minoritized groups imagine a different America, one in which participation in the public sphere did not depend on race, gender, and/or sexual identity.

PART 2

Gay Male Cultural Production

in the Cold War Era

CHAPTER FOUR

Tennessee Williams and the Politics of the Closet

You still want to know why I don't write a gay play? I don't find it necessary.
I could express what I wanted to express through other means. I would be
narrowing my audience a great deal. I wish to have a broad audience because the
major thrust of my work is not sexual orientation, it's social. I'm not
about to limit myself to writing about gay people.
—Tennessee Williams

Critics often cite Tennessee Williams's short story "Hard Candy" (1954) as
typical of the evasive and indirect way in which he treated gay male experience in his work.[1] In "Hard Candy," Williams is careful not only to avoid
explicitly stating that the elderly protagonist, Mr. Krupper, is homosexual
but also to shroud in mystery his visits to the Joy Rio, a "third-rate cinema"
situated near the waterfront where he engages in anonymous sexual encounters with young boys in exchange for a few quarters and a bag of hard
candy.[2] Before disclosing what Mr. Krupper does in the upper galleries of
the once elegant theater, Williams interrupts the story to prepare the reader
for the shock of what he is about to reveal: "In the course of this story, and
very soon now, it will be necessary to make some disclosures about Mr.
Krupper of a nature too coarse to be dealt with very directly in a work of
such brevity" (355). Although he realizes that his circumspection may confuse the reader, he refuses to deal more explicitly with the ailing Mr. Krupper's visits to the Joy Rio. If he were to approach Mr. Krupper's clandestine
sexual activities more directly, he might shock the reader, and he is determined to avoid "a head-on violence that would disgust and destroy and
which would actually falsify the story" (355) by misrepresenting the mysterious Mr. Krupper. Williams does not want the reader to come to the
reductive conclusion that Mr. Krupper is a dirty old man who preys on

innocent young boys, even though there is ample reason for the reader to do so.

Williams's desire to avoid shocking the reader by dealing openly with Mr. Krupper's anonymous sexual encounters has led a number of critics to treat "Hard Candy" as a product of his internalized homophobia.[3] According to these critics, Williams's equivocations about Mr. Krupper's surreptitious visits to the Joy Rio can be attributed to his inability to come to terms with his own sexual promiscuity, which he did not openly acknowledge until the publication of his *Memoirs* in 1975.[4] They are particularly troubled by Williams's unflattering descriptions of Mr. Krupper, which threaten to reduce homosexuality to a form of bodily corruption. Williams tells us that Mr. Krupper is "a man of gross and unattractive appearance" (353) and that he is "shameful and despicable even to those who tolerate his caresses, perhaps even more so to them than to the others who only see him" (363). But this reading ignores the way in which Williams's evasions seem designed to implicate the reader in Mr. Krupper's "mysterious" activities. The indirection and obscurity of Williams's language encourage a pornographic interest in Mr. Krupper. Despite the fact that Mr. Krupper is a dirty old man whose sexual activities are potentially exploitative, the reader eagerly devours the story. Indeed, the more evasive Williams's language becomes, the more eager the reader is to finish the story so that s/he can learn the "truth" about Mr. Krupper's pilgrimages to the Joy Rio. That Williams's evasions are intended to implicate the reader in Mr. Krupper's "mystery" becomes clear at the end of the story, when he abruptly breaks off the narrative just before Mr. Krupper is about to give a blow job to the beautiful and odoriferous "dark youth" (362) he encounters in the upper galleries on his final visit to the theater. In marking with a blank space the place in the text where the description of the blow job should occur, Williams intensifies the reader's pornographic interest in Mr. Krupper. Williams refuses to satisfy the reader's desire to experience gay male sex vicariously, thereby leaving her/him feeling cheated.

But Williams's mockery of the reader is not limited to encouraging a pornographic interest in Mr. Krupper's sexual activities, despite his gross and unattractive appearance. The obscurity of Williams's language reduces the reader to engaging in the sort of reading practices that negotiating the gay male subculture often necessitated in the Cold War era. In an influential essay on the semiotics of homosexuality, Harold Beaver has argued that gay men's marginal position in relation to the dominant culture forces them to become "prodigious consumer[s] of signs."[5] We can use Beaver's argument about gay men's privileged relation to the commodity form to speculate about the emergence in the fifties of a distinct gay male reading formation in relation to the closet. According to Beaver, gay men are constantly besieged by signs, making them particularly skillful readers. The structures of secrecy and disclosure that organize gay male experience lead them to scrutinize constantly the behavior of other men for signs of homosexuality. For them, the slightly effeminate gesture or intonation of voice becomes fraught with meaning. Moreover, practices such as cruising require them to interpret signs on multiple levels. A meaningful look, a brush of the leg, a touch of the hand—all can be interpreted as signs of sexual solicitation. Thus for gay men there is no escaping "the urge to interpret whatever transpires, or fails to transpire, between [themselves] and every chance acquaintance."[6] But gay men do not just consume signs, they also produce them. To mark their identities, they appropriate a variety of signifiers from the dominant culture (leather jackets, blue jeans, flannel shirts, key rings), which they invest with new meanings by redeploying them in a homosexual context.[7] These signifiers comprise a complex system of signs the meaning of which only those initiated into the gay male subculture are wholly capable of decoding. To negotiate the subculture, gay men must learn how to interpret signs provisionally and on multiple levels.

Beaver's analysis essentializes gay male identity by grounding it ontologically. He does not adequately consider the changes that have occurred in urban gay communities since the Stonewall rebellion in 1969, which led to the emergence of the gay liberation movement, and thus he removes gay men from the historical process.[8] Not only is contemporary gay male experience less governed by the structures of secrecy and disclosure that defined the closet in the fifties, but the AIDS crisis has radically altered gay male practices such as cruising. Still, Beaver's argument provides a fairly accurate description of the semiotics of postwar urban gay communities. In "Hard Candy," Williams foregrounds Mr. Krupper's role as both a consumer and a producer of signs. After thirty years of attending afternoon matinees at the Joy Rio, Mr. Krupper has become a particularly skillful reader of signs. Although his experiences in the upper galleries of the movie theater have taught him to exercise caution, he has also learned that "there are certain pursuits in which even the most cautious man must depart from absolute caution if he intends at all to enjoy them" (361). Thus when he discovers that the place where he usually sits has been taken by an unusually attractive boy who emits a "warm animal fragrance" (362), he carefully maps out a course of action. He initiates contact with the boy by offering him a piece of candy. Shortly before the lights come up, he jingles the quarters he has brought with him "ever so lightly in his fist so that they tinkle a bit" (363), thereby indicating to the boy that he is prepared to pay him for his sexual favors. In case he has misinterpreted the boy's presence in the upper galleries of the movie theater, he then leans toward the railing so that the boy will think that he is interested in what is happening below. When the boy remains seated after the lights go down again, Mr. Krupper interprets it as a sign that he is willing to submit to his caresses in exchange for the quarters. He then offers the quarters to the boy who, in taking them, signals that "the contract is sealed between them" (364).

Given the obscurity of Williams's language, the only way in which the reader can make sense of the story is by mastering the sort of reading practices in which Mr. Krupper has learned to engage. Williams's refusal to shock the reader by divulging the "secret" of Mr. Krupper's visits to the Joy Rio requires her/him to occupy a gay male subject-position. To understand the meaning of the story, the reader must demonstrate a mastery of gay male reading practices; that is, s/he must fill in the blanks—quite literally, as we will see shortly. Williams does not fully test the reader's ability to read as a gay man until the end of the story, where he does not explicitly state how Mr. Krupper died, but refers to it indirectly, thus shrouding it in mystery. The reader knows only that Mr. Krupper died in "an attitude of prayer" (364) and with discarded candy wrappers stuck to his clothes. Williams stresses the different ways in which Mr. Krupper's death can be interpreted. Unaware of the sort of activities the patrons of the Joy Rio engage in, the "spinsterly reporter" (364) who writes Mr. Krupper's obituary gives it unusual prominence. She is impressed by "the sentimental values of a seventy-year-old retired merchant dying of thrombosis at a cowboy thriller with a split bag of hard candies in his pocket and the floor about him littered with sticky wrappers, some of which even adhered to the shoulders and sleeves of his jacket" (364). Mr. Krupper's cousins similarly misinterpret his death. For them, it is poetic justice. Mr. Krupper has constantly pilfered their stock of hard candy. When the daughter reads his obituary in the local newspaper, she exclaims gleefully: "*Just think, Papa, the old man choked to death on our hard candy!"* (365).[9] Here it becomes apparent that deciphering Williams's veiled references to the way in which Mr. Krupper dies requires reading as a gay man. Neither the spinsterly reporter nor Mr. Krupper's cousins have mastered the codes of the gay male subculture, and so they do not know that they must read between the lines in order to interpret correctly the meaning of his death. It does not occur to them that Mr. Krupper died in a state of bliss, transfigured by his encounter with the unusually attractive boy.

Although given the position of his body there can be little doubt about the circumstances under which Mr. Krupper dies, Williams continues to shroud his homosexuality in mystery. I have already noted that he does not describe the blow job that makes possible Mr. Krupper's transfiguration but marks the place in the text where it occurs with a blank space, thus requiring the reader literally to fill in the blanks. In this respect, critics seem justified in claiming that Williams's evasions reproduce the epistemology of the closet.[10] Despite the fact that Williams encourages us to read "Hard Candy" as a narrative of disclosure, he never fully divulges the "secret" of Mr. Krupper's pilgrimages. Mr. Krupper's homosexuality remains an open secret, known only to the reader who is capable of reading between the lines. Although I agree with critics who read Williams's circumspection as an indication that he was heavily invested in maintaining the closet, I am not persuaded by the argument that his refusal to shock the reader by fully disclosing Mr. Krupper's "secret" was a product of internalized homophobia. To propose an alternative reading of Williams's relation to the closet, I want to examine more closely the structures of secrecy and disclosure embedded in his representation of gay male experience in "Hard Candy."

Until Williams interrupts the narrative to warn us that he will soon have to disclose something about Mr. Krupper that is "too coarse to be dealt with very directly," there is nothing in the text that would lead us to suspect that Mr. Krupper regularly engages in anonymous sex at the Joy Rio. Williams describes Mr. Krupper as a seventy-year-old retired businessman who is "almost like any other old man" (356) in that he spends the mornings in the park reading the newspaper. Only readers initiated into the gay male subculture would on the basis of their knowledge of Mr. Krupper's visits to the theater suspect that he is not like other old men but is a "bird of a different feather" (357). Williams remarks that even the most penetrating observer would have difficulty discovering "what it was that gave Mr. Krupper the certain air he had of being engaged in something far more momentous than the ordinary meanderings of an old man" (356). Thus even Mr. Krupper's cousins do not suspect that he leads a double life. Although their dislike of him might lead one to conclude that they had "penetrated to the very core of those mysteries" (356) that Williams insists on approaching only indirectly, they are not even curious about his activities. Indeed, they do not even speculate about what he does with the candy that he pilfers from their store: "The comments and the stares and the laughs of disgust betrayed no real interest or curiosity or speculation about him, only the fiercely senseless attention given to something acknowledged to have no mysteries whatsoever" (356). Their utter lack of curiosity about Mr. Krupper is more disturbing than their dislike of him because it reduces him to an "insensibly malign object" (356). In refusing to speculate about Mr. Krupper's activities or to show the slightest interest in them, they deny his humanity.

This may explain why in "Hard Candy" Williams did not hesitate to reproduce the epistemological structures of the closet. Although his refusal to deal more openly with Mr. Krupper's homosexuality reduces it to an open secret, the evasiveness of his language enables him to establish Mr. Krupper's subjecthood. Williams's equivocations about Mr. Krupper's homosexuality have the paradoxical effect of rendering it visible. Insofar as they transform Mr. Krupper's sexuality into an impenetrable mystery, they reverse the effects of his cousins' indifference. This is not to deny that one of the dangers of Williams's refusal to treat Mr. Krupper's visits to the Joy Rio more openly is that our interest in them will remain at the level of the pornographic. But Williams averts this possibility by breaking off the narrative at the point at which Mr. Krupper is about to give a blow job to the boy, thus arousing but not satisfying the reader's curiosity about gay male sex. Williams's hesitation to approach Mr. Krupper's homosexuality more directly guarantees that, unlike his cousins, we do not assume that we know "practically everything of any significance about him" (355). Because he refuses to describe Mr. Krupper's encounter with the anonymous youth, the "mystery" of Mr. Krupper's identity continues to elude us, forcing us to acknowledge that we can never fully know him. In reproducing the structures of the closet, in other words, Williams prevents our curiosity about Mr. Krupper from reducing him to an "insensibly malign object." Mr. Krupper's homosexuality becomes a sign not of his corruption but of his subjecthood, thereby discouraging us from positioning him as sexually other.

Many readers will no doubt object that Williams's strategies for establishing Mr. Krupper's subjecthood are as politically retrograde as his investment in the structures of secrecy and disclosure that organized gay male experience in the Cold War era.[11] In treating Mr. Krupper's homosexuality as a mystery that can never be wholly solved, Williams attributes to him a form of selfhood that in the wake of the poststructuralist critique of the subject we have learned to dismiss as an Enlightenment fiction designed to guarantee white male heterosexual privilege. Although we eventually learn Mr. Krupper's "secret," our knowledge does not provide us with the key to his subjectivity, which remains inaccessible to us. As we saw above, even after Williams makes his disclosures about Mr. Krupper's visits to the Joy Rio, he continues to equivocate about his homosexuality, merely describing the position in which his body was found, and thus he prevents us from thinking that Mr. Krupper's identity can be reduced to his homosexuality. To be sure, Williams's attempt to establish Mr. Krupper's subjecthood by shrouding his homosexuality in mystery is highly problematic from a political point of view: It reveals a liberal humanistic belief in the uniqueness and autonomy of the individual. To avert the possibility that the reader's interest in the story will remain pornographic, Williams is forced to relegate Mr. Krupper's homosexuality to the private realm where it can remain a secret. Although Mr. Krupper's encounter with the youth occurs in the public space of a movie theater, it is a private act, which, as I have already noted, not even the reader is allowed to witness.[12] Moreover, it is committed furtively and in the dark, thereby enabling Mr. Krupper and his partner to maintain their anonymity.

Despite its political limitations, however, Williams's strategy of attributing to Mr. Krupper a form of selfhood that in capitalist social formations is usually reserved for white, middle-class, heterosexual men seriously challenged the dominant understanding of gay male identity in the fifties. Williams's focus on a character whose sexual practices even many critics writing from an otherwise antihomophobic perspective see as morally reprehensible bespeaks his unwillingness to compromise his project by making his representation of gay male experience more palatable for straight middle-class readers. To clarify the politics of Williams's treatment of Mr. Krupper, it is necessary to compare his strategies in "Hard Candy" for contesting the hegemonic construction of gay male identity with those adopted by the Mattachine Society, the first gay rights organization founded in the postwar period.[13] Although, according to its charter, the Mattachine Society was established to lobby for the repeal of sodomy laws and to make "common cause with other minorities in contributing to the reform of judicial, police and penal practices," for the most part it limited its activities to the gay male equivalent of racial uplift. It wanted to see gay men assimilated into mainstream American society, and so it sought to dispel "the fears and antagonisms of the [larger] community" by establishing that gay men did not differ significantly from straight men.[14] It discouraged gay men from engaging in camp and other controversial practices that reinforced negative stereotypes and threatened to undermine the homophile movement.[15] It also insisted that only the "fringe" of the gay male community engaged in anonymous sexual encounters and that the majority of gay men were capable of sustaining long-term, monogamous relationships. By contrast, Williams was unwilling to disavow the practices and forms of identity that gay men had created in response to their oppression. Mr. Krupper is the Mattachine Society's worst nightmare, a promiscuous gay man who engages in anonymous sex in public places. Rather than repudiating his sexual practices or showing that they were not typical of the gay male community, Williams attributed to Mr. Krupper a complexity that made it difficult for the reader to see him as a stereotype.

Williams's strategies also differed from those adopted by Vidal and Baldwin, the other gay male writers we will be examining in this part of *Homosexuality in Cold War America*. As we will see in subsequent chapters, Vidal and Baldwin contested the dominant construction of homosexuality by foregrounding the construction of gay male subjectivity across variable axes of difference. They sought to define a mode of resistance that exploited gay men's fractured relation to identity. For them, the multiplicity of gay male identity did not entail a loss of agency but enabled a mobility in solidarity. The fragmentation and dispersal of their subjectivity meant that gay men could engage in opposition from multiple locations.[16] By contrast, Williams sought to reverse gay men's fractured relation to identity. On the one hand, his representation of gay male experience seemed to deny that gay male subjectivity is necessarily decentered. Because gay men must survive in the interstices of the dominant culture, they do not enjoy the luxury of having unified and coherent selves but must construct their identities from an atomized historical experience. On the other hand, Williams's treatment of Mr. Krupper as a mysterious figure whose inner world remains inaccessible to us indicates his recognition that achieving subjecthood can be a key moment in the radicalization process.[17] He understood that mobilizing gay men in opposition to postwar structures of oppression required a strategic stabilization of their identities, a stabilization that would enable them to see themselves as members of a collectivity. At the same time, however, he did not treat the achievement of a coherent self as an adequate substitute for liberation, and his investment in Enlightenment conceptions of identity should be understood as purely strategic.

I have dwelt at such length on "Hard Candy" because in this chapter I want to compare its treatment of gay male experience with that of *Cat on a Hot Tin Roof* (1954). A number of critics have recently argued that what they perceive as Williams's inability to come to terms with his homosexuality resulted in a split in his work between public and private forms of literary discourse.[18] According to them, whereas Williams did not hesitate to deal openly with gay male experience in his short stories and poetry, he refused to do so in his plays because they reached a broader audience and might expose his homosexuality to public scrutiny. The only way in which Williams was supposedly willing to express his gay identity in his plays was by refracting it.[19] We glimpse it in his treatment of sexual encounters that transgress racial, ethnic, and class boundaries; in his creation of strong female characters; and in his emphasis on the erotic in general. This argument positions Williams as a casualty of the closeted gay male subculture of the fifties and reproduces a view of his work that first gained currency in the early years of gay liberation. Following the emergence of the gay liberation movement, which led to the removal of many of the obstacles on Broadway to the production of plays that dealt openly with homosexuality, gay male critics began to attack Williams for not being more "out" in his work. In their view, Williams had not yet written a "gay" play, by which they meant a play that focused exclusively on gay male characters.[20] They saw Broadway as Williams's closet, the site where he could simultaneously reveal and conceal his gay identity, thus insuring that it remained an open secret.

What is particularly disturbing about this view is that it does not adequately consider the place of the closet in postwar gay male experience and thus seriously misrepresents Williams's hesitation to acknowledge his homosexuality publicly. Many critics are especially troubled by Williams's refusal to come out publicly until 1970, when he admitted somewhat coyly on the *David Frost Show* that he had "covered the waterfront."[21] They assume that closeted gay men are necessarily maladjusted or suffer from internalized homophobia.[22] The argument that Williams was unable to accept his homosexuality foregrounds the limitations of gay male criticism written from a narrow feminist perspective. John M. Clum, for example, argues that Williams's representation of gay male experience in "Hard Candy" is politically problematic because Mr. Krupper's anonymous sexual encounters are always with "poor, beautiful (of course) young men," as though gay male sex that cut across generational and class lines were inherently exploitative.[23] More troubling, however, from an antihomophobic perspective, is the way in which the criticism reproduces the very categories deployed by the national-security apparatus in the 1950s to position gay men as security risks. In constructing Williams as the stereotypical closeted gay man who was consumed by self-hatred, such arguments underestimate the degree to which the emergence of the national-security state made remaining in the closet a necessity for the vast majority of gay men in the postwar period. In light of the Cold War construction of homosexuality as a threat to national security, we need to avoid concluding that gay men who, like Williams, were unwilling to come out of the closet publicly suffered from internalized homophobia.

To locate Williams's work more firmly in its Cold War context, I want to compare his treatment of gay male experience in "Hard Candy" and *Cat on a Hot Tin Roof*. Many critics regard Williams's examination of the closet in *Cat on a Hot Tin Roof* as an example of the way in which his fear of public exposure led to a split in his work. Clum, for example, argues that of all of Williams's plays, *Cat on a Hot Tin Roof* provides "the most vivid dramatic embodiment of [his] mixed signals regarding homosexuality and his obsession with public exposure."[24] Clum also sees a parallel between Williams and Brick, the former athlete and heir apparent in the play who is tortured by the possibility that his relationship with his college roommate, Skipper, was homosexual. Clum reads Brick's determination to remain in the closet as an indication that "homosexuality . . . is terrifying for him because it is inevitably public."[25] Although it is true that none of Williams's plays from the fifties concerns unequivocally gay male characters, I want to show that there is more continuity in his work than critics have acknowledged. Written around the same time as "Hard Candy," *Cat on a Hot Tin Roof* manifests a similar investment in the structures of secrecy and disclosure that organized postwar gay male experience. What distinguishes *Cat on a Hot Tin Roof* from "Hard Candy" is that its examination of the closet is part of a larger critique of postwar structures of oppression. Williams seems to have understood that one of the ways in which the discourses of national security contained opposition to the Cold War consensus was by homosexualizing it. In *Cat on a Hot Tin Roof,* the closet emerges as a space in which not only gay men but also Communists and other groups targeted by the national-security apparatus can find political refuge while continuing to engage in their subversive activities.

Williams and the Political Economy of Anal Eroticism

Many critics interpret Big Daddy's confrontation with Brick in act 2 of *Cat on a Hot Tin Roof* as a deliberate reversal of the audience's expectations which is meant to highlight Brick's inability to accept his homosexuality.[26] Whereas Brick vehemently denies that "there was something not exactly right" about his relationship with Skipper, Big Daddy tries to convince him that he has no reason to feel ashamed of being homosexual.[27] Big Daddy reacts angrily when Brick derisively calls gay men "queers," "sissies," and "dirty old men" and urges him not to condemn those who are different from him. When Brick claims to be shocked by the ease with which Big Daddy discusses sodomy and the other "dirty things" (87) gay men do together, Big Daddy lectures him on the importance of tolerance: "Always . . . lived with too much space around me to be infected by ideas of other people. One thing you can grow on a big place more important than cotton!—is *tolerance!*—I grown it" (89). But perhaps the most surprising reversal occurs when Big Daddy acknowledges his own homosexual past. According to the stage directions, Big Daddy leaves "a lot unspoken" (86) when he reminisces about his youth, thereby authorizing us to fill in the blanks.[28] Big Daddy tells Brick that he was hired by Jack Straw and Peter Ochello, the gay male lovers from whom he inherited the plantation, after they found him asleep "in a wagon of cotton outside the gin" (86). In conjunction with his revelation that he "knocked around in [his] time" (85), the gaps in Big Daddy's reconstruction of his past seem intended to convey to Brick that his relationship with Straw and Ochello was sexual as well as professional. Big Daddy implies that Straw and Ochello hired him purely on the basis of his good looks and athletic build.

Despite the way in which this scene deliberately reverses the audience's expectations, however, Williams seems to have been primarily interested in establishing Brick's desire to inherit the estate on his own terms. This is not to deny that Brick's ranting about gay men is unspeakably homophobic, nor that he seems genuinely tortured by his memories of his relationship with Skipper. Rather, my point is that his refusal to acknowledge his homosexuality should be seen as an indication that he is determined to redefine the terms of his unstated contract with Big Daddy concerning the estate. Big Daddy wants to learn the "truth" about Brick's relationship with Skipper because he is afraid that Brick's homosexuality will disrupt the system of property relations he embodies. In many respects, Brick's claims to the estate are more tenuous than those of his brother, Gooper. After all, Gooper is Big Daddy's first-born son and has produced a male heir, thereby insuring that the estate will remain in the family; he has even managed the estate during Big Daddy's illness. Despite the strength of Gooper's claims, however, Big Daddy does not want to leave the estate to him and his wife, Mae, "since I hate [them] an' know they hate me" (81). Big Daddy clearly thinks that Brick is more his son than Gooper is. According to the stage directions, Brick has inherited his "virile beauty" (103) from Big Daddy and thus bears the marks of his lineage more than Gooper does. But Brick's drinking has led Big Daddy to reconsider leaving the estate to him. He asks Brick why he should "subsidize a goddam fool on the bottle" (82).

But the chief obstacle to Brick's inheriting the estate is his failure to produce an heir. Big Daddy tells Brick pointedly: "Gooper's wife's a good breeder, you got to admit she's fertile" (60). On the one hand, Big Daddy is willing to acknowledge that Maggie's exchange-value is superior to Mae's. Despite his disappointment in Maggie's failure to provide Brick with an heir, he admits: "That woman of yours has a better shape on her than Gooper's" (59). On the other hand, he compares her use-value unfavorably to Mae's. He assumes that Brick and Maggie have not yet produced an heir because Maggie is not a "good breeder," and so he urges Brick: "If you don't like Maggie, get rid of Maggie" (63). That Brick's homosexuality represents a violation of his "contract" with Big Daddy becomes clear when Big Mama pleads with him to have a son before Big Daddy dies: "Oh, Brick, son of Big

Daddy! Big Daddy does so love you! Y'know what would be his fondest dream come true? If before he passed on, you gave him a child of yours, a grandson as much like his son as his son is like Big Daddy!" (117). Brick's claim to the estate, in other words, is contingent on his willingness to reproduce the patriarchal order Big Daddy represents.

Brick's desire to remain in the closet indicates that he is unwilling to repress his homosexuality in exchange for securing his claims to the estate. Despite Big Daddy's willingness to acknowledge that he too "knocked" around in his youth, we should be careful not to confuse his homosexuality with Brick's. Big Daddy entered into a homosexual relationship with Straw and Ochello on condition that he would eventually inherit the plantation, and thus his homosexuality does not pose a threat to the patriarchal order but expresses the laws by which it operates. Although in his relationship with Straw and Ochello Big Daddy functions as an object of desire, he does not forfeit his claims to masculinity because he repairs their breach of patriarchal law. Straw and Ochello's ownership of the plantation threatens the transmission of patriarchal law, because, as gay male lovers, they cannot produce an heir. They further violate patriarchal law by failing fully to exploit the plantation's resources. They do not try to improve the planta-tion's productivity by accumulating more property but allow much of it to lie fallow. When Big Daddy becomes overseer, however, he reclaims the plantation for the patriarchal order. He not only provides Straw and Ochello with an heir, but he significantly increases the plantation's produc-tivity, eventually becoming the delta's richest cotton planter. As he proudly reminds Big Mama in act 2, under his management and with "no goddam help" (58) from her, the plantation got "bigger and bigger and bigger and bigger and bigger!" (58), demonstrating that he is its rightful owner. Thus Big Daddy's homosexuality does not prevent him from fulfilling the pa-triarchal injunction to reproduce, an injunction that is at once biological and economic.[29]

To further clarify the differences between Big Daddy's and Brick's homo-sexuality, I want to examine briefly Luce Irigaray's analysis of the patriarchal economy of exchange, in which women function as commodities. Accord-ing to Irigaray, in patriarchal societies the very foundation of the social and economic order depends on the exchange of women among men. Although men engage in the commerce of women, they do not enter into exchanges with them. Male heterosexual privilege is defined by an ability to engage in transactions with other men, and thus to retain their access to patriarchal power, men must renounce the desire to circulate as commodities. In this system of exchange, men's relations with women are governed by a homosexual economy of desire. Women have value only insofar as they "serve the possibility of, and potential benefit in, relations among men."[30] Thus heterosexuality merely provides "an alibi for the smooth workings of man's relations with himself, of relations among men."[31] To mark both the differences and the similarities between this system of exchange and homosexuality, Irigaray invents the neologism *hom(m)o-sexuality*. According to her, homosexuality differs from hom(m)o-sexuality in that it "openly interprets the law according to which society operates."[32] Moreover, in homosexual relations, the penis no longer functions symbolically but is merely a means to pleasure. For Irigaray, this is why homosexuality is so threatening to the patriarchal order and must be suppressed. Once the penis becomes a means to pleasure, *"the phallus loses its power."*[33]

Although, as a number of critics have pointed out, Irigaray does not adequately distinguish between homosexuality and hom(m)o-sexuality, her analysis provides a useful theoretical framework for understanding the differences between Brick's and Big Daddy's sexual identities.[34] Big Daddy's homosexuality is clearly grounded in a hom(m)o-sexual economy of desire. Although he enters into a relationship in which he circulates as a commodity, he retains access to patriarchal power by repositioning himself as the subject of a transaction. His willingness to function as an object of desire in exchange for inheriting the plantation transforms a homosexual relationship in which the penis does not function as a sign of patriarchal power into a hom(m)o-sexual one that is based on an exchange. Thus in Big Daddy's relationship with Straw and Ochello the penis is not a means to pleasure but provides Big Daddy with an instrument for obtaining control of the plantation. This analysis of Big Daddy's hom(m)o-sexuality casts his desire to learn the "truth" about Brick's relationship with Skipper in a wholly new light. Although Big Daddy *seems* to be more tolerant of homosexuality, he is willing to accept homosexual relations only insofar as they do not impede the reproduction of the hom(m)o-sexual system of exchange on which patriarchal property relations are based. He readily admits that he too "knocked" around in his youth because he used his homosexuality to contain the threat Straw and Ochello's relationship posed to the smooth workings of the patriarchal order.

Williams expresses the differences between Brick's and Big Daddy's homosexuality symbolically by making Big Daddy die from bowel cancer. In Williams's work, bowel cancer is a recurrent trope for gay male promiscuity. For example, in "The Mysteries of the Joy Rio," which was written in 1941 but not published until 1954, Pablo Gonzales, the gay male protagonist, visits the upper galleries of the Joy Rio theater several times a week in order to engage in anonymous sex with young boys. Like Big Daddy, he is dying from bowel cancer, a disease his late benefactor, Emiel Kroger, also died from and that he seems to have bequeathed to Gonzales along with his watch repair shop. Moreover, in "Hard Candy," a story that closely resembles "The Mysteries of the Joy Rio," we are told that Mr. Krupper suffers from "unhealthy intestines" (362), a condition that links him to Gonzales and Kroger. The recurrence of this trope has led critics to see Big Daddy's cancer as a sign of the homosexual excess of his youth. But I think it is better understood as an indication of his desire to repress his homosexuality. Big Daddy's transactions with Straw and Ochello transform the anus into a reproductive organ, thereby containing its potential to disrupt the hom(m)o-sexual system of exchange. In his relationship with Straw and Ochello, the anus functions as a means not to pleasure but to capital accumulation. We know from Freud that the genital organization of sexuality requires the repression of anal eroticism.[35] We also know from Freud that the repression of anal eroticism makes possible the accumulation of capital.[36] Freud's analysis enables us to construe Big Daddy's cancer as retribution for his betrayal of his homosexuality. Big Daddy is willing to disavow anal pleasure in exchange for the accumulation of property. Thus it seems fitting that he should be dying from a disease that Gooper describes as a "poisoning of the whole system due to the failure of the body to eliminate its poisons" (113). Big Daddy's desire to repress his homosexuality has transformed it into a "poison" that corrodes his body from within.

Big Daddy's willingness to disavow anal pleasure is key to understanding the differences between him and the other gay male characters in the play. Straw and Ochello, for example, refuse to instrumentalize the anus. Their homosexuality is not embedded in the exploitative structures of patriarchal capitalism; nor can it be reduced to the phallic binarisms that regulate the production of sexual difference. As we saw above, until Big Daddy intervenes in their relationship, they do not participate in the hom(m)o-sexual system of exchange. In their relationship, the penis does not function symbolically but is akin to the Lacanian Real. As a means to pleasure, it resists symbolization and thus threatens to disrupt the symbolic order. We know from the stage directions that their relationship "must have involved a tenderness which was uncommon" (xiii). This would seem to suggest that their desire for each other cannot be plotted along an active/passive axis in which anal penetration produces a relation of inequality. Straw and Ochello do not occupy gendered positions in relation to desire but have a relationship that is based on a reciprocity of desire and a mutual access to pleasure.

Insofar as it involves an "uncommon tenderness" that is not grounded in a phallic economy of desire, Straw and Ochello's relationship differs significantly from the other relationships in the play. Unlike those relationships, it does not provide an alibi for the smooth workings of the hom(m)o-sexual economy but represents an alternative ungoverned by the terms of the phallus. This is made clear by Williams's description of the bed-sitting-room in which the play takes place as a space that is "gently and poetically haunted [by the] pair of old bachelors who shared [it] all their lives" (xiii). The play's setting, in other words, serves as a constant reminder that the characters have betrayed Straw and Ochello's legacy, a legacy that includes an alternative mode of structuring relationships. In providing such an alternative, Straw and Ochello's relationship exposes the way in which patriarchal capitalism instrumentalizes the male body. Whereas from a hom(m)o-sexual point of view their failure fully to exploit the plantation's resources is a sign of their arrested sexual development, from a homosexual one it is a sign of their unwillingness to disavow anal pleasure.

Having clarified the differences between homosexual and hom(m)o-sexual economies of desire and their relation to patriarchal capitalism, I want to return to the point I made at the beginning of this discussion, namely, that Brick's refusal to acknowledge his homosexuality indicates his determination to redefine the terms of his "contract" with Big Daddy. Unlike Big Daddy, Brick is unwilling to repress his homosexuality in exchange for the accumulation of property. He occupies an ambiguous subject-position, one that is neither homosexual nor hom(m)o-sexual. Whereas Big Daddy bases his relationship with Straw and Ochello on a transaction, thereby insuring that it does not deprive him of access to patriarchal power, Brick refuses to hom(m)o-sexualize his relationship with Skipper. Although Maggie is willing to function as an object of exchange between him and Skipper so that their relationship will remain "one of those beautiful, ideal things they tell about in the Greek legends" (43), Brick rejects her attempt to provide a conduit for his desire. Maggie explains to Brick that she and Skipper made love not because they were attracted to each other but because "it made both of us feel a little bit closer to you" (43). Unlike Big Daddy, however, Brick has no interest in participating in the hom(m)o-sexual system of property relations, and so he refuses to triangulate his relationship with Skipper through Maggie. He resents Maggie's attempt to mediate his relationship with Skipper and blames her for Skipper's suicide. He tells Big Daddy that Maggie was jealous of Skipper and sought to destroy him: "Y'know, I think that Maggie had always felt sort of left out because she and me never got any closer together than two people just get in bed, which is not much closer than two cats on a—fence humping" (91).

At the same time, however, he also refuses to remove himself wholly from the hom(m)o-sexual economy. Because he is unwilling to relinquish access to patriarchal power, he resists entering into an unequivocally homosexual relationship with Skipper. When Skipper calls him long-distance and makes a drunken confession, Brick hangs up on him, pre-cipitating his suicide. Moreover, Brick refuses to believe that Skipper was attracted to him and blames Maggie for making Skipper doubt his sexuality. According to Brick, Skipper did not really believe he was gay but Maggie "poured in his mind the dirty, false idea that what we were, him and me, was a frustrated case of that ole pair of sisters that lived in this room, Jack Straw and Peter Ochello!—He, poor Skipper, went to bed with Maggie to prove it wasn't true, and when it didn't work out, he thought it *was* true!" (91). Brick's determination to retain access to patriarchal power pre-vents him and Skipper from experiencing the uncommon tenderness that marked Straw and Ochello's relationship. On the one hand, Brick wants to avoid forfeiting his claims to masculinity by entering into a relationship in which the penis is merely a means to pleasure and does not function as a sign of male heterosexual privilege. On the other hand, he does not want to destroy the "good, clean thing" (89) between him and Skipper by structur-ing their relationship hierarchically. Brick has no desire to enter into a homosexual relationship in which access to pleasure is not mutual. He would prefer to have a relationship with Skipper in which the phallus does not operate than one in which the anus functions purely as use-value. Thus he refuses to structure his relationship with Skipper in a way that would allow him to recuperate his masculinity.

Brick's refusal to participate in the hom(m)o-sexual economy surfaces most fully in his refusal to engage in a transaction with Big Daddy. As we saw above, Big Daddy confronts Brick about his relationship with Skipper to determine whether he is willing to hom(m)o-sexualize his desire. Unless Brick overcomes his reluctance to disavow anal pleasure, Big Daddy does not want to leave the estate to him. Brick's claim to the estate, in other words, is contingent on his willingness to instrumentalize the anus by relegating it to the status of use-value. Engaging in a transaction with Big Daddy would complete the hom(m)o-sexual system of exchange Big Daddy instituted when he inherited the plantation from Straw and Ochello. Brick's determination to remain in the closet, however, enables him to inherit the estate without fulfilling the terms of his "contract" with Big Daddy. He neither confesses his desire for Skipper nor produces a male heir in exchange for inheriting the estate. If at the end of the play he finally agrees to make love with Maggie, he does so not to show Big Daddy that he is willing to hom(m)o-sexualize his desire but rather because he is determined to remain in the closet. In the final scene, when Gooper and Mae refuse to believe that Maggie is pregnant because they "hear the nightly pleadin' and the nightly refusal" (155), Brick asks them: "How d'y'know that we're not silent lovers? Even if y'got a peep-hole drilled in the wall, how can y'tell if sometime when Gooper's got business in Memphis an' you're playin' scrabble at the country club with other ex-queens of cotton, Maggie and I don't come to some temporary agreement? How do you know that—?" (156). In producing an heir, Brick hopes to leave unresolved the question of his sexual identity. Once he has become a father, Gooper and Mae will be unable to determine whether he is homosexual or hom(m)o-sexual.

Brick's refusal to engage in a transaction with Big Daddy marks the emergence of a new social and economic order in which neither the penis nor the anus functions as use-value. By inheriting the estate without fulfilling his agreement with Big Daddy, Brick disrupts the smooth workings of the patriarchal order. His unwillingness to reduce the anus to its use-value restores the plantation to its original condition and thus makes restitution for Big Daddy's betrayal of his homosexuality, a betrayal that violates Straw and Ochello's legacy. As I have already noted, insofar as Straw and Ochello's relationship deinstrumentalizes the male body, it threatens to disrupt the hom(m)o-sexual system of exchange. As gay male subjects, Straw and Ochello do not occupy fixed positions in relation to desire but are simultaneously active and passive, desired and desiring. Thus their relationship cannot be reduced to the binary structure of heterosexual relations, as they were normativized in the Cold War era. The positions they occupy in relation to desire cannot be understood in terms of the binary opposition male/female. Nor does their desire correspond to the heterosexual mapping of the body into differentiated erotic zones coded as male or female.[37] As gay male subjects, their bodies contain multiple possibilities for achieving pleasure. In their relationship, pleasure does not remain localized at specific sites but is dispersed across the body. It is simultaneously genital, oral, and anal, and thus it cannot be understood in terms of the heterosexual economy of desire.

Although Brick and Maggie's relationship is not based on a mutual access to pleasure, it resembles Straw and Ochello's in that it undermines the binary logic of sexual difference. Like Straw and Ochello, Brick and Maggie do not occupy gendered positions in relation to desire. Unlike Big Daddy, Brick refuses to judge Maggie according to her exchange-value or her use-value. Moreover, by the end of the play he no longer tries to thwart her will but allows her to assert control over their relationship. According to the stage directions, in the final scene he watches her "with growing admiration" (157) as she throws away his liquor bottles and places his pillow on the bed next to hers, indicating her determination to make love with him. Insofar as it reverses the hierarchical structure of heterosexual relations, Brick and Maggie's relationship has the potential to impede the transmission of patriarchal law. Like Straw and Ochello's relationship, theirs cannot be understood in terms of the binary opposition male/female. Brick and Maggie's relation to desire is not fixed but constantly shifting. Brick's lack of interest in Maggie forces her to position herself as a desiring subject. Indeed, Brick seems to encourage Maggie to treat him as an object of desire. Maggie tells him that she has no interest in taking a lover because she "can't see a man but you! Even with my eyes closed, I just see you! Why don't you get ugly, Brick, why don't you please get fat or ugly or something so I could stand it?" (31). Brick's indifference seems calculated to increase Maggie's determination to have him. She tells him repeatedly that "one thing I don't have is the charm of the defeated, my hat is still in the ring, and I am determined to win!" (25), and thus he knows that she is unlikely to concede defeat.

Deinstrumentalizing the Female Body

To show more fully how Brick and Maggie's relationship disrupts the hom(m)o-sexual economy, I want to examine in some detail the construction of Maggie's subjectivity. Many critics treat Maggie as the archetypal phallic woman, claiming that she functions as a sign of both desire and castration.[38] To be sure, the stage directions consistently describe Maggie in masculine terms. They state, for example, that when Maggie's voice drops low, we "have a sudden image of her playing boys' games as a child" (18). This does not mean, however, that her subjectivity is grounded in a phallic economy of desire. As a married woman who has a better shape on her than Mae does, Maggie occupies an ambiguous position in the hom(m)o-sexual economy: she cannot be easily reduced to her exchange-value or to her use-value. Though married, she does not wholly remove herself from circulation as a commodity. As we saw above, she encourages Brick and Skipper to treat her as an object of exchange so that their relationship can remain like one of those "beautiful, ideal things" in Greek mythology. At the same time, however, she does not allow herself to be relegated to the status of exchange-value. She is well aware of her desirability as a commodity and even brags about it. She tells Brick that when she was in Memphis shopping for Big Daddy's birthday present, "there wasn't a man I met or walked by that didn't just eat me up with his eyes and turn around when I passed him and look back at me" (38). She is also proud of the fact that Big Daddy has a "lech" (19) for her, bragging that when he talks to her, he "drops his eyes to my boobs an' licks his old chops!" (19). Despite her pride in her ability to arouse male desire, however, she is determined to remove herself from the hom(m)o-sexual economy. She refuses to take a lover, even though Brick encourages her to do so.

She similarly does not allow herself to be reduced to her use-value. She resents the pressure placed on her to provide Brick with an heir and refuses to take the blame for their childlessness. She rejects the position assigned to her in the hom(m)o-sexual economy as a "breeder" whose primary function is to insure the reproduction of patriarchal property relations. She complains bitterly that the family treats her and Brick as though they were "totally useless" (16) simply because they have not yet had a child. Nor does she respect Mae, who allows the family to see her wholly in terms of her use-value. Maggie describes Mae as a "monster of fertility" (19) and makes fun of her claim that "motherhood's an experience that a woman ought to experience fully" (19), repeating it with mock solemnity. Nor does Maggie try to conceal her dislike of Mae's children, describing them as "no-neck monsters" (15) who do not know how to behave properly. As I noted above, she is even proud that she continues to have exchange-value, despite her status as a married woman. Maggie also violates patriarchal law by refusing to cede control of her body to Brick. She does not allow the hom(m)o-sexual economy to instrumentalize her body by exploiting its reproductive capacity. She insists that she has as much right to experience sexual plea-sure as Brick does. When Big Mama asks her if she makes Brick happy in bed, implying that she is to blame for their childlessness, Maggie retorts: "Why don't you ask if he makes *me* happy in bed? . . . *It works both ways!*" (37). According to Maggie, husbands and wives should have equal access to pleasure.

Maggie's ambiguous position in the hom(m)o-sexual economy can be attributed to her desire to function simultaneously as a subject and an object of desire. Insofar as Brick's sexual indifference enables her to posi-tion herself as a desiring subject, it reinforces her attraction to him. Maggie has no reason to fear that Brick will reduce her to an object of desire and thus return her to the hom(m)o-sexual system of exchange. She does not resent his indifference, because it enables her to occupy an active position in relation to desire that does not phallicize her. Maggie tells Brick that his lovemaking is "more like opening a door for a lady or seating her at a table than giving expression to any longing for her" (25) and thus does not place her in a subordinate position in relation to him. That Maggie's masculine position in relation to Brick does *not* phallicize her becomes clear at the end of the play. In the final scene, when Brick expresses admiration for her re-fusal to concede defeat, thus indicating his willingness to submit to her, she exclaims: "Oh, you weak, beautiful people who give up with such grace. What you need is someone to take hold of you—gently, with love, and hand your life back to you, like something gold you let go of" (158). Maggie's language here recalls Williams's descriptions of Straw and Ochello's uncommonly tender relationship. Although she asserts her will over Brick, she does so "gently" and "with love," suggesting that the position she occupies in their relationship is simultaneously masculine *and* feminine, active *and* passive. According to the terms of the play, such a position is gay.

Maggie's insistence on occupying a position in relation to desire that is simultaneously active and passive helps to explain why her attempt to function as an object of exchange between Brick and Skipper ultimately fails. Maggie's willingness to allow Brick to triangulate his desire for Skipper through her bespeaks her determination to dismantle the binary opposition male/female. In trying to provide a conduit for Brick's desire, she redefines her place in the hom(m)o-sexual economy. As an object of exchange, she occupies both an active and a passive position in relation to desire. Because she is the one who initiates the transaction, she does not function purely as a conduit for Brick's desire but participates in the exchange as one of the contracting parties. She readily admits that she made love with Skipper so that she could feel closer to Brick. When she recalls why she and Skipper made love, she does not exclude herself from the transaction, but stresses that she participated in it fully: "And so we made love to each other to dream it was you, *both of us*" (43; emphasis added). Thus it is hardly surprising that Skipper is unable to perform sexually when he and Maggie make love. Participating in the transaction requires him to forfeit his access to patriarchal power. In making love to Skipper, Maggie treats him as a conduit for *her* desire.[39]

In light of Maggie's desire to occupy a subject-position that is simultaneously masculine and feminine, her determination at the end of the play to provide Brick with a male heir is problematic and requires explanation. If Maggie is eager to redefine her place in the hom(m)o-sexual economy, why does she want to establish her use-value? Despite her resentment of the way in which the system of property relations relegates women to the status of use-value, why is she willing to provide Brick with a male heir in exchange for solidifying his claims to the estate? Does she want to perpetuate the system of exchange Big Daddy instituted when he inherited the plantation from Straw and Ochello or dismantle it? I think Maggie's eagerness to fulfill Big Daddy's "fondest dream" is best understood as indicating her determination to consolidate her position as a desiring subject. Her claim at the end of the play that she is pregnant shows her determination to participate in the hom(m)o-sexual economy *on her own terms*. This does not mean, however, that like Gooper and Mae, she tries to deceive Big Daddy so that he will leave the estate to Brick. She resents the way in which Gooper and Mae try to manipulate Big Daddy with their "monstrous" fertility and complains that they behave like "a couple of cardsharps fleecing a sucker" (20). Moreover, despite the fact that he embodies patriarchal law, Maggie feels an affinity for Big Daddy. Big Daddy is not ashamed of his working-class background, and she genuinely admires him because he "*is* what he *is*, and makes no bones about it. He hasn't turned gentleman farmer, he's still a Mississippi red neck, as much of a red neck as he must have been when he was just overseer here on the old Jack Straw and Peter Ochello place" (41).

That Maggie should feel an affinity for Big Daddy is hardly surprising, given the similarities between them. Like Big Daddy, Maggie comes from an impoverished background, which she is determined to overcome through the accumulation of property. She resents the way in which as a young girl she "always had to suck up to people I couldn't stand because they had money and I was poor as Job's turkey" (41). She recalls bitterly how her father's drinking forced her mother to "maintain some semblance of social position, to keep appearances up, on an income of one hundred and fifty dollars a month on those old government bonds!" (41). And she is still bitter that when she was a debutante, she had only two evening dresses, "one Mother made from a pattern in *Vogue*, the other a hand-me-down from a snotty rich cousin I hated!" (41). Thus she does not hesitate to hom(m)o-sexualize her relationship with Big Daddy. Despite her resentment of the position the hom(m)o-sexual economy assigns to women, she willingly renounces her body as a means to pleasure and exploits its reproductive capacities in order to fulfill the conditions of Brick's "contract" with Big Daddy. She does not try to conceal her determination to do so but openly declares it to Brick: "Born poor, raised poor, expect to die poor unless I manage to get us something out of what Big Daddy leaves when he dies of cancer!" (45). Here Maggie's resemblance to Big Daddy surfaces fully. Although her desire has the potential to disrupt the smooth workings of the patriarchal order, she is willing, like Big Daddy, to repress it in exchange for inheriting the estate.

But it is also here that the similarities between her and Big Daddy end. For despite her willingness to participate in the hom(m)o-sexual economy, she does not allow herself to become its instrument. She does not share Big Daddy's desire to secure the transmission of patriarchal law but enters into the system of exchange in order to subvert it from within. Her determination to establish her use-value enables her to remove herself from circulation as a commodity. To be sure, she is eager to show Big Daddy that she is as good a "breeder" as Mae is so that he will acknowledge Brick as his rightful heir. But in acting as a kind of proxy for Brick, she positions herself as the subject of a transaction. Moreover, as we saw above, Big Daddy enters into the hom(m)o-sexual system of exchange in order to contain the threat the anus poses to the reproduction of the patriarchal order. His willingness to repress his homosexuality in exchange for inheriting the plantation reduces the anus to its use-value and thus restores it to its status as a reproductive organ that guarantees the transmission of patriarchal law. Maggie, on the other hand, renounces her body as a means to pleasure *only temporarily*. Participating in the hom(m)o-sexual system of exchange enables her to occupy a masculine position in relation to desire that does not phallicize her because it is both active *and* passive. Her access to pleasure becomes contingent on her willingness to function, albeit temporarily, as pure use-value.

Elia Kazan, the Closet, and the Politics of Naming Names

Having shown that Brick and Maggie's participation in the hom(m)o-sexual economy is deceptive, I want to conclude this chapter by examining the differences between the original and the Broadway versions of the play. Clarifying the differences between the two versions will help us to locate Williams's treatment of the closet more firmly in its Cold War context. In the "Note of Explanation" Williams included in the published version of the play, he recalled that he rewrote act 3 after the director, Elia Kazan, criticized the way in which the play ended. According to Williams, Kazan objected in particular to Williams's treatment of Brick, who Kazan thought should experience "some apparent mutation as a result of the virtual vivisection that he undergoes in his interview with his father in Act Two" (124). Although Williams was eager to have Kazan direct the play and respected his opinion sufficiently to "re-examine the script from his point of view" (125), he was reluctant to have Brick experience a transformation, as he did not "believe that a conversation, however revelatory, ever effects so immediate a change in the heart or even conduct of a person in Brick's state of spiritual disrepair" (125).

Kazan's criticisms of Williams's treatment of Brick do not seem to have been motivated purely by artistic considerations. Kazan had become a controversial figure both on Broadway and in Hollywood because he had repudiated his left-wing past and named names when he appeared before the House Un-American Activities Committee in 1952.[40] He later claimed that he had cooperated with the committee in order to protect his career and avoid the blacklist.[41] Although his willingness to inform on former friends and colleagues who had been members of the Communist party in the thirties made him the target of left-wing attacks, he adamantly refused to apologize for his testimony and went to great lengths publicly to justify it. His film *On the Waterfront* (1954), for example, which won numerous Academy Awards including Best Picture and Best Director, examined union corruption and waterfront racketeering in a thinly veiled attempt to justify informing on the former Communists and fellow travelers who had been targeted by HUAC.[42] Although the film did not draw an explicit analogy between the corrupt union officials and the Communist party hierarchy, the union-busting hero, a Catholic priest played by Karl Malden, persuades one of the dockers, Terry Malloy (Marlon Brando), to testify before the crime commission about the union's corrupt activities. Malloy's willingness to confess to his criminal past and to inform on his former buddies leads to his moral regeneration, and the film ends happily with him marrying Edie Doyle (Eva Marie Saint), the film's courageous and principled heroine who encourages him to follow Father Barry's advice and inform on the union.

I have briefly summarized the plot of *On the Waterfront* in order to suggest that Kazan's criticisms of the original version of *Cat on a Hot Tin Roof* were motivated by a desire to have the play provide further justification for those who, like him, had named names before HUAC. Kazan's criticisms of the original ending indicate that he wanted Brick to experience the sort of moral regeneration Malloy experiences in *On the Waterfront* as a result of his testimony before the crime commission. Such a regeneration would justify Big Daddy's attempt to "straighten" Brick out by forcing him to acknowledge the "truth" about his relationship with Skipper and by extension exonerate former fellow travelers such as Kazan who had confessed their political "crimes." But this is clearly not what happens in the

Broadway version of the play. Although Williams insisted that he took "no attitude about [Kazan's testimony], one way or another" and partially re-wrote the play in response to Kazan's criticisms, he was unwilling to en-dorse informing on former friends and colleagues, even in the name of national security.[43] As we saw above, he stated quite clearly that he did not think it was possible for a conversation, however "revelatory," to bring about the sort of transformation that Kazan wanted Brick to undergo. Despite Williams's desire to have Kazan direct the play, Brick remains clos-eted in the Broadway version. As we saw above, Brick makes love with Maggie at the end of the play not because he has undergone a moral trans-formation and is no longer homosexual but because he refuses to relin-quish the protection afforded by the closet. Big Daddy makes clear that for Brick to inherit the estate he must hom(m)o-sexualize his desire, which he has no intention of doing.

A number of critics have noted the resemblance between the bed-sitting-room in which the play takes place and the homosexual closet.[44] Like the closet, the bed-sitting-room is a permeable space whose borders are not clearly defined but constantly shifting. According to the stage directions, it is barely distinguishable from the upstairs gallery. It includes "two pairs of very wide doors" that open onto the gallery and that provide a glimpse of "a fair summer evening that fades into dusk and night during the course of the play" (xiii). Williams also thought that the walls below the ceiling "should dissolve mysteriously into air" and that the set "should be roofed by the sky" (xiv). Moreover, the bed-sitting-room fails to protect its occupants from the intrusive gaze of others. In the scene in which he confronts Brick, Big Daddy complains that "the walls have ears in this place" (63). Although it is unusually hot, he closes the doors because "I hate eavesdroppers, I don't like any kind of sneakin' an' spyin'" (62), and he knows that Gooper and Mae are trying to overhear what he and Brick are talking about. Like the closet, in other words, the bed-sitting-room constantly exposes its occupants to public scrutiny. Family members enter it without knock-ing, complain bitterly when Brick and Maggie lock the doors, and listen through the walls to their personal conversations.

But in light of the wave of anti-Communist hysteria unleashed by the McCarthy hearings, the bed-sitting-room's permeability, its lack of fixed boundaries, has another possible meaning. Gooper and Mae's methods for exposing Brick as a homosexual who has broken his "contract" with Big

Daddy are reminiscent of the surveillance practices of the national-security apparatus. Williams renders the similarities explicit when in act 2 he has Maggie exclaim, "Sister Woman! Your talents are wasted as a housewife and mother, you really ought to be with the FBI" (54). These references to the emergence of the national-security state make possible another reading of the play, one that links it to other plays written at about the same time, such as Arthur Miller's *The Crucible* (1953), which were more explicit in their criticisms of Kazan and the other so-called friendly witnesses who testified before HUAC.[45] Williams's representation of the bed-sitting-room as a space in which Brick and Maggie are constantly threatened with exposure suggests that he too wanted to critique the emergence of the national-security state. This may explain more fully why Kazan objected to the original ending of the play. Gooper and Mae's attempts to expose Brick could be read as an indirect reference to Kazan's controversial testimony. In the play, the closet emerges as a space in which Communists, gays, and other groups targeted by the national-security apparatus can escape detection. In confronting Brick with the "truth" about his homosexuality, a truth Brick denies not because he is ashamed of it but because he does not want to forfeit his claims to the estate, Big Daddy only reinforces his determination to remain in the closet.

Williams, then, did not allow his desire to have Kazan direct the play deter him from criticizing those who had cooperated with HUAC. Despite Kazan's criticisms, Williams did not delete his allusions to McCarthyism. The few changes he did make in response to Kazan's criticisms, such as having Brick express admiration for Maggie in the final scene, did not prevent Gooper and Mae's constant spying on Brick and Maggie from recalling the McCarthy witch hunts. Williams's strategies were not unlike those Maggie and Brick adopted to subvert the hom(m)o-sexual economy from within. His "Note of Explanation" and the few minor changes he made to act 3 functioned as a kind of screen that enabled him to protest the government's violation of basic civil liberties (the right to free speech and freedom of association) without alienating Kazan. His criticisms of Kazan are sufficiently veiled that they can easily go undetected. Brick's homosexuality is not the only open secret in the play. Williams's oblique references to the national-security state simultaneously reveal and conceal his criticisms of those who, like Kazan, had betrayed former friends and colleagues in order to protect their careers.[46]

Given his exploration in *Cat on a Hot Tin Roof* of the open secret that governed gay male experience in the Cold War era, it is hardly surprising that when in the early years of gay liberation Williams was criticized for not having written a "gay" play, he responded angrily, claiming that he had not found it necessary to write one because "I could express what I wanted to express through other means."[47] Many critics have seen Williams's desire to avoid limiting his audience by focusing exclusively on gay male characters as an indication that he conceived of homosexuality as a private or civil rights issue that did not have important political and social repercussions.[48] Yet in light of his treatment of gay male experience in *Cat on a Hot Tin Roof,* this understanding of his plays seems unwarranted and ignores their thematic continuity with his more sexually explicit short stories. In *Cat on a Hot Tin Roof,* Williams explored, albeit indirectly, the linkage between homosexuality and Communism in the Cold War political imaginary. If he refused to limit his audience, that is because he understood that in the Cold War era not only gay men but also "promiscuous" women, Communists, and other groups who rejected the postwar American dream of owning a home in the suburbs were forced to inhabit the closet.

CHAPTER FIVE

Gore Vidal and the Erotics of Masculinity

In my opinion, based upon close observation, the majority of homosexuals have
some slight characteristic that will betray their inclinations to an
astute and experienced observer: an unusual inflection of the voice,
a movement of the hands or shoulders, a characteristic walk.
—Donald Webster Corey, *The Homosexual in America*

Jim was thought to be trade by most of Shaw's friends, but, as he never had affairs
with any of them, it was decided that perhaps he might be normal after all.
—Gore Vidal, *The City and the Pillar*

Convinced that gay men inevitably betrayed themselves by the inflection of
their voices or the way in which they walked, Donald Webster Corey, the
leading proponent of gay and lesbian rights in the 1950s, did not know how
to read Gore Vidal's controversial novel *The City and the Pillar* (1946), in
which the protagonist appeared to be "normal" but could not be classified
as trade.[1] Although Vidal's treatment of the gay male subculture was clearly
intended to contest the dominant understanding of gay male desire, Corey
complained that the novel's tragic ending reinforced the stereotype of the
suicidal gay man. In *The Homosexual in America* (1951), his pioneering study
of the similarities between gays and other oppressed minorities in American society, Corey speculated that the widespread acceptance of the medical model of homosexuality "may be attributed to the novelists who have
ended so many books on this subject in a mood of despair, violence, and
even suicide" and then cited *The City and the Pillar* as a case in point.[2] He
located Vidal's novel in a tradition of fictionalized gay autobiography that
ended tragically and claimed that its representation of gay male experience
was not realistic but the product of internalized homophobia. According to

Corey, Vidal used the novel to purge himself of his own self-hatred. In ending *The City and the Pillar* with a murder, Vidal resorted to the narrative technique "by which some authors, themselves homosexual and having extreme obsessions about their inclinations, persecute and punish themselves" (176). Vidal's recourse to this narrative technique supposedly enabled him to "continue to live a free life, without suffering the consequences of the physical injuries of punishment, but benefiting by the rewards of a purging chastisement" (176).

In locating him in a tradition of gay male writers who supposedly used their work to purge themselves of guilt about their homosexuality, Corey seriously distorted Vidal's project in *The City and the Pillar*. In the afterword to the revised edition of *The City and the Pillar*, published in 1965, Vidal indicated that he originally wrote the novel to undermine the set of narratives available for representing gay male experience, narratives that reduced gay male identity to a form of gender inversion. He explained that in the 1940s when *The City and the Pillar* first appeared, male homosexuality was understood medically as a form of mental illness "confined for the most part to interior decorators and ballet dancers."[3] Knowing from his limited exposure to the gay male subculture, however, that this was not the case, he deliberately "set out to shatter the stereotype by taking as [his] protagonist a completely ordinary boy of the middle class and through his eyes observ[ing] the various strata of the underworld" (156). But Vidal's project was not limited to challenging the medical model of homosexuality. Although in the afterword he made no mention of his reputation as the heir to a masculinist literary tradition that included Stephen Crane and Ernest Hemingway, his remarks indicate that he decided to write a novel about the homosexual "underworld" primarily to contest the homophobic categories of that tradition.[4] Alluding to his dissatisfaction with his acclaim as a soldier novelist, he recalled: "I was bored with playing it safe. I wanted to take risks, to try something no American had done before. I decided to examine the homosexual underworld (which I knew rather less well than I pretended), and in the process show the 'naturalness' of homosexual relations, as well as making the point that there is no such thing as a homosexual" (155). He hoped that by observing the gay male subculture through the eyes of an "ordinary" middle-class boy, he could dismantle the binary logic of sexual difference, a logic that made homosexuality seem "unnatural."

But if *The City and the Pillar* could be read, in spite of Vidal's intentions, as reinforcing the medicalization of gay male subjectivity, it could also be read as reproducing the homophobic categories of the dominant tradition of American letters. Leslie Fiedler did not believe that Vidal's novel differed significantly from the mainstream of American fiction but saw in its focus on gay male experience business as usual because it supposedly conformed to the repressed and sentimentalizing homoerotic character of American literature. To be sure, he admitted that the homoeroticism of *The City and the Pillar* was unusually explicit, but he read Vidal's representation of the homosexual "underworld" as an elaboration rather than a negation of the master tropes of the American novel. In "Come Back to the Raft Ag'in, Huck Honey!" the notorious essay in which he first expounded his argument about the centrality of male homoeroticism to American letters, he cited *The City and the Pillar* as an example of the endurance of a national myth of innocence and located it in a literary tradition that included *Two Years before the Mast, Moby-Dick,* and *Huckleberry Finn.* He saw the publication of *The City and the Pillar* as an indication that "still the dream survives: in a recent book by Gore Vidal, an incipient homosexual, not yet aware of the implications of his feelings, indulges in the reverie of running off to sea with his dearest friend."[5] In this way, Fiedler tried to contain the emergence of a distinctly gay male literary tradition by assimilating it into the dominant paradigms of American literature. We were supposed to believe that in dreaming of running off to sea, Jim Willard, the "incipient" homosexual who is the protagonist of *The City and the Pillar,* was expressing a desire to experience a merely chaste male love.

How do we account for these misunderstandings of Vidal's project? Why would Corey, the most sophisticated theorist of gay rights in the fifties, claim that Vidal's novel reinforced the stereotype of the suicidal gay man? Why would Fiedler cite Vidal's novel as an example of the endurance of the masculinist tradition of American letters? In what follows, I will try to account for these (mis)readings of Vidal's novel by arguing that they reflected the degree to which it contested the conventions that governed the representation of gay male experience in literary as well as scientific discourse. Vidal attributed to the protagonist of his novel a form of subjectivity that could not be understood in terms of the regulatory fictions that governed the production of gender in the Cold War era. For this reason, his novel challenged the set of narratives available for understanding gay male experience. Because Jim does not appear to be a woman trapped in a man's body but resembles an "ordinary" middle-class boy, his homosexuality exceeds the binary structure of sexual difference and cannot be understood as a form of gender inversion. In deviating from the conventions that governed the representation of gay male experience, Vidal's novel also called into question the self-understanding of the gay male subculture. Jim's desire for other men is rooted in a disidentification with masculinity that does not revert to or manifest itself in an identification with femininity; consequently, he continues to occupy a masculine subject-position. This subject-position does not conflict with his sexual orientation because it is grounded not in an identification with his father but in a resistance to patriarchal authority. Thus it is not reducible to the phallic binarisms that determined the relation between gender and sexuality in the postwar period. The novel's inscription of a male subject-position that is simultaneously homosexual and masculine should not be confused with the desire to escape gender, to deny it, to transcend it, or to perform it to excess that Teresa de Lauretis has recently argued characterizes lesbian fiction.[6] Rather, it should be understood as an attempt to reconceive male homosexuality by treating gender and sexuality as categories of identity that are closely related but nevertheless distinct.

Deconstructing Identity: Vidal and the Discourse of Minority Rights

Vidal's attempt to define a male subject-position that is not only homosexual but also masculine indicates why *The City and the Pillar* was misread by homophobic and antihomophobic readers alike. At least one critic has seen the centrality of masculinity in the novel's exploration of gay male subjectivity as an anticipation of the masculinization of urban gay communities in the 1970s. In a recent collection of essays devoted to reevaluating Vidal's place in American literary history, Claude Summers suggests that the novel's emphasis on the "naturalness" of homosexual relations was prescient. He links it to the emergence of the gay macho style in the 1970s, which has usually been attributed to the influence of the gay liberation movement but which, according to Summers, "began much earlier and was probably at least partly influenced by the two world wars."[7] Although I agree with Summers that a distinctly gay macho style emerged much earlier than has generally been thought and that *The City and the Pillar* can provide important insights into gay male appropriations of the signifiers of certain forms of straight masculinity, before we try to assess the significance of Vidal's masculinization of gay male subjectivity, we must first situate the novel in relation to the gay rights movement of the postwar period.[8] As Summers points out, Vidal has refused to adopt the rhetoric of mainstream gay rights activists and has insisted on using the term *homosexual* as an adjective rather than as a noun. In the afterword to the revised edition of *The City and the Pillar,* for example, Vidal states that, "despite its current usage, the word [*homosexual*] is an adjective describing a sexual action, not a noun describing a recognizable type" (155). Vidal also contends that all human beings are innately bisexual. For him, there is no shared pattern of development or common set of experiences that can explain the "etiology" of homosexuality. Again in the afterword to the revised *The City and the Pillar,* he argues that "conditioning, opportunity and habit account finally (and mysteriously) for sexual preference, and homosexualists are quite as difficult to generalize about as heterosexualists" (155). He probably would not have agreed with Corey that gays inevitably betrayed themselves to the astute and experienced observer.

In his hostility to fixed sexual categories, Vidal has more in common with gay liberationists than with the mainstream of gay rights activists, who have tended to work to consolidate the minority status of homosexuals and lesbians rather than to interrogate the disciplinary logic of identity.[9] Like Vidal, the gay liberationists of the late sixties and early seventies maintained that all human beings are innately bisexual. Drawing on Herbert Marcuse's analysis in *Eros and Civilization* (1955), which identified sexuality as a liberatory force that had the potential to counteract the reifying effects of advanced capitalism, the liberationists distinguished between *homosexuality,* which they used to indicate sexual preference, and *gayness,* which they defined as a politically subversive identity unrelated to object-choice.[10] In attacking the institutions, discourses, and practices that stabilized individual and collective identities in capitalist social formations, they looked forward to the end of "the homosexual" as a category of individual.[11]

This commitment on the part of gay liberationists to the destabilization of existing sexual categories distinguished them from more mainstream gay rights activists, who were primarily interested in extending the discourse of minority rights to homosexuals and lesbians. These activists realized that treating homosexuality and lesbianism as categories of identity similar to race and ethnicity would enable them to mobilize the mass of gay men and women, so they stressed the characteristics gay men and women supposedly had in common with one another. Influenced by Corey's pioneering work on the similarities between gay and lesbian communities and other subcultural formations, the activists sought to legitimate their demands for legal and other reforms by claiming that homosexuals and lesbians constituted an oppressed minority and therefore were entitled to the same legal protections as other minorities.[12] Their project should be seen as assimilationist. In contrast to gay liberationists, they were primarily interested in making the postwar culture of consumption more accessible to homosexuals and lesbians. They treated sexuality as a personal or civil rights issue and refused to interrogate the normative status of heterosexuality.

Situating Vidal's anti-essentialist project in relation to the postwar gay rights movement helps to clarify the relationship between *The City and the Pillar* and the emergence of a gay macho style in Cold War America. Although in *The City and the Pillar* Vidal tried to define a gay male subject-position that was masculine and thus can be said to have participated in the masculinization of urban gay communities, he sought to complicate the narratives available for understanding the construction of gay male subjectivity by extricating them from the binarisms that structured heterosexual relations in the Cold War era. If, throughout his career as a writer Vidal has rejected the rhetoric of mainstream gay rights activists, refusing to use the term *homosexual* as a noun, that is because he has tried to avoid fixing or stabilizing gay male identity and has chosen instead to demonstrate that gay men simultaneously occupy a multiplicity of potentially contradictory subject-positions. Vidal uses the novel to show that men can be simultaneously gay and masculine. They may experience a conflict between these subject-positions, but that does not mean that masculinity and homosexuality are fundamentally incompatible. This is not to say that, for Vidal, the construction of gay male subjectivity automatically exceeds the binary logic of gender. Despite their relative autonomy, sexuality and gender function in *The City and the Pillar* as mutually constitutive categories of identity. The dominant understanding of gay male desire influences how the gay male characters in *The City and the Pillar* experience the relation between their gender and their sexuality. Still, although the construction of gay male subjectivity in Vidal's novel reflects the binary oppositions that regulate the production of gender, it cannot be reduced to them.

Overcoming the Limits of Camp:
Urban Gay Communities and the Erotics of Masculinity

Because it tries to show that masculinity and homosexuality are compatible, we can use *The City and the Pillar* to gain insight into the masculinization of postwar urban gay communities. The emergence of a gay macho style is usually understood as representing a politically subversive appropriation of the signifiers of male heterosexuality. Richard Dyer argues that the gay macho style should be seen as a form of "semiotic guerilla warfare"—a term he borrows from Umberto Eco—in which gay men self-consciously try to undermine the signifying practices that naturalize the production of gender in capitalist social formations. Dyer claims that the gay macho style helps to demystify masculinity by eroticizing it in an explicitly homosexual context. Gay male appropriations of masculinity show that it is not the exclusive property of straight men but that its meaning is historically contingent. The adoption of a theatrically masculine appearance by gay men has supposedly done "much mischief . . . to the security with which 'men' are defined in society, and by which their power is secured. If that bearded, muscular beer drinker turns out to be a pansy, how ever are they going to know the 'real' men any more?"[13] From this perspective, the prevalence of a macho style in urban gay communities does not indicate an erotic investment in masculinity or an identification with it. Rather, it should be seen as part of a struggle to undermine the discourses and institutions that regulate the production of gender. The adoption of a theatrically masculine appearance represents a counter-deployment of the signifying practices that naturalize male heterosexual privilege.

Recent discussions of the gay bathhouses that flourished in the seventies before the onslaught of the AIDS epidemic have demonstrated a similar tendency to identify urban gay communities as utopian spaces in which the counter-deployment of the signifying practices that stabilize gender disrupts them. Many gay male intellectuals have seen the bathhouses as the institutional embodiment of the gay macho style and its emancipatory potential. Dennis Altman, for example, claims that the bathhouses were utopian spaces in which the willingness to engage in sex spontaneously and with multiple partners represented "a sort of Whitmanesque democracy, a desire to know and trust other men in a type of brotherhood far removed from the male bonding of rank, hierarchy and competition that characterizes much of the outside world."[14] In an interview conducted in 1978, Michel Foucault similarly stressed the utopian possibilities of the bathhouses. He suggested that the anonymity of the sexual encounters in the bathhouses enabled gay men to divest themselves of their identities as social subjects and to maximize the erotic possibilities of the body. In their willingness to engage in sex with multiple partners, gay men functioned purely as bodies, providing each other with the instruments for obtaining mutual pleasure. For Foucault, there existed in the bathhouses "the exceptional possibility of being desubjectified, of being desubjugated . . . perhaps not in the most radical way, but in any case, with sufficient intensity for one to take note of it."[15] In other words, one of the more controversial aspects of the masculinization of postwar urban gay communities, namely, the practice of engaging in anonymous sex, promised to disrupt the logic of identity. In promoting the pursuit of pure bodily pleasure, the bathhouses supposedly functioned as sites for the production of a collective gay male subject.

The tendency to identify the gay macho style with the utopian possibility of transcending the binary structure of sexual difference has not gone uncontested. Leo Bersani claims that rather than being a subversive parody, the gay macho style indicates an identification with masculinity that reinforces the very signifying practices that oppress gay men. Because gay men tend to adopt a theatrically masculine appearance to attract other gay men, Bersani questions whether straight men see the gay macho style as a threat to their identities: "nothing forces [straight men] to see any relation between the gay-macho style and their image of their own masculinity (indeed, the very exaggerations of that style make such denials seem plausible)."[16] He also believes that male homosexuality necessarily entails an erotic investment in masculinity. In his view, the desire for men "can't be merely a kind of culturally neutral attraction to a Platonic Idea of the male body; the object of desire necessarily includes a socially determined and socially pervasive definition of what it means to be a man."[17] This does not mean, however, that Bersani does not see gay male desire as potentially subversive. He challenges Dyer's and Altman's analyses of the masculinization of the gay male subculture because he believes that the most threatening aspect of male homosexuality is precisely its relation to femininity.[18] Stressing the link between the anus and the vagina in the symbolic order, he argues that "to be penetrated is to abdicate power."[19] If gay male desire has the potential to disrupt the regulatory fictions that govern the production of gender, that is because it evokes "the intolerable image of a grown man, legs high in the air, unable to refuse the suicidal ecstasy of being a woman."[20] Given this understanding of the erotics of anal penetration, it is hardly surprising that Bersani thinks that gay men should embrace the link between homosexuality and femininity rather than try to deny it by strategically redeploying the signifiers of masculinity.

Although it is more compelling than Dyer's and Altman's, there are several problems with Bersani's argument. He seems unable to conceive of male homosexuality apart from the discourses, institutions, and practices that regulate the production of gender. Rather than treating gender and sexuality as distinct categories of identity, he assumes that the relation between them is causal. According to the logic of his argument, an individual's gender necessarily expresses or reflects her/his sexuality and her/his sexuality necessarily expresses or reflects her/his gender.[21] Thus he not only naturalizes the phallic economy of heterosexual desire but assumes that it is constitutive of gay male subjectivity. Feminizing the anus, he contends that as a point of reception, its relation to desire is passive rather than active, and thus it resembles the vagina. In this way, he reduces gay male subjectivity to a form of gender inversion. Indeed, the only difference between his argument and the medical model of homosexuality is that in foregrounding the gay man's pleasurable relation to the anus, he locates the gay man's identification with femininity at the level of the body rather than at the level of the psyche.

Another problem with Bersani's argument is that it follows the example of Dyer and other gay male critics in claiming that the adoption of a theatrically masculine appearance by many gay men as a marker of their identities represented an abrupt departure from earlier gay male practices. But this distorts the history of the gay male subculture in Cold War America. Both Dyer and Altman assume that, until the emergence of a distinctly gay macho style in the seventies, urban gay communities were organized around the link between male homosexuality and femininity. Perceiving themselves as women trapped in men's bodies, gay men adopted a self-consciously effeminate mode of behavior to mark their identities. Mainstream gay rights activists have attacked camp as politically retrograde, but both Dyer and Altman contend that gay male appropriations of straight femininity are politically subversive. Dyer, for example, states that they indicate "a great sensitivity to gender roles *as* roles and a refusal to take the trappings of femininity too seriously."[22] But this argument seems contradictory. The emergence of a style of dress and mode of behavior meant to parody masculinity can be said to demonstrate the endurance of camp, not a repudiation of it. In adopting a theatrically masculine appearance as a marker of their identities, gay men continue to try to transcend gender by performing it to excess. But there is a more serious problem with the argument that the appropriation of the signifiers of masculinity deviated sharply from the earlier practices of the gay male subculture. There is ample evidence to suggest that both Dyer and Altman exaggerate the hegemonic role of camp in postwar urban gay communities. In addition to Vidal's representation of gay male experience in *The City and the Pillar*, which I examine in detail below, there is also Corey's claim in *The Homosexual in America* that the presence in gay bars of homosexuals who self-consciously parodied femininity was "discouraged not only by the proprietors, but by the gay clientele" (123). Such a claim indicates that camp encountered significant opposition and that its hegemonic role was not a given but had to be renewed continuously.

If Bersani misrepresents the masculinization of gay male subjectivity, that is because he overlooks its origins in the crisis of masculinity precipitated by the rise of the "organization man." As I noted in the introduction, despite the financial benefits of conforming to the domestic model of masculinity, the rise of the "organization man" was vigorously contested. In stressing the importance of postwar oppositional forms of masculinity, I do not mean to romanticize them. As I indicated in chapter 1, they are best understood as responses to a set of government policies designed to consolidate the postwar shift from production to consumption. Rooted in a desire to return to an earlier stage of capitalism when the entrepreneurial spirit still flourished, these forms of masculinity did not adequately challenge existing social and economic arrangements. Moreover, they were complicitous with the Cold War construction of "the homosexual" as a national-security risk. Because male homosocial bonds were objects of intense scrutiny and suspicion in the Cold War era, the men who rejected the postwar American dream of owning a home in the suburbs were under considerable pressure to distinguish themselves from gay men. Such pressure was one of the causes of the fragmentation and dispersal of the New Left, and thus it worked to contain opposition to the Cold War consensus. Annoyed by its project to dismantle the logic of identity, a project that conflicted with their pursuit of an "authentic" masculinity, the leaders of the New Left dismissed the gay liberation movement as trivial and distracting. Their macho posturing alienated lesbian and gay members, who eventually broke with the New Left in 1969 in order to found the Gay Liberation Front.[23]

Still, in order to clarify the masculinization of postwar urban gay communities, it is necessary to situate it in relation to the proliferation of oppositional forms of masculinity. The resistance to the rise of the "organization man" indicates that rather than being a monolithic entity, as Bersani implies, masculinity was a site of intense ideological struggle throughout the postwar period. My aim in relating the emergence of a distinctly gay macho style to the reorganization of masculinity in the forties and fifties is to suggest that in adopting a theatrically masculine appearance, gay men identified themselves with an oppositional form of masculinity. Appropriating the signifiers of a masculinity that defined itself in opposition to white-collar America allowed gays to signal their rejection of the domesticated values of the white suburban middle class. This is not to suggest that the adoption of a theatrically masculine appearance has merely been a way for gay men to mark their difference from mainstream white America. Although Bersani, by being unable to conceive of homosexuality apart from the regulatory fictions that govern the production of gender, misinterprets the masculinization of the gay male subculture, he is nonetheless right to suggest that the emergence of a distinctly gay macho style indicates an erotic investment in masculinity.

I want to use *The City and the Pillar* to propose an alternative understanding of the gay macho style. Vidal's masculinization of Jim Willard's subjectivity indicates that the style represents a fantasy rather than a parody of straight masculinity. According to psychoanalytic theory, fantasy is not the object of desire but its setting or *mise-en-scène*.[24] It contains the potentially endless dispersal and displacement of the individual's desire by organizing and regulating it. In the fantasy scenario, the individual's desire is not performed or fulfilled so much as it is constituted, which is to say that it is through fantasy that the individual learns how to desire. Fantasy grounds the individual's desire by determining which objects s/he invests in libidinally and seeks gratification from.[25] Applying the psychoanalytic theory of fantasy to the gay macho style enables us to avoid reducing it to the heterosexual economy of desire. The emergence of a distinctly gay macho style was contingent on the availability of a form of masculinity that signified resistance to the containment of sexuality within the privatized space of the nuclear family. In expressing a fantasy about masculinity, the adoption of a masculine appearance as the setting or *mise-en-scène* of gay male desire first emerged in the fifties in opposition to the rise of the "organization man," not as an identification with straight masculinity. In other words, I am proposing that the gay macho style neither represents a purely subversive parody of masculinity in which gay men have no erotic investment, nor indicates an identification with straight masculinity that reflects an internalization of the signifying practices that oppress gay men. Rather, the gay macho style represents the use of an oppositional form of masculinity that first emerged in the fifties as a means of staging a desire that does not conform to the domesticated values of the white suburban middle class. The appropriation of the signifiers of an oppositional form of masculinity should be understood as functioning not only as the setting or *mise-en-scène* of gay male desire but as a marker of its difference from more traditional forms of desire. To elaborate this understanding of the gay macho style, I want to turn to *The City and the Pillar* and examine in more detail Vidal's masculinization of gay male subjectivity.

Eroticizing Gay Male Identity: Vidal and the Contested Terrain of Masculinity

Shortly after Jim Willard begins working as a ballboy at the Garden Hotel in Beverly Hills, he discovers, through the hotel's bellhops, the existence of the homosexual "underworld." Despite his own attraction to other men, he does not make a connection between himself and the bellhops who introduce him to the "underworld," and he is even appalled by the discovery that many of them are exclusively attracted to other men. He begins to think that he can readily identify the bellhops who are gay by the characteristics they have in common. Echoing the observations Corey makes in the passage from *The Homosexual in America* that serves as an epigraph for this chapter, he remarks: "They walked with a tight slightly mincing and completely self-conscious manner. Their voices had a curious quality, a feminine intonation, and their eyes were searching but wary, continually defending, asking."[26] In other words, the theatrically feminine appearance these men have adopted to mark their identities allows Willard to distinguish his desire from theirs. Because he does not behave in an effeminate manner but is an accomplished athlete, he must not be gay, and thus he can participate in the homosexual "underworld" without identifying himself with it. Unable to deny his own exclusive attraction to other men, he would sometimes "study himself in a mirror to see if there was any trace of the woman in his face or manner; he was pleased always that there was not. Then [he] decided that he was unique. He was the only one who had done what he had done, felt the way he did, and acted the way he had acted" (100). Jim's exposure to the homosexual "underworld" has precipitated a crisis in which he is unable to reconcile his desire for other men with his masculinity. He seems to assume that the relation between his gender and his sexuality is causal. At the same time, however, his discovery that there are many men who, like him, desire other men enables him to distance himself from the bellhops who define themselves wholly in terms of their membership in the homosexual "underworld." Having internalized the dominant understanding of gay male desire, he tells himself that he must not be gay, despite his exclusive attraction to other men. Unlike the bellhops who have adopted a theatrically feminine appearance as a sign of their participation in the gay male subculture, he does not resemble a woman trapped in a man's body and therefore must be "unique."

Jim does not acknowledge the similarities between him and other gay men until Paul Sullivan, the left-wing writer who becomes his lover, describes to him the "typical" pattern of gay male development. Sullivan explains that most gay men begin their sexual lives when they are adolescents by having "erotic dreams of a certain boy and you get to know him and you often become friends and if he's sufficiently ambivalent and you're sufficiently aggressive you'll have a wonderful time experimenting with each other; there it begins" (125). Like Jim, Sullivan has internalized the dominant construction of homosexuality, and so he does not see Jim as gay. He describes the set of experiences that gay men supposedly have in common with one another because he feels certain that Jim's development has not been typical. Since Jim's desire for other men cannot be reduced to a form of gender inversion, his experiences must not correspond to the pattern Sullivan has been describing. Sullivan concludes by telling Jim: "There are many types and many different patterns but there are certain similar beginnings. *You're not like the others* because you started rather late and I don't think you have much feeling about your relationships" (125). Yet Jim recognizes in Sullivan's description of the "typical" pattern of gay development his own experiences with Bob Ford, the high school friend he fantasizes about running off to sea with. Listening to Sullivan, he realizes that he is "a man not unlike these others, varying only in degree from a basic pattern. Jim, who had never really thought of himself as one, now regarded himself with wonder and fear and doubt" (126). Jim's willingness to identify himself as gay manifests itself most fully when Sullivan tells him that he should have an affair with Maria Verlaine because it might "rescue" him from the gay male subculture. Jim responds angrily, "Why should I be rescued?" (171). Jim no longer refuses to acknowledge the similarities between him and other gay men but accepts that he is a "member of the submerged world of the homosexual" (171).

At first glance the set of experiences I have been mapping can be said to correspond to a typical coming-out story, in which Jim gradually learns to accept his homosexuality as the essential core, or "truth," of his identity. Despite the fact that he appears to be "normal" and can pass as straight, Jim becomes increasingly willing to identify himself with other gay men and no longer tries to repress his "real" self. This is certainly how many critics have understood *The City and the Pillar.* Claude Summers, for example, sees Jim as a "homosexual Everyman" and claims that Vidal's novel represents "an ambitious attempt to trace realistically a homosexual's awakening in a particular time and place, while also locating this experience in the vast expanses and repetitive patterns of myth."[27] In this way, Summers locates *The City and the Pillar* in a tradition of Anglo-American gay male fiction that includes E. M. Forster's *Maurice* (1914) and Edmund White's *A Boy's Own Story* (1982). But reading Vidal's novel as a "typical" coming-out story does not seem wholly warranted. To begin with, such a reading does not adequately interrogate the narrative trope of coming out, which tends to function as a regulatory fiction that fixes or stabilizes gay male identity. On the one hand, the coming-out story makes available to gays a set of narratives that enables them to make sense of their personal histories and to locate them within a larger collective history. On the other hand, it reduces gay male desire to a minority experience that is supposedly grounded in a shared pattern of development.

But locating *The City and the Pillar* in a tradition of Anglo-American gay male fiction is also problematic because it requires reading Vidal's novel according to a fixed set of narrative conventions that makes Jim's experiences seem more linear and coherent than they really are. The narrative trope of coming out encourages a normative, teleological understanding of the construction of gay male subjectivity.[28] According to the narrative logic of the coming-out process, as it has been defined by mainstream gay rights activists, the gay man's acceptance of the "truth" of his identity constitutes a fixed point of arrival from which he then interacts with the world as a wholly self-present individual who is able to lay claim to his rights as a citizen.[29] But there is no single moment of self-discovery in *The City and the Pillar* in which Jim can be said to acknowledge the essential core of his identity or in which he successfully resolves the conflict between his gender and his sexuality. To be sure, he becomes increasingly willing to accept the exclusivity of his attraction to other men. But he continues to distance himself from the gay male subculture because of its appropriation of the signifiers of straight femininity.

His resistance to identifying fully with other gay men is perhaps most obvious in his continuing devotion to Bob. The intensity of his desire for Bob reflects "the fact that Bob had been drawn to him as a person, in spite of the object, and the original force would not have diminished over the years, could not have diminished" (292). Thus he longs to renew his affair with Bob because it supposedly does not conform to the binary organization of gender relations. Jim thinks that because Bob made love to him as a "person" and not as a man, they do not occupy gendered positions in relation to desire. This is not to say that Jim's understanding of the organization of his sexuality does not shift over the course of the novel. As I noted above, Jim does not feel that his desire for other men is incompatible with the masculinization of his subjectivity until he begins working at the Garden Hotel and discovers the existence of a homosexual "underworld" whose members mark their identities by adopting a theatrically feminine appearance.

Insofar as it cannot be understood as a form of gender inversion, Jim's subjectivity threatens to destabilize the binary oppositions that govern the construction of masculinity. His attraction to other men is rooted in a disidentification with his father that cannot be traced to an identification with his mother. Jim dislikes his father intensely and considers him a "bitter pompous little man" (29). Mr. Willard seems vaguely jealous of Jim's relationship with Bob, which he does not approve of, and he tries to prevent him from spending the weekend at the cabin with Bob before Bob ships out to sea. Jim's reaction to Mr. Willard's tirade about his plans for the weekend is typical: "He could not understand [his father], his temper and his bitterness. He wished sometimes that his father was like Bob's, uncaring, absorbed in drinking and being alive. He looked at his father, hating him at this moment: these moments of hatred seemed to increase the older he got" (30).

Jim's antagonistic relationship with his father can be traced to the rise of the "organization man" and the emergence of competing models of masculinity in the postwar period. Mr. Willard dislikes Jim almost as intensely as Jim dislikes him. Mr. Willard seems to sense Jim's lack of identification with him and resents him because "he was tall and handsome and not at all the sort of son [he] would like to have had" (27). Jim, who is an accomplished athlete, embodies a different type of masculinity from his father's, which indicates why his father does not understand him and prefers John, the youngest son whose masculinity is more like his own. Like Mr. Willard, John asserts his masculinity primarily by pursuing a career and raising a family. The emergence of competing models of masculinity divides Jim from his brother as well as from his father. Unlike Jim, John respects patriarchal authority, as it is embodied by his father, and is the son Mr. Willard wants to have. When John enters the dining room shortly after Jim does, Mr. Willard looks at him "satisfied in some strange way with what he saw" (28), despite the fact that he is not as handsome or athletic as Jim. John does not share Jim's desire to be independent and self-reliant but intends to follow in Mr. Willard's footsteps and enter politics after graduating from college. Like Mr. Willard, he does not approve of Jim's plans to spend the weekend at the cabin with Bob and considers fishing and camping, traditional masculine activities that Jim and Bob pursue avidly, a "waste of time" (28).

Because Jim's lack of identification with his father does not revert to or express itself in an identification with his mother, his sexuality does not automatically conflict with his gender, and he continues to occupy a masculine subject-position. Jim's homosexuality marks his difference from his father and the white middle-class values he embodies. Jim's desire for Bob can be attributed to the oppositional form of masculinity Bob represents. Bob does not care whether his father approves of him, and he does as he pleases, regardless of the consequences. He tells Jim that he has no intention of going to college, since "there isn't a thing they could teach me that I want to know. I guess I want to have a good time and travel more than anything else" (43). Jim admires Bob's refusal to submit passively to patriarchal authority and wishes that he could be more like him. When Bob calls Jim's father a "stuck-up bastard," Jim is grateful to him "for having said what he himself had always wanted to say" (44). He envies Bob's independence and self-reliance, which provides him with a model, and wishes that he did not have to please his father and go to college. When Bob tells Jim about his decision to enlist in the merchant marine, Jim replies, "I wish I was going with you up North. I'd really like to see New York and do as I please for once" (45). But at first Jim lacks Bob's courage to rebel against patriarchal authority, and he stammers that he cannot run off to sea with him because "I think I ought to wait till next year. I'll be eighteen then and I'll have a high-school diploma and that's important to have. My father wants me to go to college . . . you know that, and I don't want to disappoint him and . . ." (43). Despite his desire to be like Bob, Jim continues to depend on his father's approval and is unwilling to assert his independence from him.

Although Bob's willingness to defy middle-class expectations by refusing to go to college and pursue a career eventually provides Jim with a model, we should be careful not to confuse Jim's resistance to the domestication of masculinity with Bob's. Bob's opposition to the rise of the "organization man" is based on a form of male identity that was no longer ideologically dominant but had become residual because it conflicted with the new corporate order. Bob wants to do as he pleases, unencumbered by domestic responsibilities, and he later refuses to settle down with his wife, Sally, and raise a family. Although Sally constantly pressures him to resign his commission in the merchant marine so that he can become a partner in her father's insurance company, he insists that life at sea is a "career like any other" (296) and accepts a promotion to first mate. He perceives his responsibilities to his family as incompatible with his manhood. He seems to think that providing for his family necessitates becoming an "organization man" who submits to a corporate hierarchy. When Jim returns home at the end of the novel to try to renew their affair, Bob tells him that his decision to run off to sea was a mistake and that he wishes that "I had had sense enough to go to college. . . . Maybe I wouldn't have gone to sea. Then I wouldn't have to make this choice. I could have become a lawyer or something" (298). His career in the merchant marine has not adequately prepared him for his role as a breadwinner.

In contrast, Jim's growing opposition to the rise of the "organization man" cannot be attributed to a nostalgia for an ideologically outmoded form of straight male identity. Insofar as it is rooted in a rejection of patriarchal values, his masculinity corresponds neither to the residual nor to the dominant models of masculinity but represents an alternative to them. Although he shares Bob's desire to recover forms of male homosocial bonding that are discouraged because they conflict with the Fordist organization of production and consumption, his subjectivity cannot be reduced to a phallic economy of desire. Whereas Bob resists the domestication of masculinity by escaping into the male homosocial world of the sea, Jim does so by seeking relationships with other men that are based on a mutual access to pleasure. He eventually leaves the actor Shaw, for example, because Shaw insists on structuring their relationship hierarchically. Shaw, who is older and more experienced, expects Jim to be "the admirer and the pupil" (116) who learns from him how to negotiate the gay male subculture. Although Jim eventually becomes the dominant sexual partner in their relationship, he continues to occupy a subordinate position in relation to Shaw, who treats him "as though he were a possession and not a man" (115). Despite the fact that he continues to feel attracted to Shaw, he becomes dissatisfied with their relationship because Shaw refuses to treat him as an equal, and he eventually leaves him for Sullivan: "He did not want a father as much as he wanted a brother; he did not want sex in this unnatural way as much as he wished to have it incidental to a large emotion, to a mingling of his identity with an equal" (116). Sullivan, who is not as egotistical as Shaw, promises to fulfill Jim's desire for "a companion, a brother, another of his age with whom he could share himself" (116).

To show that Jim's resistance to the reorganization of masculinity does indeed differ from Bob's, I would like to examine briefly a passage that, somewhat surprisingly, Vidal deleted when he revised the novel in 1965. This passage helps to clarify the relation between the masculinization of

Jim's subjectivity and the postwar proliferation of oppositional forms of masculinity. In the passage we learn that when Jim was a boy, he covered his bedroom walls with pictures of his favorite baseball and tennis players. Despite the fact that his admiration for these players has since waned, he "left the pictures up anyway because he didn't like the rosebud wallpaper" (31) his mother had placed on the walls. Here it becomes clear that the masculinization of Jim's subjectivity reflects not an identification with masculinity but a resistance to the signifying practices that gender sexuality. If Jim seems to identify with masculinity, that is because the alternative would entail identifying with femininity. This does not mean that he devalues his mother and the domesticity she represents. At one point in the novel, when Sullivan attributes Jim's homosexuality to a fear of the female body, Jim protests that his desire for other men "was not the result of negation, of hatred or fear of women; it came, rather, from a most affirmative love" (271).[30] Yet insofar as it would reduce his homosexuality to a form of gender inversion, identifying with femininity would legitimize the dominant construction of homosexuality. In occupying a masculine rather than a feminine subject-position, Jim calls into question the set of narratives available for understanding gay male subjectivity. He does not identify fully with either masculinity or femininity. The pictures on the walls merely signal his refusal to occupy the feminine subject-position assigned to gay men by patriarchal discourse.

In conveying Jim's lack of identification with either masculinity or femininity, this passage allows us to construe the masculinization of his subjectivity as a form of resistance. Politically strategic, it demonstrates his refusal to submit to the feminization of gay male subjectivity. Jim's investment in a model of masculinity that had been displaced by the rise of the "organization man" is more erotic than identificatory. Inhabiting an outmoded form of masculinity allows him not only to mark his difference from his father but also to stage his desire for other men. That is, his appropriation of the signifiers of an oppositional form of masculinity functions as the setting or *mise-en-scène* of his desire and not its object. Despite his growing lack of interest in sports in high school, he continues to compete in tennis matches because in doing so he is able to solidify his relationship with Bob. Although he does not become fully conscious of his desire for Bob until they make love by the river, he realizes that "to consummate [his desire for Bob] they played tennis together and talked about the girls Bob liked" (39). Jim enjoys playing tennis with Bob and talking about the girls he likes because it increases intimacy between them and enables him to express his desire for Bob in a way that does not threaten Bob's masculinity: "Games had been very important to both of them. Jim found it difficult to talk to Bob and the games helped: the hitting of a white ball back and forth across a net formed a better communication than words" (23). Jim senses that a more open declaration of his love would drive Bob away. Because Jim appears to be an "ordinary" middle-class boy who does not resemble the stereotype of the effeminate homosexual, Bob does not perceive their intimacy as "un-natural" and even encourages it.

Jim's strategic deployment of his masculinity indicates that his relation to the dominant and residual models of masculinity is more complicated than Bob's. Whereas Jim's attraction to Bob reflects his longing for a male companion, or "brother," with whom he can share himself, Bob's attraction to Jim reflects his desire to recover forms of male homosocial bonding that were increasingly pathologized in the postwar period. Unlike Jim's, Bob's subjectivity *can* be reduced to a phallic economy of desire. He treats their encounter by the river as an immature form of heterosexuality. Whereas Jim is not afraid to acknowledge that he has enjoyed having sex with Bob, Bob tries to deny the significance of their encounter by dismissing it as "awful kid's stuff" (49); in so doing, he tries to show that he does not confuse it with the "real" thing. While he has clearly enjoyed having sex with Jim and is willing to continue to have sex with him so long as they remain at the cabin, he feels threatened by the encounter and tells Jim that "guys aren't supposed to do that with each other. It's not natural" (49). Despite Jim's recollection of it, the encounter by the river confirms rather than challenges the medical model of homosexuality. Bob conceives of homosexuality as a form of gender inversion. When he and Jim have sex, he repeats "the movements and subtleties that he had learned with girls" (48), thereby positioning Jim as a woman.

Whereas Bob's resistance to the domestication of masculinity can be attributed to a desire to recover displaced forms of male homosocial bonding by running off to sea, Jim's can be attributed to a rejection of patriarchal values. Bob diminishes their lovemaking by dismissing it as "kid's stuff," but Jim experiences it as "his first completion, his first discovery of a twin: the half he had been searching for" (48). Jim's desire for Bob reflects a longing to experience solidarity with another man and not a misogynistic desire to escape the domestic sphere. Convinced that Bob shares his fantasies of defying patriarchal authority, Jim assumes that Bob's desire for him cannot be reduced to the binary structure of heterosexual relations. Unlike Bob, who envies Jim's body, which is more muscular than his, and constantly competes with him to show that he is stronger, Jim admires Bob's body "with a strange, different emotion that had no envy in it" (39). Moreover, when Jim looks at Bob's body, he experiences a "twinship, a similarity, a warm emotion which he could not name" (39). Jim has sex with Bob neither to subdue a powerful competitor, nor to submit passively to a "real" man.

That Jim's subjectivity does indeed exceed the phallic economy of heterosexual desire is made clear in the series of disturbing dreams he has when he becomes seriously ill while in the army and almost dies. Sometimes he dreams of a "menacing, subtly distorted Bob who would never come near him, who always retreated when he tried to touch him" (200). At other times, he dreams of being held by his mother and feeling safe and secure until his father appears. Then he would "slip out of her arms and his father would beat him and all the time there would be a brown river roaring in his ears" (201). Insofar as it literalizes the psychic violence inflicted on the subject by her/his traumatic entry into the symbolic order, this dream restages the Oedipal scenario. Jim's father intervenes in his relationship with his mother not only by barring his access to her but by brutally beating him as well. At the same time, however, this dream indicates that the organization of Jim's sexuality cannot be reduced to the either/or structure of the Oedipus complex, which forces the subject to negotiate identifications at the expense of object-choices. The roaring river Jim hears while his father beats him complicates the dream's restaging of the Oedipal scenario by indicating the presence of Bob, who provides an alternative to the set of identifications and object attachments that are the usual product of the Oedipal crisis. The river in the dream not only recalls the river by the cabin where Jim and Bob had sex, but its color—brown—evokes the anal eroticism of their encounter. Its presence in the dream links Jim's desire for other men to a disidentification with his father and not to an identification with his mother. Jim responds to the crisis precipitated by his father's barring of his access to his mother not by identifying with him but by rejecting him. This does not mean, however, that he compensates for his rejection of his father by identifying with his mother. The roaring river he hears in the dream is linked not only to the homoeroticism of his relationship with Bob but to a form of masculinity that defines itself in opposition to patriarchal authority. It recalls the site where he openly indulges in his fantasies of defying his father's wishes and running off to sea with Bob.

Remystifying Gender: Corey and the Minoritizing of Gay Male Identity

In attributing to Jim a form of gay male subjectivity that is not grounded in the Oedipal structure of the nuclear family, Vidal's novel not only contested the dominant construction of homosexuality but provided an alternative understanding of gay male experience that was potentially more subversive than Corey's extension of the discourse of minority rights to gay man. Jim's resistance to the feminization of gay male subjectivity conflicted with the self-understanding of the gay male subculture. Corey, for example, could not conceive of male homosexuality apart from the either/or structure of Oedipal desire. The only way in which he could demonstrate that homosexuality was a category of identity similar to race and ethnicity was by grounding it ontologically.[31] Although he objected to the medicalization of gay male subjectivity and was careful to distinguish between those gay men who self-consciously parodied femininity and those who appeared to be "normal" and could pass as straight, he continued to think of homosexuality as a form of gender inversion. At the same time that he recognized the heterogeneity of urban gay communities and conceded that generalizing about gay men was difficult, if not impossible, he argued that male same-sex desire could be traced to an identification with the mother that manifested itself in a desire "to be like her in every respect" (72). In this way, he tried to show that homosexuality represented a fixed minority identity rather than a medical condition requiring treatment. Despite the heterogeneity of urban gay communities, gay men had certain characteristics in common that distinguished them from other Americans and that preexisted their mobilization as gay men. Thus they could legitimately lay claim to the same legal protections as other oppressed minorities.

Because it refuses to essentialize gay male identity, we can use Vidal's novel to clarify the limitations of Corey's minoritarian construction of homosexuality. Given the essentializing logic of the discourse of minority rights, as it was deployed in the postwar period, the only way in which Corey could legitimately claim that homosexuality constituted a minority identity rather than a form of psychopathology was by reifying the category *homosexual* and arguing that it preexisted social relations rather than was a product of them. At the same time, however, in suppressing the heterogeneity of gay male experience, Corey sacrificed the ability to interrogate the discourses and practices that gendered sexuality. Whereas Vidal tried to identify a form of gay male subjectivity that was rooted in a resistance to both the residual and the dominant models of masculinity, Corey tried to consolidate gay men's minority status by locating the source of their sexual orientation in a shared pattern of development. For this reason, he inadvertently contributed to the mystification of the production of gender. If male same-sex desire could be traced to an identification with the mother, the relation between gender and sexuality was causal rather than mutually determining.

In using *The City and the Pillar* to clarify the limitations of the minoritarian, or subcultural, model of male homosexuality pioneered by Corey, I do not mean to exaggerate the significance of Vidal's anti-essentialist project in *The City and the Pillar*. Vidal's attempt to define a form of gay male subjectivity that transcended the binary logic of gender was utopian. Despite its inscription of a gay male subject-position that was not grounded in Oedipal structures, Vidal's novel makes clear that occupying such a position was virtually impossible in the Cold War era. In the novel, the medical model of homosexuality prevents Jim from reconciling his gender and his sexuality. As we saw above, Jim longs to renew his affair with Bob because he thinks that it will enable him to occupy a position in relation to desire that is not gendered. Yet when he tries to renew the affair at the end of the novel, Bob rejects him, projecting his own self-hatred onto him. Bob tells him: "You're a queer . . . you're nothing but a damned queer!" (306). Here the novel emphasizes Jim's inability to evade or transcend the gendering of his sexuality. The novel's tragic ending, in which Jim rapes and murders Bob, reverses their encounter by the river, in which they wrestle one another before making love, and it indicates that their relationship cannot escape the rigid hierarchies structuring male homosocial bonds. Jim resorts to raping and murdering Bob in order to dominate him.

Despite the utopian aspect of his project, however, Vidal's masculinization of gay male subjectivity represented a more serious challenge to existing arrangements than did Corey's minoritarian model. In attributing to Jim a form of gay male subjectivity that exceeded the either/or structure of Oedipal desire, Vidal showed that masculinity was not a monolithic entity but a contested terrain in which different models of masculinity competed for dominance. Thus his critique of postwar American society was more far-reaching than Corey's. Whereas Corey limited his political demands to official recognition of gays as a piece of the postwar cultural mosaic, Vidal called into question the basic design of that mosaic. For Vidal, the primary source of gay male oppression was not the inaccessibility of the American dream but the discourses and institutions that regulated the production of gender.

Kaja Silverman has recently tried to define the place of femininity within gay male subjectivity by arguing that gay men are women at the level of their unconscious identifications.[32] Elaborating Bersani's critique of the gay macho style, she claims that the adoption of a theatrically masculine appearance by many gay men indicates an internalization of the very signifying practices that oppress them. Like Bersani, she does not see how the redeployment of the signifiers of a certain form of straight masculinity in an explicitly homosexual context might be politically subversive or indicate resistance to patriarchal discourse. For this reason, she elaborates a theory of gay male subjectivity that stresses its potentially subversive relation to femininity. She tries to show that the appropriation of the signifiers of femininity by some gay men indicates that an unconscious identification with women provides the very foundation of all gay identities, as well as the position from which they desire. Silverman's analysis is clearly motivated by a desire to establish the basis for a political alliance between gay men and women. If gay men are women at the level of their unconscious identifications, they too have a stake in disrupting the reproduction of patriarchal discourse. But in stressing the potentially subversive relation between male homosexuality and femininity, Silverman denies the alterity of gay male subjectivity. Her desire to valorize marginal or "deviant" masculinities that not only acknowledge but embrace castration, alterity, and specularity in many respects requires her to subsume gay male subjectivity under the category *woman*. Although she makes a point of acknowledging the heterogeneity of gay male experience as well as claiming that she has no intention of providing a totalizing theory of male homosexuality, she is unwilling to entertain the possibility that the emergence of a distinctly gay macho style may have indicated resistance to, rather than inscription within, patriarchal discourse.

The City and the Pillar indicates the possibility of establishing a coalition between gay men and women that does not subsume gay male subjectivity under the category *woman* but acknowledges its alterity. As we have seen, appropriating the signifiers of an oppositional form of masculinity (independence, self-reliance, sexual promiscuity) enables Jim to mark his difference from his father. The masculinization of his subjectivity demonstrates his resistance to the signifying practices that oppressed gay men in the fifties, not an internalization of them. He disrupts patriarchal operations by refusing to contain his sexuality within the privatized space of the nuclear family. In this way, Vidal's novel shows that, although gay male subjectivity is constituted differently from straight female subjectivity, gay men, like straight women, nevertheless have a stake in dismantling the discourses and institutions that regulate the production of gender. Along with his masculinization of Jim's subjectivity, Vidal makes clear that patriarchal forms of masculinity provide the greatest obstacle to gay liberation.

CHAPTER SIX

A Negative Relation to One's Culture:

James Baldwin and the Homophobic

Politics of Form

The negative relation to one's culture has great validity in certain periods;
at others, it is simply sterile, even psychopathic, and ought to give way,
as it has done here, in the last decade, to the positive relation. Anything else
suggests too strongly the continuation of the negative Oedipal relations of
adolescence—and in much of the alienation of the 20s and 30s there was
just that quality of immaturity.
—Newton Arvin, *Partisan Review* (1952)

When *Another Country* was first published in 1962, many critics dismissed it
as a failed attempt at a social-protest novel, claiming that Baldwin was
vulnerable to the very criticisms he had leveled against Richard Wright in
"Everybody's Protest Novel," the controversial 1948 *Partisan Review* essay in
which he attacked Wright for reducing literature to a weapon in the struggle against racism.[1] Irving Howe's criticisms of the novel in "Black Boys and
Native Sons," an essay on African American writers that first appeared in
Dissent in 1963, were typical. Howe suggested that "anyone vindictive
enough to make the effort, could score against [*Another Country*] the points
Baldwin scored against Wright," and he derogatorily described Rufus Scott,
the novel's black male protagonist, as a "sophisticated distant cousin of
Bigger Thomas."[2] Despite the similarities between *Another Country* and
Wright's *Native Son* (1940), however, Baldwin's model seems to have been
less Wright than Henry James, the writer many postwar critics regarded as
the "master" of novelistic discourse. Baldwin included James among the list

of writers who had helped him "break out of the ghetto," and the epigraph of *Another Country* is an unidentified passage from James.[3] At least one critic has cited the epigraph as evidence that the novel's thematic concerns were inspired by James, but Baldwin's debt to the "master" seems to have been more formal than thematic.[4] For Baldwin adopts a Jamesian narrative strategy, relying on what James in his prefaces to the New York edition of his novels called "successive reflectors," or multiple centers of intelligence, through which he filters the novel's action.[5]

Baldwin was one of a handful of postwar writers who willingly acknowledged a debt to James.[6] Although postwar writers were often criticized for neglecting matters of form and were encouraged to imitate James's style, by and large they resisted using him as a model, claiming that his narrative techniques could not adequately capture the complexity of postwar experience.[7] Ralph Ellison, for example, when he received the National Book Award in 1953, explained his innovative use of the autobiographical form in *Invisible Man* (1953) by stating that "the diversity of American life with its extreme fluidity and openness seemed too vital and alive to be caught for more than the briefest instant in the tight well-made Jamesian novel, which was, for all its artistic perfection, too concerned with 'good taste' and stable areas."[8] This does not mean, however, that Baldwin's use of a Jamesian mode of narration in *Another Country* should be interpreted as evidence that he thought the complexity of postwar experience could be caught in a tight, well-made Jamesian novel. Granted, Howe's criticisms of Baldwin were unfounded and bordered on racist. He refused to read *Another Country* on its own terms and insisted on comparing it to Wright's *Native Son*, whose representation of black experience was supposedly more authentic because it expressed "the violence that gathers in the Negro's heart as a response to the violence he [*sic*] encounters in society" (358). But he was right to suggest that *Another Country* represented Baldwin's attempt at a social-protest novel; Rufus Scott can indeed be described as a "distant cousin" of Bigger Thomas.

But if *Another Country* may be read as a social-protest novel, how do we explain Baldwin's use of narrative techniques that could not have been more different from Wright's in *Native Son*? Did Baldwin want to deny his debt to his African American literary antecedents, which is the way Howe interpreted his formal strategies, or was his use of a Jamesian mode of narration better suited to his project? In what follows, I will argue that

Baldwin's use of multiple centers of intelligence should be understood as a creolizing appropriation of James's narrative techniques, in which he combined the formal strategies of the Jamesian novel with the thematic concerns of the naturalistic novel, the form of novelistic discourse postwar critics tended to think was most appropriate for representing African American experience.[9] By filtering the action of *Another Country* through the characters' consciousnesses, Baldwin was able to foreground issues of subjectivity that many postwar critics thought the naturalistic mode of narration marginalized. Although the construction of subjectivity in Baldwin's novel is partially determined by the material conditions of existence, it cannot be reduced to them. Moreover, by frequently shifting the novel's point of view, Baldwin was able to stage a series of dialogic encounters between characters of different races, classes, and genders which showed that such categories were mutually constitutive and could not be understood apart from one another. Thus one of the advantages of his use of a Jamesian mode of narration was that it racialized whiteness. It demonstrated that white subjectivity was grounded in racist constructions of blackness.[10] In *Another Country,* whiteness does not indicate an absence of color but is a product of a racialized social formation in which the construction of white and black subjectivity are mutually determining. Baldwin's project to creolize James's formal strategies is expressed symbolically in *Another Country* in the scene in which we learn that the two favorite novels of Eric Jones, the gay male protagonist, are *The Wings of the Dove* and *Native Son.*[11]

Cold War Liberals and the Homosexualization of Left-Wing Political Activity

In addition to creolizing a form of novelistic discourse that many postwar critics thought could not adequately capture African American experience, Baldwin's project in *Another Country* also included recovering James from a theory and tradition of American letters that was deeply homophobic, not only in its political implications, but also in its application to specific texts. Postwar critics of the novel as a form such as Lionel Trilling and Richard Chase defined the novel as a journey from innocence to experience in which the hero gained a more realistic view of the world. Chase, for example, in a review of Ellison's *Invisible Man* published in *Kenyon Review* in

1952, argued that the typical novel plot involved "the passage, or the failure of passage, from innocence to experience."[12] For Chase, this passage required the hero to abandon a view of the world that was unrealistic and that underestimated its complexity. The hero who successfully negotiated this passage gained a maturity of vision that enabled her/him to accept the world as it was. Chase argued that, in narrativizing the hero's loss of innocence, the novelist properly assumed that "life is in need of 'clarifying'— that is, of being clearly seen in its reality and complication—and of 'justification'—that is, of being grasped in its inner meaning and fashioned into a controlling image by the imagination" (679). In defining the novel in this way, Chase echoed the views of his friend and colleague in the Columbia English department, Lionel Trilling. Trilling also defined the novel as a passage from innocence to experience. In "Manners, Morals, and the Novel," an essay that originally appeared in *Kenyon Review* in 1948, Trilling described the novel as a "perpetual quest for reality, the field of its research being always the social world, the material of its analysis being always manners as the indication of the direction of man's [sic] soul."[13]

What is particularly striking about this definition of the novel is that Trilling and Chase tended to describe their political trajectories in precisely the same terms. They tried to justify the increasing conservatism of their cultural politics by ascribing it to a political loss of innocence. Like other Cold War liberals, they identified the Moscow show trials of the 1930s and the Ribbentrop treaty as decisive events in their personal histories that made them realize that their faith in the "common man" was misplaced.[14] Not wanting their repudiation of left-wing politics to be interpreted as a betrayal but as a sign of their intellectual and emotional maturity, they claimed that they no longer viewed the world through the distorting lens of Marxist ideology but as it really was. In so doing, they reinforced the view expressed by Newton Arvin in the epigraph to this chapter that left-wing political activity could be attributed to an inability to resolve the Oedipus complex. In claiming that their faith in the "common man" reflected an unrealistic view of the world that they eventually outgrew, Trilling and Chase implied that left-wing politics represented an adolescent refusal to accept the world as it was and was best understood as a continuation of the negative Oedipus complex into adulthood. Moreover, in equating left-wing politics with a lack of a maturity of vision, they marginalized alternative traditions of the novel. Writers such as Dreiser, Dos Passos, Steinbeck, and

Wright whose fiction was explicitly political did not belong in the canon because they failed to represent the world accurately and lacked insight into its complexity. The tendency of these writers to focus on the material conditions of existence at the expense of issues of subjectivity indicated their failure to negotiate successfully the passage from innocence to experience and thus was a sign that they suffered from an arrested sexual development.

Although in the twenties and thirties left-wing critics such as V. L. Parrington and Granville Hicks had deliberately neglected Henry James, relegating him to the "genteel" tradition of American fiction, Trilling and Chase regarded him as the only American writer who had successfully mastered the novel form, and they sought to reclaim him for their theory and tradition of American letters.[15] In his highly influential essay "Reality in America," for example, Trilling complained that even if James had intended his novels "to be understood as pleas for co-operatives, labor unions, better housing, and more equitable taxation, the American critic in his liberal and progressive character would still be worried by James because his work shows so many of the electric qualities of mind" (13). To revive scholarly and critical interest in James, Trilling and Chase stressed his technical contributions to the development of the novel, which they claimed equaled those of Balzac and Flaubert, as well as his powers of social observation.[16] In "Manners, Morals and the Novel," Trilling argued that "in America in the nineteenth century, Henry James was alone in knowing that to scale the moral and aesthetic heights in the novel one had to use the ladder of social observation" (212). In *The American Novel and Its Tradition* (1957), Chase went even further, claiming that James's novels were "the most complete and admirable . . . yet produced by an American."[17] Yet Trilling's and Chase's attempts to establish James's reputation as a master of novelistic discourse were not always easy to reconcile with their definition of the novel. Trilling's reading of *The Princess Casamassima,* in which he praised the historical accuracy of its portrait of British working-class life, provides a case in point, for it conflicted with his criticisms of the naturalistic novel in "Reality in America."

Trilling was convinced that the populist aesthetic of the Popular Front continued to influence criticism of American literature, and in "Reality in America" he used Parrington's *Main Currents in American Thought* (1927) as an example of the way in which left-wing critics unnecessarily politicized the study of American letters. Although Parrington's admittedly partisan reconstruction of American literary history owed more to the Progressive Era than to the Popular Front, Trilling attacked him as though he were an unreconstructed Stalinist, seriously distorting his cultural politics.[18] According to Trilling, Parrington's positivistic assumptions about the nature of reality reduced American literature to a superstructural expression of the capitalist mode of production. Like other left-wing critics, Parrington refused to accept the idea that "there is any other relation possible between the artist and reality than this passage of reality through the transparent artist" (5). As I have shown elsewhere, Trilling tried to counter the influence of Parrington's history of American letters by defining reality in such a way that it did not lend itself readily to a materialist critique.[19] For Trilling, reality did not exist independently of the individual but was experienced subjectively; consequently, the individual's relation to reality was not transparent but highly mediated.

Trilling's reading of *The Princess Casamassima,* originally published as the introduction to an edition of the novel issued in 1948, was difficult to reconcile with these criticisms of Parrington. Trilling emphasized the historical accuracy of James's representation of British working-class life and thus seemed to suggest that, at least in James's case, the artist's relation to reality *was* transparent. He assured readers that "there is not a political event of *The Princess Casamassima,* not a detail of oath or mystery or danger, which is not confirmed by multitudinous records" (68) and summarized the ideas of Bakunin and other anarchists to prove his point. In so doing, he sought to convince readers that the anarchists in the novel were not an exaggeration but represented "with complete accuracy the political development of a large part of the working class of England" (71). Thus, despite his criticisms of Parrington's partisan readings of the classics of American literature, Trilling approached James's novel from an overtly political perspective. He did not hesitate to judge *The Princess Casamassima* on the basis of its politics, arguing that it should be included in the canon because it could be read as a "brilliantly precise representation of social actuality" (74).

I want to examine Baldwin's project to creolize the Jamesian novel by combining its narrative techniques with the thematic concerns of the naturalistic novel in the context of the Cold War construction of James as a master of the novel form. I will show that Baldwin's use of multiple centers of intelligence in *Another Country* should be understood as an attempt to reclaim James from a theory of the novel that was deeply homophobic in its political implications. To be sure, Trilling and Chase never explicitly state that left-wing intellectuals were homosexuals, but in reinforcing the association of left-wing politics with an inability to resolve the Oedipus complex, they enabled gay male writers such as Baldwin to construe their claims about the novel as homophobic. Their equation of left-wing political activity with a lack of a maturity of vision reproduced the homophobic categories of Cold War political discourse. In the 1950s, both Communism and homosexuality were generally considered immature forms of heterosexuality in which the Communist or the homosexual remained fixated on the mother.[20] Like the Communist who was thought to have betrayed the nation's security by passing classified documents to the Soviet Union, the homosexual was supposedly unable to resolve the Oedipus complex and suffered from an arrested sexual development. Thus in claiming that writers such as Dreiser and Wright who focused on the material conditions of existence lacked a maturity of vision, Trilling and Chase helped to underwrite the connection between Communism and homosexuality in the Cold War imaginary. Baldwin's creolizing appropriation of James's narrative techniques challenged this attempt to pathologize left-wing politics by linking it to homosexuality. Despite the oppositional content of *Another Country*, Baldwin's use of a Jamesian mode of narration demonstrated his mastery of the novel form, as defined by Trilling and Chase. Thus he could not be accused of lacking a maturity of vision, despite the fact that he was both openly gay and politically engaged.

Cold War Liberals and the Denial of Difference

Trilling and Chase's legitimation of the discourses of national security was not limited to equating left-wing politics with a lack of maturity of vision. In defining the novel in such a way as to exclude politically engaged writers such as Wright from the canon, Trilling and Chase legitimated the Cold War construction of "the homosexual" as a national-security risk. To understand more fully the place of James in Trilling and Chase's theory and tradition of American letters, it is necessary to review briefly what is perhaps their most famous contribution to American studies, namely, their distinction between the novel and the romance, which they regarded as the characteristically American form of novelistic discourse.[21] Echoing a long line of American writers that included Cooper, Hawthorne, and James, they complained that American society lacked the dense social texture that conditioned the rise of the novel in Europe. The romance had become the characteristic form of novelistic discourse in America, they argued, because the class structure was too fluid to function as the hero's antagonist. In "Art and Fortune," an essay that first appeared in *Partisan Review* in 1948, Trilling explained that "in this country the real basis of the novel has never existed—that is, the tension between a middle class and an aristocracy which brings manners into observable relief as the living representation of ideals and the living comment on ideas" (260). In other words, the permeability of class boundaries had hindered the development of the American novel, which was not as "thickly textured" (212) as its European counterpart.

Chase elaborated these views into a fully developed theory of the differences between the novel and the romance in his classic study, *The American Novel and Its Tradition*. Although he did not agree with Trilling that American fiction was inferior to European fiction, he also tried to show that the basis of the novel did not exist in America and that a distinctive form of novelistic discourse, the romance, had emerged in its place. For him, what distinguished the romance was the nonreferentiality of its language and its oblique relation to society. Whereas the novel mirrored the tensions between the bourgeoisie and the aristocracy, the romance was anti-mimetic and ignored "the spectacle of man [*sic*] in society" (ix) or addressed it only indirectly. For this reason, it could be said to promote freedom. According to Chase, the novel sought to appropriate reality "with the high purpose of bringing order to disorder" (4), and thus was imperialistic. The romance, on the other hand, was "free" to render reality in "less volume and detail" (4), and thus was democratic. Unlike the novel, it explored, rather than appropriated, "the remarkable and in some ways unexampled territories of life in the New World" and "reflect[ed] its anomalies and dilemmas" (5). Thus Chase privileged the romance over the novel because he thought that it expressed the democratic values that defined American political culture. Insofar as it ignored the "spectacle" of man in society, the romance represented a more authentic expression of the American national character.

As several critics have pointed out, Trilling and Chase's distinction between the novel and the romance is best understood as an extension of the discourse of American exceptionalism to literary history.[22] Their claim that the basis of the novel did not exist in the United States overlooked its history of class struggle and can be traced to the consensus model of American history that reemerged in the postwar period.[23] They accepted the view of historians that what distinguished the United States was that it was composed of special interest groups rather than classes struggling for control over the production and distribution of material goods and re-sources. Trilling provided the most explicit statement of this position in "Art and Fortune," in which he tried to minimize the labor unrest of the forties, even though it threatened to disrupt the postwar economic recov-ery. Such unrest, he asserted, represented a "contest for the possession of the goods of a single way of life, and not a cultural struggle" (261). He refused to believe that a person's class position might influence how s/he thought and lived her/his relation to the world. American workers might strike for higher wages and better benefits, but they remained fundamen-tally committed to the American way of life.

Trilling also refused to believe that Americans were deeply divided along racial and ethnic lines and that such divisions might serve as the basis for the novel. Despite the fact that he was Jewish and had earlier in his career written for the *Menorah Journal,* the publication of the International Men-orah Society, an organization founded at Harvard in the 1920s to combat the anti-Semitism of university life, the only differences he was willing to ac-knowledge were those of class.[24] In "Art and Fortune," he claimed that race and ethnicity could not be compared to class because they played only an insignificant role in the formation of identity. Thus they were of no legiti-mate concern to the novelist. For him, one of the consequences of the economic prosperity of the postwar period was that it had impaired "our ability to see people in their difference and specialness" (262). Given this privileging of class, it is hardly surprising that Trilling refused to acknowl-edge the importance of the postwar liberation movements of minoritized groups. In a footnote in which he addressed the question of whether race and ethnicity could be considered equivalent to class, he claimed that such movements could not be compared to the labor movement because they involved "no real cultural struggle, no significant conflict of ideals . . . the excluded group has the same notion of life and the same aspirations as the excluding group" (261), a statement that would seem to contradict his claims about the labor unrest of the forties. Nor could racial and ethnic conflict replace class conflict as the basis of the novel. Without explaining why, he stated that "for the purposes of the novel [such conflict] is not the same thing" (261). In trivializing the role of race and ethnicity in American life, Trilling marginalized a whole tradition of American literature that in foregrounding racial and ethnic conflict problematized his and Chase's claims about the Americanness of the romance. This tradition, which included such writers as Frederick Douglass, Richard Wright, and Zora Neale Hurston, provided an alternative vision of American society, one that challenged the consensus model of American history that Trilling and Chase's literary criticism indirectly ratified.

Reclaiming American Letters:
Cold War Liberals and the Deployment of Homophobia

To show that Trilling and Chase's theory of the novel was deeply homophobic not only in its political implications but also in its application to specific texts, I want to examine in some detail Chase's reading of *Billy Budd* in his influential study *Herman Melville* (1949). Geraldine Murphy has recently shown that in the forties *Billy Budd* became an important site of struggle between anti-Stalinist intellectuals such as Trilling and Chase who regarded liberalism as the only legitimate alternative to the forces of reaction in postwar American society and intellectuals such as F. O. Matthiessen who remained committed to the left-wing politics of the thirties.[25] Whereas Matthiessen saw Billy Budd as a Christ figure victimized by an authoritarian society, Chase saw him as a maladjusted youth who had failed to negotiate the passage from innocence to experience. I agree with Murphy that postwar readings of *Billy Budd* can tell us a great deal about the sexual politics of literary criticism in the Cold War era, but where she sees deep-seated fears about women and the dissolution of ego boundaries, I see a project to consolidate the connection between Communism and homosexuality. This is not to ignore the misogyny of Chase's reading, which is critical of Billy's passivity in relation to authority because it supposedly feminizes him. But I want to stress the way in which Chase's reading helped to underwrite the construction of "the homosexual" as a national-security risk. Linking Chase's reading to the discourses of national security will enable us to speculate that its real target was Matthiessen, who, as both a gay man and a fellow traveler, could be said to embody the link between Communism and homosexuality in Cold War political discourse.

Like other postwar critics, Chase read *Billy Budd* as a political allegory in which the forces of democracy struggled against and eventually defeated the forces of totalitarianism. But whereas other postwar critics approached the novel from the perspective of myth criticism, he approached it from the perspective of psychoanalysis.[26] He described a Billy who was unable to resolve the Oedipus complex. According to him, Billy was "fatally passive" and sought "his own castration."[27] He explained Billy's passive submission to authority in Oedipal terms, stating that he "has identified himself with the mother at a pre-Oedipean [sic] level and has adopted the attitude of harmlessness and placation toward the father in order to avoid the hard struggle of the Oedipus conflict" (270). He also argued that Billy tried to evade the threat of castration "by symbolically castrating himself (by being consciously submissive and by repressing his rage and hostility against the father in order to placate him)" (270). In short, he considered Billy a homosexual. The pattern of development he attributed to Billy corresponded to postwar constructions of homosexuality: Billy overidentified with his mother and sought to placate his father by passively submitting to him. In this respect, Chase's use of Freudian theory reproduced the homophobic categories of the discourses of national security. In suggesting that Billy was a homosexual who remained fixated on his mother, Chase's reading pathologized left-wing political activity, reducing it to a form of homosexuality. Chase read *Billy Budd* not as a tragedy of the "common man," which is how left-wing critics such as Matthiessen read it, but as a sort of Blakean journey in which Billy failed to negotiate successfully the passage from innocence to experience.

Chase was clearly less interested in challenging a tradition of left-wing criticism than in impugning Matthiessen's authority as one of the leading critics of American literature. Chase blamed Matthiessen for inaugurating a tradition of reading *Billy Budd* as a testament of acceptance. In *Herman Melville,* he accused Matthiessen of contributing "an unresolved religious strain" (ix) to the Progressive Era reading of *Billy Budd.* In *The American Novel and Its Tradition,* he complained that postwar critics "have followed the lead of F. O. Matthiessen in *The American Renaissance* and have viewed Melville's novel as a drama of religious revelation" (113). But the continuing influence of Matthiessen's "Christian" reading of Melville's novel only partially explains Chase's criticisms of him. Chase's remarks in "Art, Nature, Politics," an essay that appeared in *Kenyon Review* in 1950, indicate that the real object of his criticism was Matthiessen's continuing involvement in left-wing politics. Unlike Chase and other Cold War liberals, Matthiessen remained committed to the populist aesthetic of the Popular Front, and thus his cultural politics undermined their claims that their repudiation of the Left should be seen as a sign of their intellectual and emotional maturity. Chase claimed in this essay that the individual who had read and understood Melville "would not vote for Henry Wallace . . . because Melville presents his reader with a vision of life so complexly true that it exposes the ideas of Henry Wallace as hopelessly childish and superficial."[28] Here Chase was clearly referring to Matthiessen, who had actively campaigned for Wallace, the 1948 Progressive party presidential candidate.

Chase's tendency to identify left-wing political activity with a lack of maturity of vision enables us to construe his reading of *Billy Budd* as a veiled attack on Matthiessen. Chase clearly associated Matthiessen with the "fatally passive" Billy of his reading of the novel. His disparaging remarks about Wallace implied that, as a Wallace supporter, Matthiessen was himself childish and could be said to resemble Billy. Like Billy, Matthiessen had failed to negotiate the passage from innocence to experience and was unable to see the world as it really was. According to Chase, reading and understanding Melville should have discouraged Matthiessen from supporting Wallace because "literature tells us that life is diverse, paradoxical, and complicated, a fateful medley of lights and darks, and it tells us this with a dramatic forcefulness which we seldom meet outside of literature."[29] Although Matthiessen was widely regarded as one of Melville's most authoritative critics, Chase implied that he did not understand Melville's novel. Lacking maturity of vision, he was unable to see through Wallace's populist rhetoric.

But Chase had other reasons for associating Matthiessen with Billy. As a gay fellow traveler, Matthiessen could be said to suffer from an arrested sexual development.[30] His homosexuality could be seen as proof that a commitment to left-wing politics did indeed represent a continuation of the negative Oedipus complex into adulthood. Moreover, his tragic suicide shortly before he was to appear before the House Un-American Activities Committee in 1950 could be interpreted as a "fatally passive" act that duplicated Billy's passive submission to authority. In light of these possible constructions of Matthiessen's personal history, all authorized by the discourses of national security, the Billy who seeks his own castration in Chase's reading of Melville's novel can be construed as a figure for Matthiessen. Like Matthiessen, Chase's Billy embodied all of the characteristics Chase most disliked about left-wing intellectuals.

Wright and the Homophobic Politics of the Naturalistic Novel

Having shown why Baldwin might have interpreted Trilling and Chase's claims about American literature as deeply homophobic, I now want to examine the relation of his literary criticism to their project to identify Communism and other forms of left-wing politics as unacceptable alternatives to Cold War liberalism. Baldwin's contribution to the debate over the politicization of literary culture that had begun in the thirties was limited to two essays on Richard Wright, "Everybody's Protest Novel" and "Many Thousands Gone," which appeared in *Partisan Review* in 1948 and 1951, respectively. At first glance, Baldwin's criticisms of Wright bear a striking resemblance to Trilling and Chase's criticisms of the naturalistic novel and seem to express an equally hostile view of politically engaged writing. In "Everybody's Protest Novel," for example, Baldwin criticized Wright for treating literature as a weapon in the struggle against racism, claiming that Wright was a failure as a novelist because he did not understand that the proper domain of literature was "freedom which cannot be legislated, fulfillment which cannot be charted."[31] Moreover, like Trilling and Chase, Baldwin tended to use the critical vocabulary of the New Critics, stressing the paradox, ambiguity, and tension of postwar experience.[32] In his view, *Native Son* did not accurately represent race relations in America because its stark vision did not acknowledge that "only within this web of ambiguity, paradox, this hunger, danger, darkness, can we find at once ourselves and the power that will free us from ourselves" (15). Baldwin also seemed to agree with Trilling and Chase that left-wing critics simplified the relation between literature and society by reducing literature to a superstructural expression of the capitalist mode of production. In "Everybody's Protest Novel," he reminded critics that literature was not a form of sociology and warned that "our passion for categorization, life neatly fitted into pegs, has led to an unforeseen, paradoxical distress; confusion, a breakdown of meaning" (19).

Despite these similarities, however, Baldwin's criticisms of Wright should not be confused with Trilling and Chase's project to marginalize left-wing intellectuals. If Baldwin criticized Wright for reducing literature to propaganda, that is because Wright had become the paradigmatic African American writer against whom all other African American writers were judged and found wanting. Although *Native Son* is generally recognized as a masterpiece of literary naturalism indebted to the novels of Dreiser and Dos Passos, a number of postwar left-wing critics praised it for deviating from the conventions of the naturalistic novel. Irving Howe, for example, regarded the novel as "a work of assault rather than withdrawal" (356) that overcame the formal limitations of the naturalistic mode of narration. Whereas most naturalistic novels were written "as if by a scientist survey-ing a field of operation" (356), Wright did not try to conceal his anger toward white America but instead allowed himself to succumb to "a vision of nightmare" (356). His use of the naturalistic mode of narration was more complex than that of his models and resembled a "kind of expression-ist outburst, no longer a replica of the familiar social world but a self-contained realm of grotesque emblems" (357). Howe's tendency to read *Native Son* as an "authentic" expression of black male rage inscribed racist fantasies about black masculinity. Howe's essay needs to be read in the context of the postwar rebellion against the domestication of masculinity. Like many white left-wing intellectuals in the postwar period who deplored the rise of the "organization man," Howe tended to see black men as em-bodying an especially phallic form of masculinity.[33] Indeed, his celebration of *Native Son* as a work of "assault" resembled nothing so much as Norman Mailer's notorious essay "The White Negro," which as we saw in chapter 1 tended to romanticize black male rage as a form of oppositional conscious-ness.

Baldwin's criticisms of Wright are best understood as a reaction against the tendency of Howe and other critics to praise *Native Son* as an authen-tic expression of black male rage, a tendency that reinforced racist con-structions of black male identity. In "Everybody's Protest Novel," Baldwin stressed the relation of *Native Son* to Harriet Beecher Stowe's *Uncle Tom's Cabin,* ignoring its participation in a tradition of naturalistic writing. In locating *Native Son* in a tradition of social-protest fiction that included

Uncle Tom's Cabin, Baldwin challenged Wright's status as a representative African American writer whose novels supposedly captured "the black experience." According to Baldwin, Wright's naturalistic representation of African American life was no more authentic than Stowe's sentimental one. Like Stowe, Wright wrote for a predominantly white liberal readership. Baldwin complained that social-protest fiction in general tended to provide white liberal readers with "a very definite thrill of virtue from the fact that [they] are reading such a book at all" (19). In locating *Native Son* in the same literary tradition as *Uncle Tom's Cabin*, Baldwin stressed the way in which Wright's novel reinforced the myth of the threatening black phallus. Baldwin's admittedly outlandish claim that Wright should be seen as a direct literary descendant of Stowe was meant to call attention to the racism inherent in the assumption that Bigger was representative of black masculinity. Baldwin saw Bigger and Uncle Tom as opposite sides of the same racist coin. Whereas Bigger embodied the stereotype of the criminalized black male youth, Uncle Tom, who Baldwin complained had been "robbed of his humanity and divested of his sex" (18), embodied the stereotype of the obedient and nonthreatening "plantation darky."

Baldwin's criticisms of Wright have usually been construed as staging an Oedipal struggle in which he tried to "kill off" or displace the more established Wright.[34] But this reading ignores the legitimacy of Baldwin's criticism that Wright's use of a naturalistic mode of narration did not lend itself to an examination of African American subjectivity. Although Baldwin agreed with Wright that African American subjectivity could not be understood apart from the material conditions of existence, he did not feel that it could be reduced to them. Despite his emphasis on Bigger's identity as a social being, Wright was unable to explain how Bigger had become a social being. Baldwin complained that there was no place in Wright's novel for "the complex techniques [blacks] have evolved for their survival," nor for "the relationship that [they] bear to one another, that depth of involvement and unspoken recognition of shared experience which creates a way of life" (35). Because of this oversight, Wright was unable to clarify the complex process whereby blacks became social beings. Not only did we know as little about Bigger at the conclusion of *Native Son* as at the beginning, but we also knew "almost as little about the social dynamic which we are to believe created him" (35). By ignoring the construction of African American subjectivity across multiple axes of difference, Wright encouraged the tendency of white Americans to think of African Americans not as fellow citizens but as a "social problem" involving "statistics, slums, rapes, injustices, remote violence" (25). Moreover, Wright's use of a naturalistic mode of narration hindered him from showing that whiteness and blackness were not binary oppositions but mutually constitutive categories. He did not seem to realize that "Negroes are Americans and their destiny is the country's destiny" (42).

But Baldwin was also critical of Wright because he thought that Wright reinforced racist constructions of black male identity, which as a gay African American writer he was eager to see dismantled. Wright's criticisms of African American writers in "Blueprint for Negro Writing," an essay that appeared in *New Challenge* in 1937, could be construed as misogynistic and homophobic. In a famous passage, Wright dismissed his black literary antecedents as "prim and decorous ambassadors who went a-begging to white America. They entered the Court of Public Opinion dressed in the knee-pants of servility, curtsying to show that the Negro was not inferior, that he [*sic*] was human, and that he had a life comparable to that of other people."[35] The terms Wright uses here indicate that he rejected earlier black writers as models because he did not think they were sufficiently masculine. Ignoring the tradition of black women's writing, he claimed that these writers sought to convince white Americans that they were fully human, and so they "curtsyed" and behaved in ways that were "prim" and "decorous" and that positioned them as women.

That these criticisms of his black literary antecedents could also be read as homophobic becomes clear in the passage in which he describes the Harlem Renaissance as "that foul soil which was the result of a liaison between inferiority-complexed Negro 'geniuses' and burnt-out white Bohemians with money" (315). Granted, Wright did not explicitly mention that many of the writers associated with the Harlem Renaissance, such as Langston Hughes, Alain Locke, Claude McKay, and Countee Cullen, were gay. But his description of the Harlem Renaissance as "that foul soil" echoed contemporary constructions of homosexuality and could be interpreted as a homophobic reference to their sexual liaisons with white male intellectuals as well as with one another. Baldwin undoubtedly knew of the sexual orientation of these writers—Countee Cullen was one of his boyhood teachers—and he was certainly familiar with the homoeroticism of their work. My point is that, as a gay African American writer whose style did not conform to Wright's masculinist prescriptions but could be described as prim and decorous, Baldwin would have been offended by Wright's description of Harlem Renaissance writers.

We can gauge Baldwin's reaction to Wright's literary blueprint by examining his response to Mailer's "The White Negro." In "The Black Boy Looks at the White Boy," an essay that originally appeared in *Esquire* in 1961, Baldwin criticized Mailer for trying to exploit white male anxiety about black male sexual prowess. Baldwin complained that Mailer's essay reinforced the myth of the threatening black phallus while ignoring the way in which it was used to make black men feel sexually inadequate. According to Baldwin, since black men could not possibly live up to such a myth, they were reduced to questioning their manhood. Moreover, the myth was often used to exclude gay black men from the black community because their sexuality supposedly did not conform to it. Alluding to his own problematic relation to the black community, Baldwin remarked that "it is still true, alas, that to be an American Negro male is also to be a kind of walking phallic symbol: which means that one pays, in one's own personality, for the sexual insecurity of others."[36] Baldwin claimed that Mailer himself used the myth to marginalize gay black men. Mailer did not consider Baldwin truly black because his sexual orientation "inevitably connected, not to say collided, with the myth of the sexuality of Negroes which [Mailer], like so many others, refuses to give up."[37] Judging from these criticisms, it seems likely that Baldwin would have objected to Wright's valorization of an aggressive black masculinity. Such a valorization could be used to marginalize him and other gay black writers—as indeed it was in the sixties when Eldridge Cleaver and other black nationalist intellectuals viciously attacked him because he was gay.[38]

Wright's legitimation of the myth of the threatening black phallus was not the only aspect of his blueprint for black writers that Baldwin would have found problematic. Wright argued that black cultural production in general should have an organic relation to the black community, shaping the lives and consciousnesses of black people and providing them with a "guide" (315) to everyday life. Emphasizing the importance of the black vernacular tradition, he explained that "Negro writers who seek to mould or influence the consciousness of the Negro people must address their messages to them through the ideologies and attitudes fostered in this warping way of life" (319). Implicit in Wright's prescriptions was an understanding of black identity that conflicted with Baldwin's. Although Wright acknowledged that the aims of black nationalism were "unrealizable within the framework of capitalist America" (320), he maintained that "the nationalist character of the Negro people" (318) was unmistakable and urged black writers to display a "nationalist spirit" (320) in their writing. It is important to stress that Wright wrote "Blueprint for Negro Writing" when he was still a member of the Communist party and that he may not have been expressing his own views but rather those of the party when he claimed that black writers should encourage the nationalist aspirations of black people.

Still, his views concerning the cultural impoverishment of black people did not differ significantly from those he expressed later in his career after he had broken with the Communist party, and we can use "Blueprint for Negro Writing" to highlight the differences between him and Baldwin.[39] Unlike Wright, Baldwin located the roots of the black vernacular in both African and American culture and stressed the hybridization of black identity.[40] He also challenged the way in which nationalists privileged blacks' ties to Africa over their ties to America. In an essay written for *Encounter* in which he reported on the Conference of Black Writers and Artists held in Paris in 1956, he questioned the underlying assumptions of the pan-Africanism of the American delegation, which included Wright, and explained that he returned to the United States convinced that "our relation to the mysterious continent of Africa would not be clarified until we had found some means of saying to ourselves and to the world, more about the mysterious American continent than had ever been said before" (21). Nor did he think that the conference had adequately addressed the question, "Is it possible to describe as a culture what may simply be, after all, a history of oppression?" (28). For Baldwin, African American culture was the product of peculiar circumstances and could only be tenuously connected to the diverse cultures of postcolonial Africa.

Creolizing the Jamesian Novel:
Baldwin and the Politics of Subjectivity

In the remainder of this chapter, I want to read Baldwin's *Another Country* as a critique both of Wright's tendency to valorize an aggressive black masculinity and of Trilling and Chase's homophobic theory and tradition of American letters. Although I will not undertake a full-scale reading of the novel, I will try to clarify the politics of its formal strategies by examining them in the context of the postwar backlash against the left-wing political activity of the thirties. Baldwin's focus on racial, ethnic, and gender differences indirectly challenged Trilling and Chase's claim that the basis of the novel did not exist in America. In filtering the action of *Another Country* through the characters' consciousnesses, he showed that racial, ethnic, and gender differences could legitimately replace those of class as the basis of the Jamesian novel. His use of multiple centers of intelligence enabled him to stage the construction of subjectivity across multiple axes of difference. The frequent shifts in the novel's point of view make clear that identity is necessarily constituted through a dialogic encounter with otherness. Because race, class, and gender function in the novel as mutually constitutive categories of identity, they cannot be understood apart from one another. Thus in using a Jamesian mode of narration, Baldwin sought to broaden the definition of the political by extending it to issues of subjectivity that, according to the Cold War consensus, transcended politics.

This is not to suggest that Baldwin's project was limited to challenging the homosexualization of left-wing political activity by the discourses of national security. In filtering the action of *Another Country* through the characters' consciousnesses, Baldwin sought to promote a model of political solidarity that was rooted in a collective experience of oppression rather than membership in a homogeneous community. The frequent shifts in the novel's point of view encouraged identifications across racial, class, and gender lines. Insofar as they conflicted with the organization of identity under the Cold War consensus, such identifications were potentially subversive. Baldwin rejected models of political solidarity that were patterned on kinship relations. Such models tended to reinforce the differences among women, African Americans, gays, and other disenfranchised groups, thereby preventing them from forming the broadly based coalitions that were needed to overcome the racist, sexist, and homophobic structures of postwar American society. This explains more fully why Baldwin used a Jamesian mode of narration in *Another Country*. In frequently shifting the novel's point of view, he sought to encourage a mobility in solidarity. He wanted to promote a form of resistance that exploited the subaltern's fractured relation to identity. For him, the fragmentation and dispersal of the subaltern's identity did not entail a loss of agency but enabled her/him to engage in opposition from multiple locations. Because the characters belong to a plurality of overlapping communities (gay, African American, working-class, and so on), they have the potential to shift their identities to accommodate a variety of changing political needs, possibilities, and opportunities.

The character in the novel who is most representative of postwar structures of oppression is Richard, the commercially successful writer who is married to Cass. Richard is one of three main characters who do not function as a center of intelligence. (The other two are Ida and Leona, Rufus's white lover; I discuss the significance of the inaccessibility of their consciousnesses below.) In denying us access to Richard's consciousness, Baldwin discourages us from identifying with him. Richard's relationship with Steve Ellis, a slick white television producer, shows how the imbrication of racism and sexism tended to benefit straight white middle-class men. At first glance, Richard seems to occupy a position in relation to Ellis that is not unlike Ida's. Both he and Ida depend on Ellis to promote their careers, Richard as a screenwriter, Ida as a jazz singer. Moreover, like her, he is reduced to prostituting himself in exchange for Ellis's patronage. Ida becomes sexually involved with Ellis, and Richard forsakes his ambition to become a "serious" writer so that he can work full-time for Ellis. Despite these parallels, however, their positions in relation to Ellis are not symmetrical. Whereas Richard becomes a writer for a popular television series and thus benefits materially from his relationship with Ellis, Ida's relationship with Ellis nearly destroys her career. She becomes known in Harlem as a "white man's whore," and jazz musicians refuse to work with her.

Baldwin uses his characterization of Richard to suggest that the role of racism, sexism, and homophobia in the construction of white male subjectivity is originary. Richard's identity as a straight white man depends on the subordination of blacks, women, and gays. This becomes clear in the scene in which he beats Cass after she reveals that she is having an affair with Eric. Richard seems less disturbed by the fact that Cass is having an affair than by the fact that her lover is a gay man. He refuses to believe that she initiated the affair and assumes that her role in it has been wholly passive: "He pulled her head forward, then slammed it back against the chair, and slapped her across the face, twice, as hard as he could. The room dropped into darkness for a second, then came reeling back, in light; tears came to

[Cass's] eyes, and her nose began to bleed. 'Is that it? Did he fuck you in the ass, did he make you suck his cock? Answer me, you bitch, you slut, you *cunt!* ' "[41] Richard feels threatened by the affair because it challenges his manhood. He does not understand why Cass would prefer to have sex with a gay man, and he imagines that Eric has forced her to engage in practices that homosexualize her. The violence of his reaction foregrounds the mutually determining relation between sexism and homophobia. Richard projects himself into the affair, fantasizing that he and not Cass is the object of Eric's desire. When Cass tries to defend Eric by claiming that she knows him better than Richard does, Richard responds, "I guess you do—though *he* may have preferred it the other way around. Did you ever think of that?" (376). Richard refuses to relinquish his authority to regulate the sexuality of women and gays. Convinced that Eric is a woman trapped in a man's body and thus could not possibly desire Cass, Richard reduces his affair with Cass to the binary structure of heterosexual relations.

This scene is particularly significant because it links Cass to Leona, Rufus's battered white lover who eventually suffers a mental breakdown and must be institutionalized. Although Cass and Leona seem to have little in common with one another, their experiences of patriarchal oppression are remarkably similar. Before Leona comes to New York, her husband physically abuses her, accusing her of having an affair with another man, and he eventually divorces her, gaining custody of their child. The parallels in their personal histories are expressed symbolically in the scene in which Richard beats Cass. After the beating, Cass staggers to the bathroom where "she ran the water, [and] the bleeding slowly began to stop. Then she sat down on the bathroom floor. Her mind swung madly back and forth, like the needle of some broken instrument" (376). This passage recalls an earlier passage in the novel in which Vivaldo visits Rufus and Leona in their apartment and finds Leona "sitting on the bathroom floor, her hair in her eyes, her face swollen and dirty with weeping. Rufus had been beating her" (55). In foregrounding the similarities of Cass's and Leona's experiences of patriarchal oppression, these passages make clear that these women have certain interests in common, despite the differences in their class positions. True, Cass is relatively privileged in comparison to Leona, but she is no less vulnerable to patriarchal violence.

Despite its stress on the similarities of their situations, however, the novel shows how the differences in their class positions prevent them from forming an alliance with one another. For Baldwin, women's experiences of patriarchal oppression are differentiated by their race and class. As a poor white southern woman, Leona is less able than Cass to negotiate sexist structures. She does not understand the extent to which racism and sexism are mutually reinforcing but thinks that Rufus's desire to humiliate her sexually is purely racial. This is not to deny that Cass experiences a particularly brutal form of patriarchal oppression. Her refusal to contain her sexuality within the privatized space of the nuclear family makes her vulnerable to misogynistic constructions of female sexuality. As we saw above, when she tells Richard about her affair with Eric, he beats her and calls her a "slut" and a "cunt." Still, her position as a white middle-class woman shields her from the sort of oppression Leona experiences. Cass has a better understanding of patriarchal structures. When Richard tells her that he does not believe in female intuition because it is something women have dreamed up, she responds, "Something women have dreamed up. But *I* can't say that—what men have 'dreamed up' is all there is, the world they've dreamed up is the world" (108). She also has a better understanding of the mutually determining relation between racism and sexism. She realizes that as a middle-class white woman she is relatively privileged in relation to blacks and other disenfranchised groups, and she questions the adequacy of white liberal views of race. When Vivaldo draws an analogy between his experiences growing up in a working-class Italian neighborhood in Brooklyn and Rufus's experiences growing up in Harlem, Cass points out that Vivaldo's experiences "did not happen to you because you were white. They just happened. But what happens up here [in Harlem] . . . happens *because* they are colored. And that makes a difference" (113–14).

By contrast, Leona is unable to make a connection between her identity as a woman and America's political and social institutions. Her oppression as a white working-class woman is compounded by her limited understanding of the imbrication of racism and sexism. Because her lover is black, she is more vulnerable than Cass to misogynistic constructions of female sexuality. Rufus views her solely in terms of the stereotype of the sexually insatiable white woman who prefers black men. He enjoys humiliating her in front of others by reminding her, "You told me yourself that [your husband] had a thing on him like a horse. You told me yourself how he did you—he kept telling you how he had the biggest thing in Dixie, black *or* white" (57). He also tells Vivaldo, "Man, this chick can't get enough" (57). Leona fails to understand that Rufus's attempts to humiliate her are sexually as well as racially motivated. She thinks that Rufus abuses her because he is black and "don't think he's good enough for *me*" (56). Leona's inability to see that Rufus's treatment of her is inextricably linked to misogynistic fantasies about female sexuality reinforces her oppression. She is unable to leave him, despite the fact that he abuses her, because she is convinced that they can overcome their differences through love. Unlike Cass, who recognizes the inadequacy of white liberal views, Leona minimizes the extent to which experience is differentiated by race. She responds to Rufus's taunts by repeating white liberal pieties. Whenever Rufus becomes abusive, she tells him, "Rufus . . . ain't nothing wrong in being colored" (52).

In stressing that Cass's and Leona's experience of patriarchal oppression are differentiated by class, the novel raises important questions about the ability of women to organize politically across class barriers. Despite the fact that they are both victims of misogynistic constructions of female sexuality, Leona's problems are compounded by her lack of cultural capital and require a different solution from Cass's. Cass's nascent feminist consciousness links her to the middle-class housewives Betty Friedan described in her highly influential book *The Feminine Mystique* (1963). Like those housewives, Cass resents her confinement to the domestic sphere and rebels against the rigidly defined gender roles of the Cold War era. In linking her to these housewives, Baldwin calls attention to the limitations of the postwar women's movement, which failed to address the problems of women of color, lesbians, and white working-class women. The white middle-class housewives who, largely in response to Friedan's book, began to organize politically in the early 1960s tended to universalize their own set of experiences.[42] They were primarily interested in contesting the sexism of the media and in opening up the professions to women, an agenda that reflected their oppression as educated middle-class housewives. In refusing to filter the novel's action through Leona's consciousness, Baldwin questions the relevance of such an agenda to white working-class women. The fact that Leona does not function as one of the novel's centers of intelligence underscores her lack of cultural capital. Although, like Cass, she is white, her problems are only tangentially related to the confinement of women to the domestic sphere, and it does not seem likely that they can be solved through consciousness-raising.

But the novel does not just raise questions about women's ability to organize across class barriers; it also demonstrates how racial differences hindered them from forming an alliance on the basis of their gender. Ida, for example, tries to use her knowledge of the imbrication of racism and sexism to bridge the differences between her and Cass, but Cass refuses to acknowledge the interests they have in common as women who are unwilling to restrict their sexuality to the domestic sphere. When she and Cass are alone in a taxi, Ida reminds Cass that in having an affair with Eric, she stands "to lose everything—your home, your husband, even your children" (351). But Cass insists that she will never lose her children, which prompts Ida to reply, "It happened . . . to my ancestors every day" (352). For Ida, there is a historical basis for forming an alliance with Cass; she thinks that the similarities between her and Cass are greater than the differences. But Cass resents her expressions of solidarity, detecting in them "the very faintest hint of blackmail" (345). Indeed, she insists that their situations are different, despite the fact that they are both having affairs. She is convinced that as a white middle-class wife and mother, she is more vulnerable than Ida to public censure, and she tells herself that if the world were to discover that she is having an affair with Eric, it would "condemn [her] yet more cruelly than Ida. For Ida was not white, nor married, nor a mother. The world assumed Ida's sins to be natural, whereas those of Cass were perverse" (345–46).

This scene is particularly ironic because it reverses the scene discussed above in which Cass objects to Vivaldo's claim that his experiences growing up in Brooklyn were comparable to those of Rufus growing up in Harlem. In that scene, which also takes place in a taxi, Cass correctly argues that experience is differentiated by race and that Vivaldo's experiences are not comparable to Rufus's. But in the scene with Ida, Cass's claim that her and Ida's situations are different is racially motivated. She shares the world's view that black women are naturally sexual and does not approve of Ida's affair with Ellis, which she sees as a form of prostitution. Her subjectivity is grounded in racist constructions of black sexuality, and she rejects Ida's expressions of solidarity because she feels threatened by the similarities between them. While returning home from the jazz club in a taxi, she becomes sexually aroused by the Latino driver and realizes that until her affair with Eric, her marriage protected her "not only against the evil in the world, but also against the wilderness of herself. And now she would never be protected again. She tried to feel jubilant about this. But she did not feel jubilant. She felt frightened and bewildered" (362). Cass's racially coded language here suggests that she is unwilling to acknowledge the similarities between her and Ida because to do so would be to admit that she can no longer claim that she is morally superior to her. She seems to experience her desire for the taxi driver, a working-class man of color, as an indication that her sexuality has been African Americanized by her affair with Eric. She no longer views her "sins" as perverse but natural: they are a product of a "wilderness" inside her.

Cass's racially coded description of her sexuality confirms Ida's view that the role of racism in the construction of white subjectivity is originary. When, during a particularly heated exchange, Vivaldo defends Eric's relations with Rufus, insisting that they were not sexually exploitative, Ida responds, "I know how white people treat black boys and girls. They think you're something for them to wipe their pricks on" (324). Despite this knowledge, however, she is less able than Cass to negotiate the racist and sexist structures of postwar American society. She does not understand the extent to which African Americans are divided along gender lines and thus is more vulnerable than Cass to patriarchal violence. Although Cass and the rest of the white world may see Ida's "sins" as natural, the black world sees them as a betrayal of the race and expects her to subordinate her identity as a woman to her identity as an African American. After one of her performances, a musician who knew her brother, Rufus, slaps her on the bottom and whispers, "You black white man's whore, don't you never let me catch you on Seventh Avenue, you hear? I'll tear your little black pussy *up*. . . . I'm going to do it twice, once for every black man you castrate every time you walk, and once for your poor brother, because I loved that stud. And he going to thank me for it, too, you can bet on that, black girl" (425). Despite the fact that she is oppressed not only because she is black but also because she is a woman, Ida is expected to close ranks with black men against a racist society.

Ida's vulnerability to sexism as well as racism indicates why she does not function as one of the novel's multiple centers of intelligence. In denying us access to her consciousness, the novel underscores the inadequacy of white liberal views of racial and sexual difference. Baldwin's formal strategies hinder white liberal readers from thinking that they can understand Ida's motives, particularly as they relate to her affair with Ellis, or that they can know what it means to be an African American woman simply from reading the novel. The character who most fully embodies white liberal views is Vivaldo, who remains blind to the ways in which experience is differentiated by race and gender. Like Leona, who assumes that Rufus feels inferior to her because he is black, Vivaldo thinks that he and Ida can overcome their differences through love. He fails to see the relation between his love for Ida and a history of racial and gender oppression that includes the use of rape as an instrument of terror. He responds to her criticisms of whites by repeating white liberal pieties about the power of love to overcome racial and gender differences. Convinced that his love for her transcends issues of race, he muses at one point in the novel: "Oh, Ida . . . I'd give up my color for you, I would, only take me, take me, love me as I am! Take me, take me as I take you" (308). But Ida does not share his faith in the power of love to overcome their differences, and she insists on seeing their relationship in the context of America's history of racial and gender oppression. When Vivaldo claims that his love for her shows that not all whites exploit blacks sexually, she responds, "Our being together doesn't change the world, Vivaldo" (324). Unlike Vivaldo, she realizes that the racism and sexism of America's political and social institutions cannot be overcome individually but only through collective action.

Vivaldo's views of racial and gender differences were typical of white male left-wing intellectuals in the postwar period. As noted earlier, writers such as Irving Howe and Norman Mailer tended to romanticize a criminalized black male identity. Convinced that black men had replaced the working class as the privileged agents of history, Howe and Mailer embraced the myth of the threatening black phallus and identified black male rage as a form of oppositional consciousness. Although Vivaldo does not romanticize a criminalized African American male identity, he nevertheless tends to view African American men through the lens of racist stereotypes. His subjectivity is grounded in racist constructions of black male identity. He constantly measures his masculinity against that of black men and finds it wanting. We learn that while he was in the army, he and a "colored buddy" (134) once got drunk and exposed themselves to a German woman who was sitting at a table near them. Despite the fact that he was relieved to discover that his black friend's penis was "just like his, there was nothing frightening about it," Vivaldo continued to have nightmares in which his buddy "pursued him through impenetrable forests, came at him with a knife on the edge of precipices, threatened to hurl him down steep stairs to the sea. In each of the nightmares, he wanted revenge" (134). The fear of castration inscribed in these nightmares suggests that Vivaldo tends to project onto black men his own sexual anxieties. On one level, the nightmares indicate that he feels guilty about his complicity as a white man with a history of racial oppression that includes the lynching of black men and the mutilation of their genitals: his buddy threatens to avenge this history by castrating him. But on another level, the nightmares indicate that he is afraid that black men are more sexually potent than he is and that he is already castrated. He is unable to elude his buddy, and the forests in which he is pursued are "impenetrable," suggesting that he simultaneously fears and desires penetration by his buddy.

Vivaldo's tendency to project his own sexual anxieties onto black men helps to explain the tensions between him and Rufus. His view of Rufus is colored by racist stereotypes, and he constantly competes with him sexually. In foregrounding the racial dynamics of Vivaldo's relationship with Rufus, the novel emphasizes the extent to which postwar working-class men were divided along racial lines. Vivaldo's relationship with Rufus seems to be motivated by a desire to establish that he is sexually more potent than Rufus is. Just as Vivaldo refuses to acknowledge that his relationship with Ida must be understood in the context of America's history of racial and gender oppression, so too does he refuse to acknowledge that his relationship with Rufus has been shaped by racist stereotypes. Rather, he tells himself that "they were friends, far beyond the reach of anything so banal and corny as color. They had slept together, got drunk together, balled chicks together, cursed each other out, and loaned each other money" (133). Yet just as Vivaldo and Ida are unable to overcome their differences through love, so too are he and Rufus. Despite their friendship Vivaldo and Rufus continue to see one another in purely racial terms. Vivaldo realizes that "somewhere in his heart the black boy hated the white boy because he was white. Somewhere in his heart Vivaldo had feared and hated Rufus because he was black" (134).

Foregrounding the racial dynamics of Vivaldo's relationship with Rufus enables Baldwin to demonstrate how the mobilization of racist stereotypes in the postwar period hindered working-class men from organizing across racial barriers, despite the interests they had in common as members of an exploited class. Both Vivaldo and Rufus can be understood as oppressed by racist stereotypes because such stereotypes virtually guarantee that they will remain divided along racial lines. The myth of the threatening black phallus places pressure on them to compete with one another sexually, and "they balled chicks together, once or twice the same chick" (134), in order to prove their masculinity to one another. Vivaldo's tendency to project his sexual anxieties onto Rufus prevents him from showing Rufus how much he loves him, and he feels partially responsible for Rufus's suicide. He tells Eric that when he spent the night with Rufus shortly before he committed suicide, "I had the weirdest feeling that [Rufus] wanted me to take him in my arms. And not for sex, though maybe sex would have happened. I had the feeling that he wanted someone to hold him, to hold him, and that, that night, it had to be a man" (342). But he refrained from holding Rufus because he was afraid that Rufus might think he was "queer": "I still wonder, what should have happened if I'd taken him in my arms, if I'd held him, if I hadn't been—afraid. I was afraid that he wouldn't understand that it was—only for love" (342). In other words, Vivaldo's insecurities about his masculinity prevent him from expressing solidarity with Rufus.

Redefining the Meaning of Community

Baldwin, then, stressed the potentially insurmountable obstacles women and other disenfranchised groups faced in building the broadly based coalitions that were necessary for overcoming postwar structures of oppression. Deeply divided along racial, class, and gender lines, the characters in *Another Country* are unable to form alliances with each other, despite the fact that they occupy similar positions in American society. This does not mean, however, that Baldwin thought that it was impossible for minoritized groups to express solidarity with each other in ways that did not require them to suppress their differences. He used a set of narrative techniques that enabled him to stage the construction of subjectivity across variable axes of difference because he wanted to promote a model of political solidarity that was not patterned on kinship relations. Each of the characters occupies a multiplicity of contradictory subject-positions, and thus their identities constantly threaten to become unstable. Eric provides perhaps the most obvious example of this multiple positioning. He occupies a position of alterity in relation to his own identity. His ability to identify with other gay men is limited not only by racial and class differences but by internalized homophobia as well. At one point in the novel, he becomes self-conscious when he sees "two glittering, loud-talking fairies" (263) approach him on a path in Central Park, and he "pulls in his belly, looking straight ahead" (263). At another point, he describes the gay bar on his street as a "cemetary" behind which a lot of "back-alley cock-sucking" (333) takes place.

William Cohen has recently claimed that Eric's inability to identify fully with other gay men should be seen as evidence that Baldwin thought of homosexuality as a limiting category that needed to be transcended. Cohen is particularly troubled by Eric's description of the gay bar and argues that it "might be unremarkable were it not for the fact that [it] tends to define and condemn anonymous gay figures as a class."[43] Although I agree with Cohen that Eric's blanket condemnation of anonymous sexual encounters is deeply homophobic, I also think his criticism that Baldwin was a liberal humanist who thought of sexuality as a personal or civil rights issue misses the point. Eric's limited ability to identify fully with other gay men should be seen as part of Baldwin's project to identify forms of resistance that exploited the dispersal and fragmentation of the subaltern's subjectivity. For Baldwin, the sort of narrowly conceived identity politics Cohen advocates militates against forms of solidarity that are grounded in a collective experience of oppression rather than membership in a homogeneous community.[44] Insofar as it requires the constant policing of borders to determine who does and does not legitimately belong to the gay community, Cohen's kinship model tends to hinder the building of broadly based coalitions. To be sure, Eric's fractured relation to identity prevents him from identifying fully as a gay man and raises questions about his loyalty to the gay community. But it also enables him to engage in opposition from a multiplicity of locations. The fragmentation and dispersal of his subjectivity enhances his ability to identify with African Americans and other minoritized groups. He is able to shift his identity depending on the kinds of oppression (racial, economic, sexual, and so on) he is forced to confront.

Baldwin's distrust of kinship models of solidarity must be seen in the context of the marginalization of his work by left-wing intellectuals. As we saw above, Baldwin experienced firsthand the sort of border policing to which a narrowly conceived identity politics could lead. Writers such as Irving Howe and Eldridge Cleaver did not regard him as a legitimate

spokesman for the black community because he was gay, and they compared his work unfavorably to that of Wright, who they thought more
accurately represented "the black experience." Baldwin expressed his distrust of forms of community that refused to acknowledge difference perhaps most fully in "Here Be Dragons," an essay he wrote shortly before his
death in 1987. His remarks about the multiplicity of identity are worth
quoting in full because they help to clarify his project in *Another Country:*
"Each of us, helplessly and forever, contains the other—male in female,
female in male, white in black, and black in white. We are a part of each
other. Many of my countrymen appear to find this fact exceedingly inconvenient and even unfair, and so very often do I. But none of us can do
anything about it."[45] Henry Louis Gates Jr. has read these remarks as an
indication that shortly before his death, Baldwin experienced an "intellectual resurgence."[46] According to Gates, despite a noticeable decline in the
quality of his work since the seventies, Baldwin had finally found "his
course, exploring the instability of all the categories that divide us."[47] This
reading would seem to corroborate Cohen's criticism that Baldwin conceived of homosexuality and other categories of identity as limiting. Although, unlike Cohen, Gates does not seem especially troubled by the
liberal humanism inherent in such a view, he too clearly believes that
Baldwin thought that racial and other categories of identity needed to be
transcended because they divided Americans.

Yet it can also be argued that Baldwin was making precisely the opposite
point. His belief that the multiplicity of identity constitutes a "fact" that we
must learn to accept because there is nothing we can do about it would
seem to indicate that, for him, racial and other differences are a permanent
fixture of America's multicultural landscape and can never be transcended.
Granted, his argument that we are a part of one another partakes of the
rhetoric of liberalism, with its dream of a "color-blind" society in which
racial and other differences are eventually eliminated. But it can also be said
to challenge the dominant understanding of the categories that organize
identity. Although the categories *white* and *black* and *male* and *female* are
usually understood as polar opposites, Baldwin's remarks suggest that they
subsist in a more dynamic relation to one another and constantly threaten
to become destabilized. If he is right in claiming that we are a part of one
another, the categories *white* and *black* and *male* and *female* must be understood not as distinct entities but as conditioning one another. To be sure,

this understanding of identity is "inconvenient" insofar as it limits the ability of blacks and other disenfranchised groups to mobilize politically on the basis of a single axis of difference. But it makes possible forms of solidarity that are grounded in a mobility of identity and thus provides a more effective basis for collective action.

Although Baldwin never responded directly to the sort of border policing left-wing intellectuals such as Howe and Cleaver engaged in, Ralph Ellison did, and I would like to conclude this chapter by quoting him. His remarks are applicable to Baldwin's project and will help us to link it to similar projects undertaken by African American writers in the Cold War era. In "The World and the Jug," an essay that originally appeared in the *New Leader* in 1963, Ellison defended his narrative strategies in *Invisible Man* against charges that he had betrayed his black literary antecedents by refusing to use the naturalistic mode of narration. Responding to Howe's criticism in "Black Boys and Native Sons" that he and Baldwin did not adequately acknowledge their debt to Wright, Ellison stated that "protest is an element of all art, though it does not necessarily take the form of speaking for a political or social program. It might appear in a novel as a technical assault against the styles which have gone before, or as a protest against the human condition."[48] I have tried to show that the element of protest in *Another Country* was not limited to speaking for a particular political or social program but included a "technical assault" on both the Jamesian and the Wrightian novel, as they were defined by critics such as Trilling and Chase. In combining James's formal strategies with Wright's thematic concerns, Baldwin did not just extend the definition of the political to domains of experience postwar left-wing intellectuals thought were apolitical. He also demonstrated the importance of contesting the dominant theory and tradition of American letters, a theory and tradition that reproduced the homophobic categories of the discourses of national security.

CONCLUSION

The Work of Transformation

I believe that it is very important when one wants to do a work of transformation
to know not only what are the institutions and their real effects, but
equally what is the type of thought that sustains them: what can one still accept
of this system of rationality? What part, on the contrary, deserves to be
set aside, transformed, or abandoned?
—Michel Foucault, "What Calls for Punishment?"

If in this study I have emphasized the potential of Williams's, Vidal's, and
Baldwin's work to disrupt the Cold War consensus, that is because I have
wanted to contest the received narrative of the postwar gay rights movement. The tendency of historians to treat the Stonewall rebellion as an
epochal event that gave birth to the modern gay rights movement has
positioned the fifties as the Dark Ages of gay male identity and politics.
Although it is generally acknowledged that in the fifties the gay male subculture thrived and grew more extensive, it is also assumed that the construction of "the homosexual" as a national-security risk drove gay men
from the public sphere and into hiding. For this reason, the fifties have
come to embody the disciplinary regime of the closet. But this understanding of postwar gay male identity and politics overlooks both film noir,
which as we saw in part 1 undermined the project undertaken by the
national-security state to render gay men invisible, and the work of the gay
male writers we examined in part 2. As we have seen, Williams, Vidal, and
Baldwin contested the Cold War consensus in ways that, unlike film noir,
did not reinforce homophobic stereotypes. Their work provided an alternative understanding of gay male identity that laid the foundation for the gay
liberation movement. Unlike liberal gay rights activists, these writers did
not seek to align gay men with racial and ethnic minorities; nor did they

treat gay male identity as a unitary, unproblematic given. Rather, they stressed the construction of gay male subjectivity across variable axes of difference. For them, the source of gay men's oppression lay not in their exclusion from the nation's political, economic, and cultural life, but in the institutions, discourses, and practices that regulated the production of gender and sexual identity. Thus their work provided the social movements of the sixties with a particularly useful knowledge of postwar structures of oppression. Unlike the cultural workers we examined in the first part of this study, Williams, Vidal, and Baldwin did not engage in a politics of nostalgia. Rather, they helped to undermine the Cold War consensus by politicizing domains of experience even left-wing intellectuals tended to assume were apolitical.

But I have also emphasized the emancipatory potential of Williams's, Vidal's, and Baldwin's work because I feel that it can help us to develop new and more effective strategies for intervening in the political public sphere. In light of the recent anti-gay backlash orchestrated by the Christian Right, the work of transformation facing gays and lesbians seems not only more urgent but also more daunting. Since the collapse of gay liberation in the early seventies, the minoritarian understanding of gay and lesbian identity pioneered by Donald Webster Corey has dominated the political and rhetorical strategies of the gay rights movement.[1] Through the organization of public events such as the annual Gay Pride Parade, which marks the anniversary of the Stonewall rebellion, activists have been able to mobilize the mass of gay men and women, instilling in them a sort of ethnic pride in their history and culture. Although until recently the commemoration of Stonewall as a sort of Independence Day for *all* gay men and women necessitated the suppression of the role of the street queens, transvestites, and female impersonators who initiated it, it has provided activists with a particularly effective tool for persuading gays and lesbians to conceive of themselves as part of an oppressed minority.[2] Moreover, the minoritarian understanding of gay and lesbian identity has enabled gay rights organizations to open up new avenues of legal and political recourse by appropriating the strategies of the civil rights movement. Such organizations have applied to the courts for equal protection and the right to privacy; participated in coalitions to design, pass, and enforce civil rights laws; pressured public officials into supporting legislation designed specifically to protect gays and lesbians; and lobbied the news media for more balanced and "objective" reporting of gay and lesbian issues.

These strategies are laudable and should not be abandoned. They have not only transformed public debates about homosexuality but also enabled many of us to live and work openly as lesbians and gay men. Still, recent events have shown that they are incapable of countering the anti-gay backlash. Gay rights organizations have had only limited success in extending the discourse of minority rights to gay men and lesbians. Indeed, our minority status has become increasingly contested and unstable. The early nineties saw a proliferation of anti-gay initiatives designed specifically to exclude us from existing civil rights legislation. For the most part, the courts have upheld these initiatives, rejecting the arguments of gay rights organizations that they violate our right to equal protection and therefore deserve heightened judicial scrutiny.[3] In the wake of *Bowers v. Hardwick*, the 1986 Supreme Court ruling upholding the Georgia sodomy law, the lower courts have become unwilling to extend to us status as a suspect class.[4] Meanwhile, the Christian Coalition and other right-wing religious groups have developed a set of strategies that have rendered ineffective the civil rights discourse upon which the gay rights movement has traditionally relied for mobilizing public support for the gay and lesbian agenda. One of the ways in which these groups have gained entry into the political mainstream, despite their extreme right-wing views, has been by conceding the privacy arguments that have been the cornerstone of the liberal gay rights movement. Shifting the political terrain, they claim that they have no desire to interfere with "private" expressions of homosexuality and lesbianism. Rather, they only want to block passage of legislation that promotes or legitimates the gay and lesbian "lifestyle" (for example, publicly funded AIDS education materials that describe safe sex practices) and that accord gay and lesbian relationships the same status as heterosexual marriages.

Given its limited ability to respond effectively to the current crisis, it is hardly surprising that the civil rights model has come under increasing attack from within our communities. In the early nineties, organizations such as Queer Nation emerged to challenge the liberal strategies pursued by the gay rights movement.[5] Inspired by the militancy of ACT-UP but frustrated by its exclusive focus on AIDS, these organizations rejected the politics of assimilation and pursued a militantly nationalistic or "in-your-face" strategy to achieve greater visibility for gays and lesbians. They adopted a more aggressive and confrontational political style than that of liberal gay rights activists anxious to show the public that we do not differ significantly from mainstream Americans. The members of Queer Nation, for example, dressed and behaved in ways that made a spectacle of their homosexuality and lesbianism and that advanced their project "to make trouble and have fun" by disrupting the signifying practices that naturalize heteronormativity.[6] Their tactics included appropriating public space through Queer Nights Out and Kiss-Ins in which gay and lesbian couples invaded straight bars and shopping malls and scandalously made out.[7] They also "outed" closeted public figures like Jodie Foster and Malcolm Forbes to demonstrate that many famous and successful Americans are lesbian or gay.[8] Through such tactics, these organizations sought to challenge the notion, recently given new life by the Christian Right, that homosexuality and lesbianism are shameful and should remain hidden from public view. Although their militancy represented a promising new direction in gay and lesbian politics and culture, these organizations avoided interrogating the ethnic model of gay and lesbian identity, and thus their strategies were no more satisfactory than those of liberal gay rights organizations. Like those organizations, they tended to privilege the experience of white middle-class gay men. Their militantly nationalistic position stressed the primacy of sexual identity; differences such as race, class, and gender were not considered constitutive elements of gay and lesbian identity and experience. In this way, the new militancy ignored the needs and interests of those of us who are multiply positioned and are unable or unwilling to privilege our sexuality over other aspects of our identities.

A more satisfactory challenge to the dominance of the civil rights model has emerged from the social constructionism that has dominated historical scholarship in lesbian and gay studies since the early eighties.[9] Inspired by Foucault's work on the history of sexuality, this scholarship has problematized the identity claims that have traditionally grounded the gay rights movement, showing that insofar as such claims treat homosexuality and lesbianism as universal, transhistorical categories of identity that pre-exist social relations, they are essentialist. Following Foucault's example, this scholarship has focused primarily on the discourses, signifying practices, and modes of intelligibility that have governed the construction of "the homosexual" as a category of individual. Recently, scholars working at the cutting edge of gay and lesbian studies have used the Foucauldian perspective to shift the focus of lesbian and gay studies from the politics of identity to the politics of culture. Deeply indebted to the poststructuralist critique of the subject, these scholars have gone even further in challenging the ethnic model of gay and lesbian identity and culture. They stress the mobility of desire and claim that the dislocating operations of the unconscious render the achievement of a fixed, stable identity virtually impossible.[10] They also claim that a logic of exclusion and hierarchy governs the production of *all* identity.[11] Appropriating the techniques of deconstruction, they have shown that heterosexuality depends for its meaning and coherence on the exclusion, repression, and disavowal of homosexuality; thus the hierarchical relation between the two categories is unstable and susceptible to reversal.

The poststructuralist turn represents a particularly promising development in gay and lesbian studies and has several advantages over the nationalistic strategies of organizations such as Queer Nation. First, it places the emergence and consolidation of the binary opposition heterosexual/homosexual at the very core of Western thought and culture. Because this opposition structures Western modes of thought and knowledge, no cultural theory can afford to ignore its production and circulation. As Eve Kosofsky Sedgwick has powerfully put it, "an understanding of virtually any aspect of modern Western culture must be, not merely incomplete, but damaged in its central substance to the degree that it does not incorporate a critical analysis of modern homo/heterosexual definition."[12] Second, the new direction in gay and lesbian studies promises to dismantle the phallocentric regime of sexuality that limits or constrains the pleasures of the body. Recalling the sexual utopianism of the gay liberation movement, gay and lesbian critics influenced by poststructuralism seek to promote an eroticization of everyday life, in which sexuality is no longer centered around the genitals but is dispersed across the body. Finally, the poststructuralist turn in gay and lesbian studies has the potential to produce modes of resistance and identity that do not privilege white gay male experience. Gay and lesbian studies has incorporated the poststructuralist critique of identity politics and begun to foreground race, class, and gender as constitutive elements of gay and lesbian identity and experience. Discarding sexual object-choice as a master category of social and sexual identity, many theorists have adopted the term *queer* as more inclusive than the terms *gay* and *lesbian*, which reinforce the binary opposition between heterosexuality and homosexuality and cannot accommodate sexual identities that do not fall under either category (for example, bisexuality, transvestism, and sadomasochism).[13] Their use of the more fluid and ambiguous *queer* is governed partly by a desire to construct a community that is no longer defined by the sexual object-choice of its members. Like the gay male writers we have examined, "queer" theorists seek to identify modes of solidarity and collectivity that acknowledge difference and that depend primarily on opposition to normalizing, disciplining social forces.

Despite its insistence on problematizing gay and lesbian identities, however, the ability of queer theory and activism to counter the anti-gay backlash also seems limited. To begin with, queer theorists have been slow to translate their knowledge into a political language that can be understood and mobilized at the grassroots level. Indeed, they have all but abandoned the legislative and judicial arenas to liberal gay rights activists, overlooking the work that still needs to be done at the level of the state.[14] Moreover, queer theory's project to destabilize identity as a grounds of politics and theory in order to open up alternative modes of solidarity and resistance does not adequately acknowledge the political and social achievements of the liberal gay rights movement. Gay and lesbian identity politics have not just been exclusionary and regulatory; they have also been personally and politically enabling for the mass of gay men and women. Insofar as queer theory and activism ignores the way in which queerness itself functions as a disciplinary technology, especially with respect to those of us who continue to treat identity as the grounds of our activism, whether for strategic or deeper reasons, this blindness seems particularly problematic and needs to be rectified. But perhaps the most serious problem with queer theory and activism is that it does not adequately address the political needs and aspirations underlying identity politics.[15] The tendency of both liberal and nationalistic gay rights activists to treat gay and lesbian identities as fixed and unitary seems rooted not in a lack of theoretical sophistication but in a desire to achieve the sort of subjecthood that white heterosexual men have traditionally enjoyed in Western cultures. Because they have been denied a history and a culture that affirms rather than negates them, gay men and lesbians have a fragmented relation to identity that has been politically and personally disabling. The dominance of the minoritarian understanding should be seen as a desire to repair or reverse this relation.

In this study, I have tried not only to clarify Williams's, Vidal's, and Baldwin's cultural politics but also to highlight those aspects of their understanding of gay male identity and experience that might help to rectify the gaps, blindnesses, and omissions that threaten to disable queer theory and activism. As I have already noted, insofar as it stressed the fragmentation and dispersal of gay male subjectivity, the work of these writers anticipated the poststructuralist turn in gay and lesbian studies. This is hardly surprising. Many queer theorists and activists have expressed a desire to recover the utopian project of the gay liberation movement, a project that was deeply indebted to Williams's, Vidal's, and Baldwin's work. But queer theorists and activists limit the work of transformation facing us primarily to the cultural sphere. They have not shown much interest in heterosexuality as a material practice that shapes and is shaped by existing political and economic arrangements. Rather, they have sought to disrupt the cultural practices that construct subjectivities, as though they could transform the world by transforming the dominant representation of it.[16] Given the present historical conjuncture, in which the Christian Right is pressuring Congress to revive the patriarchal family through government programs and policies, we need a politics that is less culturalist, a politics that does not confuse our increasing visibility at the level of mass culture with our political and economic enfranchisement.[17] Thus it is my hope that this study will not only revive scholarly interest in Williams, Vidal, and Baldwin, but will also help reclaim their work for contemporary gay and lesbian politics and culture. For as I have tried to show, these writers understood that gender relations are reproduced at the political and economic, as well as the cultural level.

NOTES

Introduction: I'm Really a Queen Myself

1. Leslie Fiedler, "The Un-Angry Young Men: America's Post-War Generation," in *The Collected Essays of Leslie Fiedler,* 2 vols. (New York: Stein & Day, 1971), 1:405. Hereafter cited by page number.

2. Fiedler elaborates his argument about the repressed and sentimentalizing homoerotic character of American letters most fully in *Love and Death in the American Novel* (New York: Anchor, 1992 [1960]).

3. Robert J. Corber, *In the Name of National Security: Hitchcock, Homophobia, and the Political Construction of Gender in Postwar America* (Durham, N.C.: Duke Univ. Press, 1993).

4. For an important exception to the sort of institutional forgetting to which these writers have been subjected, see David Savran, *Communists, Cowboys, and Queers: The Politics of Masculinity in the Work of Arthur Miller and Tennessee Williams* (Minneapolis: Univ. of Minnesota Press, 1992), 76–174. It is significant, however, that Savran's appreciation of the complexities of Williams's cultural politics does not extend to Vidal, whom he dismisses as "impudent" and "aristocratic" (84). This assessment is typical among left-wing academic critics. Eve Kosofsky Sedgwick, for example, has criticized Vidal for engaging in a "hypervigilance for the lapses of the tough-mindedness of others [which] can only suggest he in turn must be, as they say, insecure about his own." Eve Kosofsky Sedgwick, *Epistemology of the Closet* (Berkeley and Los Angeles: Univ. of California Press, 1990), 153. For an important corrective of these dismissive views, see Donald E. Pease, "Citizen Vidal and Mailer's America," in *Gore Vidal: Writer against the Grain,* ed. Jay Parini (New York: Columbia Univ. Press, 1992), 247–77. Baldwin has not fared much better in academic criticism. Although he is widely acknowledged as one of the most important essayists of the postwar period, left-wing academic critics tend to dismiss his novels as liberal humanist and politically retrograde. See, for example, William A. Cohen, "Liberalism, Libido, Liberation: Baldwin's *Another Country,*" *Genders* 12 (winter 1991): 1–21.

5. I have borrowed the term *oppositional consciousness* from Chela Sandoval, "U.S. Third World Feminism: The Theory and Method of Oppositional Consciousness in the Postmodern World," *Genders* 10 (spring 1991): 1–24. Sandoval argues that indi-

viduals achieve oppositional consciousness through active political engagement in which their identities shift to accommodate specific tactical and strategic needs, possibilities, and limits. She contends that individuals "othered" by the dominant social formation are not so much decentered as they have a multiplicity of tactical centers from which they can resist both marginalization and co-optation.

6. My critique of forms of political solidarity that are based on kinship models or that are grounded in fixed notions of identity and/or homogeneous communities is indebted to Iris Marion Young, "The Ideal of Community and the Politics of Difference," in *Feminism/Postmodernism,* ed. Linda J. Nicholson (New York: Routledge, 1990), 300–323, and Biddy Martin and Chandra Talpade Mohanty, "Feminist Politics: What's Home Got to Do with It?" in *Feminist Studies/Critical Studies,* ed. Teresa de Lauretis (Bloomington: Indiana Univ. Press, 1986), 191–212. See also Cindy Patton, *Inventing AIDS* (New York: Routledge, 1990), 5–24, and Chandra Talpade Mohanty, "Cartographies of Struggle: Third World Women and the Politics of Feminism," in *Third World Women and the Politics of Feminism,* ed. Chandra Talpade Mohanty, Ann Russo, and Lourdes Torres (Bloomington: Indiana Univ. Press, 1991), 1–47.

7. For a discussion of Williams's, Vidal's, and Baldwin's influence on the gay liberation movement, see Dennis Altman, *Homosexual: Oppression and Liberation* (New York: New York Univ. Press, 1993 [1971]).

8. On the divisions within the postwar gay rights movement, see John D'Emilio, *Sexual Politics, Sexual Communities: The Making of a Homosexual Minority in the United States, 1940–1970* (Chicago: Univ. of Chicago Press, 1983); Dennis Altman, *The Homosexualization of America* (Boston: Beacon, 1983), 108–45; and Jeffrey Weeks, *Sexuality and Its Discontents: Meanings, Myths and Modern Sexualities* (London: Routledge, 1985), 185–201.

9. For an excellent discussion of the Christian Right's assault on the so-called rainbow curriculum in New York City, see N'Tanya Lee, Don Murphy, and Juliet Ucelli, "Whose Kids? Our Kids! Race, Sexuality, and the Right in New York City's Curriculum Battles," *Radical America* 25, no. 1 (January–March 1991): 9–21.

10. The literature on the postwar domestication of masculinity is vast and growing. For the most comprehensive accounts, see Barbara Ehrenreich, *The Hearts of Men: American Dreams and the Flight from Commitment* (Garden City, N.J.: Doubleday, 1983); Elaine Tyler May, *Homeward Bound: American Families in the Cold War Era* (New York: Basic, 1988); Elizabeth Long, *The American Dream and the Popular Novel* (Boston: Routledge & Kegan Paul, 1985); Lynn Spigel, *Make Room for TV: Television and the Family Ideal in Postwar America* (Chicago: Univ. of Chicago Press, 1992), 36–98; Elizabeth Traube, *Dreaming Identities: Class, Gender, and Generation in 1980s Hollywood Movies* (Boulder, Colo.: Westview Press, 1992); and Savran, *Communists, Cowboys, and Queers,* 20–75.

11. These studies were C. Wright Mills, *White Collar* (1952), William Whyte, *The Organization Man* (1956), and David Riesman, *The Lonely Crowd* (1950).

12. One such survey was the Kelly Longitudinal Study, conducted by E. Lowell Kelly, a psychologist at the University of Michigan. In the late 1930s Kelly began gathering data on six hundred white middle-class men and women. He was interested in studying their attitudes toward marriage, careers, homeownership, and childrearing. For a detailed discussion of Kelly's study and what it reveals about postwar American culture, see May, *Homeward Bound*, 11–14, 175–82.

13. For a detailed discussion of the postwar reorganization of the economy along Fordist lines, see Mike Davis, *Prisoners of the American Dream: Politics and Economy in the History of the U.S. Working Class* (London: Verso, 1986), 181–230. See also David Harvey, *The Condition of Postmodernity: An Inquiry into the Origins of Cultural Change* (Cambridge, Mass.: Blackwell, 1990), 121–97.

14. For a discussion of the impact of the GI bill of rights on the class formation of postwar American society, see Davis, *Prisoners of the American Dream*, 181–230.

15. I have taken the statistics in this paragraph from May, *Homeward Bound*, 165–66.

16. For a detailed account of the devastating impact of the Interstate Highway Act of 1956 on the inner cities, see Kenneth T. Jackson, *Crabgrass Frontier: The Suburbanization of the United States* (New York: Oxford Univ. Press, 1985), 248–51. For a more personal account of this devastation, see Marshall Berman's discussion of New York real estate developer and urban planner Robert Moses in *All That Is Solid Melts into Air: The Experience of Modernity* (New York: Penguin, 1988), 290–348. For a discussion of the impact of the Interstate Highway Act on Los Angeles, see Mike Davis, *City of Quartz: Excavating the Future in Los Angeles* (New York: Vintage, 1991), and Edward Soja, *Postmodern Geographies: The Reassertion of Space in Critical Social Theory* (London: Verso, 1989), 157–221.

17. For a detailed discussion of the racially discriminatory policies of the Federal Housing Administration, see Jackson, *Crabgrass Frontier*, 190–218, and May, *Homeward Bound*, 162–82.

18. This is a quotation from the 1939 *Underwriting Manual* of the Federal Housing Administration, which was used throughout the postwar period. Quoted in Jackson, *Crabgrass Frontier*, 206.

19. On the Housing Act of 1949, see Jackson, *Crabgrass Frontier*, 219–30.

20. On the shifting identifications of postwar ethnic minorities and the refraction of class struggle through the lens of race, see Michael Omi and Howard Winant, *Racial Formation in the United States: From the 1960s to the 1980s* (New York: Routledge, 1986), 89–135. See also Howard Winant, *Racial Conditions: Politics, Theory, Comparisons* (Minneapolis: Univ. of Minnesota Press, 1994), 57–68.

21. The argument that the decay of inner-city neighborhoods reflects the breakdown of the black family and other cultural "pathologies" in the black community is usually attributed to Daniel Patrick Moynihan's notorious "*Report* on the Negro Family," which he wrote in 1965 when he was Undersecretary of Labor in the

Johnson administration. But Moynihan drew his notion of the "culture of poverty" from Gunnar Myrdal's *An American Dilemma* (1944), a highly influential study of African Americans and their "failure" to assimilate.

22. On the role of *Playboy* in promoting resistance to the domestication of masculinity, see Ehrenreich, *The Hearts of Men*, 42–51.

23. On the relation between the emergence of the New Left and the resistance to the postwar reorganization of masculinity, see Alice Echols, "We Gotta Get out of This Place: Notes towards a Remapping of the Sixties," *Socialist Review* 22 (1992): 9–33. See also Van Gosse, *Where the Boys Are: Cuba, Cold War America, and the Making of a New Left* (London: Verso, 1993). Gosse argues that for a brief time in the late fifties before the Cuban revolution began to drift leftward Fidel Castro and his guerrilla fighters functioned as icons of *machismo* for disaffected white middle-class college students who were rebelling against white-collar America.

24. For a detailed discussion of film noir's political genealogy, see Brian Neve, *Film and Politics in America: A Social Tradition* (London and New York: Routledge, 1992), 145–70.

25. Quoted in Neve, *Film and Politics in America*, 150.

26. For a summary of the debates in film studies over whether film noir constitutes a genre or a cycle of films, see Frank Krutnik, *In a Lonely Street: Film Noir, Genre, Masculinity* (London and New York: Routledge, 1991), 3–32. Film scholars are reluctant to treat film noir as a genre primarily because it was not one of the genres officially recognized by the film industry. (These included the western, the crime thriller, the melodrama, the horror film, the musical, and the romantic comedy.) But the fact that we can specify the typical noir hero would seem to justify treating film noir as a genre.

27. Richard Dyer, "Homosexuality and Film Noir," in *The Matter of Images: Essays on Representations* (London: Routledge, 1993), 52–72. It is particularly surprising that Krutnik, whose study discusses film noir's homoerotic component in some detail, does not include the presence of gay male characters among his list of film noir's defining characteristics.

28. Examples of gay male characters in film noir include but are not limited to Gutman (Sidney Greenstreet) and Cairo (Peter Lorre) in *The Maltese Falcon* (John Huston, 1941); Marriott (Douglas Walton) in *Murder, My Sweet* (Edward Dmytryk, 1944); Lydecker (Clifton Webb) in *Laura* (Otto Preminger, 1944); Ballen (George Macready) in *Gilda* (Charles Vidor, 1946); Geiger and Carroll, gay male lovers in *The Big Sleep* (Howard Hawks, 1946); Cathcart (Clifton Webb) in *The Dark Corner* (Henry Hathaway, 1946), a reprise of Webb's role in *Laura;* and Bruno Anthony (Robert Walker) in *Strangers on a Train* (Alfred Hitchcock, 1951).

29. Corber, *In the Name of National Security*, 56–82.

30. On the impact of the Kinsey report on postwar American culture, see John

D'Emilio and Estelle B. Freedman, *Intimate Matters: A History of Sexuality in America* (New York: Harper & Row, 1988), 239–300.

31. Alfred Kinsey et al., *Sexual Behavior in the Human Male* (Philadelphia: Saunders, 1948), 627.

32. See my discussion of the 1950 Senate hearings on the government employment of homosexuals and lesbians in *In the Name of National Security,* 61–69.

33. Examples of postwar films that do not clearly distinguish the gay male characters from the straight male characters include *Gilda* (Charles Vidor, 1946); *Strangers on a Train* (Alfred Hitchcock, 1951); *The Wild One* (1954); *Rebel without a Cause* (Nicholas Ray, 1955); *Tea and Sympathy* (Vincente Minnelli, 1956); *North by Northwest* (Alfred Hitchcock, 1959); and *Advise and Consent* (Otto Preminger, 1962). I discuss both *Strangers on a Train* and *North by Northwest* in *In the Name of National Security.* In calling attention to the differences between film noir's system of representation and that of other forms of postwar cinematic discourse, I do not mean to overlook the examples of film noir that also created a climate of suspicion and paranoia by failing to distinguish clearly between the gay male characters and the straight male characters. After all, *Strangers on a Train* is often classified as a film noir.

34. For a discussion of the left-wing populism of Frank Capra's "middle-period" films, see Neve, *Film and Politics in America,* 35–55. For a discussion of the sentimental optimism of the Popular Front, see Walter Kalaidjian, *American Culture between the Wars: Revisionary Modernism and Postmodern Critique* (New York: Columbia Univ. Press, 1993), 160–87.

35. On the postwar retreat from the New Deal, see Davis, *Prisoners of the American Dream,* 52–101; George Lipsitz, *Rainbow at Midnight: Labor and Culture in the 1940s* (Urbana: Univ. of Illinois Press, 1994), 157–225; and John Patrick Diggins, *The Proud Decades: America in War and Peace, 1941–1960* (New York: Norton, 1988), 14–22.

36. On the relation between the Fair Deal and the New Deal, see Lipsitz, *Rainbow at Midnight,* 157–225, and Diggins, *The Proud Decades,* 109–10.

37. On the impact of McCarthyism in general on Hollywood's left-wing community, see Larry Ceplair and Steven Englund, *The Inquisition in Hollywood: Politics in the Film Community, 1930–1960* (Berkeley and Los Angeles: Univ. of California Press, 1979).

38. I want to be clear that in claiming that Williams, Vidal, and Baldwin were unencumbered by a history of involvement with the Communist party and thus were better able to judge postwar developments, I am merely trying to foreground the limitations of the party's treatment of the "woman question" and am not engaging in red-baiting. Discussions of the literary leftism of the thirties continue to be governed by the polarities of Cold War political discourse. Both Paula Rabinowitz and Walter Kalaidjian, for example, seem unable to discuss the role of the Communist party in the intellectual culture of the Depression era without vilifying it. They see literary

proletarianism as an unmitigated Stalinist failure and celebrate the populist aesthetic of the Popular Front era as more progressive. See Rabinowitz, *Labor and Desire: Women's Revolutionary Fiction in Depression America* (Chapel Hill: Univ. of North Carolina Press, 1991), 18–62, and Kalaidjian, *American Culture between the Wars*, 59–159. Barbara Foley, on the other hand, seems unable to discuss the cultural production of the Popular Front era without treating it as a sellout of the working class. She minimizes the role of Stalinism and treats literary proletarianism as truly an art of the working class. See Foley, *Radical Representations: Politics and Form in U.S. Proletarian Fiction, 1929–1941* (Durham, N.C.: Duke Univ. Press, 1993), 126–28. For a more balanced view of these issues, see James F. Murphy, *The Proletarian Moment: The Controversy over Leftism in Literature* (Urbana: Univ. of Illinois Press, 1991).

39. It is important to point out that critics attacked William Inge and Edward Albee, playwrights also rumored as gay, on the same grounds, claiming that the women with whom their protagonists were romantically involved were really men. Critics called the alleged deception the "Albertine strategy." For a discussion of this critical tactic, as it was used against Williams, see Savran, *Communists, Cowboys, and Queers,* 115–20.

40. For an example of the way in which this view of postwar urban gay communities informs recent work in gay studies, see Gilbert Herdt, " 'Coming Out' as a Rite of Passage: A Chicago Study," in *Gay Culture in America: Essays from the Field,* ed. Gilbert Herdt (Boston: Beacon, 1992), 29–67. See also Savran, *Communists, Cowboys, and Queers,* 84–88. According to this view, gay men did not begin to resist their oppression until the Stonewall rebellion of 1969, which led to the birth of the gay liberation movement.

41. There is considerable disagreement over whether camp should be seen as a strategy of survival or an oppositional practice. See, for example, Andrew Ross, "The Uses of Camp," in *No Respect: Intellectuals and Popular Culture* (New York: Routledge, 1989), 135–70. For a more sympathetic view of camp, see David Bergman, "Strategic Camp: The Art of Gay Rhetoric," in *Gaiety Transfigured: Gay Self-Representation in American Literature* (Madison: Univ. of Wisconsin Press, 1991), 103–21. Camp has recently attracted a great deal of attention in queer studies. Although I think such attention is merited, I fear that it will overshadow the other forms of gay male resistance that emerged in the postwar period.

42. See, for example, Elizabeth Lapovsky Kennedy and Madeline D. Davis's ethnographic study of Buffalo's postwar working-class lesbian community, *Boots of Leather, Slippers of Gold: The History of a Lesbian Community* (New York: Penguin, 1993). Kennedy and Davis similarly question the received narrative of postwar gay and lesbian activism. They trace the emergence of the gay liberation movement to postwar gay and lesbian working-class communities that rejected the dominant constructions of gendered identity.

43. The recent commemoration of the twenty-fifth anniversary of the Stonewall

rebellion has exaggerated the tendency to suppress the roots of the gay liberation movement in the work of postwar gay male writers. See, for example, Andrew Kopkind, "After Stonewall," *Nation,* 4 July 1994, 4–5. Kopkind's essay provides moving testimony of the place of the Stonewall rebellion in the gay male political imaginary, but like so many other such essays, it constructs the 1950s as the Dark Ages of gay male identity and culture. Kopkind ends his essay by celebrating Stonewall for ending "the years of gay men and lesbians locking themselves inside windowless, unnamed bars; writing dangerous, anonymous novels and articles; lying about their identity to their families, their bosses, the military; suffering silently when they were found out; hiding and seeking and winking at each other, or drinking and dying by themselves" (5).

44. This view of the gay liberation movement is particularly prevalent among left-wing scholars who should know better. See, for example, Stanley Aronowitz, "The Situation of the Left in the United States," *Socialist Review* 23, no. 3 (spring 1995): 5–79.

45. Kennedy and Davis, *Boots of Leather, Slippers of Gold.*

1 Masculinizing the American Dream: Discourses of Resistance in the Cold War Era

1. C. L. R. James, *American Civilization,* ed. Anna Grimshaw and Keith Hart (Cambridge, Mass.: Blackwell, 1993), 274. Hereafter all references are to this edition and will be cited by page number.

2. James's desire to link his project to that of the American studies movement was perhaps most apparent in his use of the term *American civilization.* As David R. Shumway has shown, one of the chief aims of the American studies movement was to establish that there was such a thing as American civilization. See David R. Shumway, *Creating American Civilization: A Genealogy of American Literature as an Academic Discipline* (Minneapolis: Univ. of Minnesota Press, 1994), 299–344.

3. See Robert A. Hill, "Literary Executor's Afterword," in James, *American Civilization,* 350–51.

4. Jonathan Arac, "F. O. Matthiessen and American Studies: Authorizing a Renaissance," in *Critical Genealogies: Historical Situations for Postmodern Literary Studies* (New York: Columbia Univ. Press, 1989), 157–75.

5. For a more detailed discussion of the relation between the emergence of American studies and the Cold War, see Shumway, *Creating American Civilization,* 299–344. See also Russell Reising, *The Unusable Past: Theory and the Study of American Literature* (New York: Methuen, 1986), and Geraldine Murphy, "Romancing the Center: Cold War Politics and Classic American Literature," *Poetics Today* 9, no. 4 (1988): 737–47.

6. On Matthiessen's desire to synthesize the populist aesthetic of the Popular Front and the formalism of the New Criticism, see Arac, "F. O. Matthiessen and American Studies," 169–71.

7. I do not mean to suggest that James owed his emphasis on the importance of mass culture to Matthiessen, but rather that his belief that American democracy had produced an art that expressed the people's aspirations derived from Matthiessen. Where he differed from Matthiessen was in claiming that in the twentieth century mass culture had replaced high literary discourse as the most accurate reflection of the people's needs and expectations.

8. An important exception to this view of mass culture was Henry Nash Smith's *Virgin Land* (1950), which used dime novels and other forms of mass culture to examine the myth of the frontier. But American studies scholars in general refused to acknowledge the importance of mass culture. Indeed, the tendency to treat mass culture as a debased form of art eventually led to a split in the American Studies Association between populists and elitists, and in 1969 disgruntled members of the ASA founded the Popular Culture Association as an alternative. For a discussion of this split, see Shumway, *Creating American Civilization*, 312–18.

9. The similarities were not limited to James's emphasis on the collective forms of reception made possible by the mechanical reproduction of art. His belief that the violence of film noir functioned therapeutically recalled Benjamin's claims about the therapeutic effects of slapstick comedy, particularly the linking of violence and comedy in the Mickey Mouse and Silly Symphony cartoons of the thirties. For a discussion of Benjamin's argument about the significance of these cartoons, see Miriam Hansen, "Of Mice and Ducks: Benjamin and Adorno on Disney," *South Atlantic Quarterly* 92, no. 1 (winter 1993): 27–61.

10. Although French film critic Nino Frank coined the term film noir in 1946 to indicate the resemblance of these films to the detective fiction published in Gallimard's *Serie noire*, it was not widely used by American film critics until the late 1960s.

11. Fredric Jameson, "Reification and Utopia in Mass Culture," in *Signatures of the Visible* (New York: Routledge, 1992), 9–34.

12. I have borrowed the term *political preconscious* from Donald E. Pease. See his "Leslie Fiedler, the Rosenberg Trial, and the Formulation of an American Canon," *boundary 2* 17, no. 2 (1990): 155–98. I mean to distinguish film noir's political preconscious from its political unconscious. I am not interested here in the fantasies and desires that constituted film noir's "unsaid," or that which it could not acknowledge without precipitating a crisis of meaning, but in those that *consciously* shaped its oppositional content. On the political unconscious, see Fredric Jameson, *The Political Unconscious: Narrative as a Socially Symbolic Act* (Ithaca: Cornell Univ. Press, 1981).

13. C. Wright Mills, *White Collar* (New York: Oxford Univ. Press, 1956 [1951]), xx. Hereafter all references are to this edition and will be cited by page number.

14. For a discussion of Mills's relation to the Old and New Lefts, see Richard H. Pells, *The Liberal Mind in a Conservative Age: American Intellectuals in the 1940s and 1950s* (Middletown, Conn.: Wesleyan Univ. Press, 1989), 249–51. See also Neil Jumonville, *Critical Crossings: The New York Intellectuals in Postwar America* (Berkeley and Los Angeles: Univ. of California Press, 1991), 58–59.

15. Mills lists works by Erich Fromm, Leo Lowenthal, and Herbert Marcuse as important sources for his understanding of the impact of the processes of routinization and rationalization on the construction of postwar subjectivity. He also claims to have derived his understanding of such concepts as class, status, and bureaucracy from Max Weber, who was an important figure for the Frankfurt school. See *White Collar,* 357.

16. Despite the similarities between his understanding of mass culture and that of Max Horkheimer and Theodor Adorno, Mills does not list *Dialectic of Enlightenment* (1944) among his sources. He seems to have owed his understanding of mass culture primarily to Leo Lowenthal.

17. The Marxist critics most closely associated with this theory of mass culture were Max Horkheimer and Theodor Adorno, although as I indicated in note 16 Mills does not seem to have been familiar with their *Dialectic of Enlightenment,* in which they elaborated this view.

18. For my understanding of Mills's macho image, I am indebted to Alice Echols, who discusses its influence on the New Left in "We Gotta Get out of This Place: Notes towards a Remapping of the Sixties," *Socialist Review* 22 (1992): 9–33.

19. Here is how a reviewer glowingly described C. Wright Mills in 1956:

"C. Wright Mills, a tall, husky, hard-driving Texan of forty, has made a professor's dream come true: his scholarly monographs . . . are also hot sellers on the trade-book market. . . . [S]omewhere during this period he found time to acquire professional architectural training and awesome competence with machinery, tools, and photographic equipment. He lives . . . in an old farmhouse that he completely rebuilt with his own hands. . . . Once a sports-car enthusiast, he has now graduated to motorcycles, and owns a German BMW. Weather permitting, he commutes on this thoroughbred machine to his Columbia classes, thus neatly solving the parking problems at Morningside Heights, and asserting his own independent personality."

Thomas E. Cooney, "Sociologist on a Motorcycle," *Saturday Review,* 28 April 1956, 9. I am indebted to Jonathan Arac for bringing this review to my attention.

20. Todd Gitlin, *The Sixties: Years of Hope, Days of Rage* (New York: Bantam, 1987), 34.

21. Several historians have confirmed Mills's description of the impact of the rise

of monopoly capitalism on the definition of success and the frustration the emphasis on "personality" as opposed to "character" caused many men. See, for example, Warren Susman, *Culture as History: The Transformation of American Society in the Twentieth Century* (New York: Pantheon, 1987), 274–84. See also T. J. Jackson Lears, *No Place of Grace: Antimodernism and the Transformation of American Culture, 1880–1920* (Chicago: Univ. of Chicago Press, 1994 [1981]), 59–96, and E. Anthony Rotundo, *American Manhood: Transformations in Masculinity from the Revolution to the Modern Era* (New York: Basic, 1993), 167–221.

22. The association of mass culture with femininity was not unique to Mills but has a long history that can be traced at least to the nineteenth century and middle-class fears of the masses. See Andreas Huyssen, "Mass Culture as Woman: Modernism's Other," in *After the Great Divide: Modernism, Mass Culture, Postmodernism* (Bloomington: Indiana Univ. Press, 1986), 44–62.

23. For a discussion of Miller's relation to the Old Left, see Pells, *The Liberal Mind in a Conservative Age*, 324–28. See also David Savran, *Communists, Cowboys, and Queers: The Politics of Masculinity in the Work of Arthur Miller and Tennessee Williams* (Minneapolis: Univ. of Minnesota Press, 1992), 22–26.

24. Quoted in Savran, *Communists, Cowboys, and Queers*, 20.

25. This is why Savran's tendency to group Miller with Cold War liberals does not seem warranted. Savran exaggerates Miller's conservatism, although it is important to point out that his desire to recuperate Tennessee Williams, whose work has been unjustly dismissed by left-wing intellectuals as apolitical in comparison to Miller's, in many respects requires him to do so.

26. Robert Warshow, "The Movie Camera and the American," in *The Immediate Experience: Movies, Comics, Theatre, and Other Aspects of Popular Culture* (New York: Doubleday, 1962), 121.

27. Arthur Miller, *Death of a Salesman* (New York: Penguin, 1976). Hereafter all references are to this edition and will be cited by page number.

28. It is important to point out that it would not have been historically possible for Willy and Linda to have weathered a twenty-five-year mortgage in 1949, when the play was written. Until 1933, when the Home Owners Loan Corporation was signed into law, the typical length of a mortgage was between five and ten years, and homeowners were at the mercy of unpredictable forces in the money market, which tended to prevent them from securing renewals of their mortgages. On this aspect of homeownership, see Kenneth T. Jackson, *Crabgrass Frontier: The Suburbanization of the United States* (New York: Oxford Univ. Press, 1985), 190–218. It does not seem likely that Miller would have been unaware of this historical impossibility. But by distorting the history of homeownership, he was able to stress the way in which the government policies we examined in the introduction boosted and consolidated the reorganization of masculinity that began with the shift from industrial to monopoly capitalism in the late nineteenth century.

29. Paul Rabinowitz, "Women and U.S. Literary Radicalism," in *Writing Red: An Anthology of American Women Writers, 1930–1940*, ed. Charlotte Nekola and Paul Rabinowitz (New York: Feminist Press, 1987), 1–25. See also Walter Kalaidjian, *American Culture between the Wars: Revisionary Modernism and Postmodern Critique* (New York: Columbia Univ. Press, 1993), 138–59. Kalaidjian argues that the phallicization of the American worker in the cultural production of the Popular Front era served less as an image of working-class power than as a symptom of its absence.

30. As we saw in the introduction, many postwar civil rights organizations such as the Mattachine Society were dedicated to securing the right of such groups to become white-collar workers so that they could achieve the postwar American dream of homeownership.

31. Savran overlooks the tension between Miller's interest in the material forces that conditioned male subjectivity and his desire to adhere to classical conventions, which may explain why he tends to exaggerate Miller's conservatism. Because he wants to highlight Tennessee Williams's oppositional politics, Savran tends to suppress Miller's materialist understanding of postwar American culture, an understanding that calls into question his construction of Miller as a Cold War liberal.

32. The incoherence of Miller's critique of the rise of the white-collar worker can also be attributed to the influence the dominant mode of representation in the Cold War era exerted on even the most progressive cultural workers. As I show in *In the Name of National Security,* this mode of representation tended to discourage a materialist understanding of American culture by psychologizing social relations. See my *In the Name of National Security: Hitchcock, Homophobia, and the Political Construction of Gender in Postwar America* (Durham, N.C.: Duke Univ. Press, 1993), 19–55.

33. Andrew Ross, *No Respect: Intellectuals and Popular Culture* (New York: Routledge, 1989), 87.

34. Norman Mailer, "The White Negro: Superficial Reflections on the Hipster," in *Advertisements for Myself* (New York: Putnam, 1959), 326. Hereafter all references are to this edition and will be cited by page number.

35. Mailer's optimism about a social explosion explains why his implicit criticisms of the Communist party in "The White Negro" should not be confused with the anti-Communist hysteria of Cold War liberals.

36. The view that gayness and blackness were mutually exclusive categories of identity was hardly unique to Cleaver. Amiri Baraka (Leroi Jones) and other black nationalists expressed a similar view. For a discussion of this view and its prevalence in the black power movement, see Michele Wallace, "Black Macho," in *Black Macho and the Myth of the Superwoman* (London: Verso, 1990), 62–69. It is important to point out, however, that not all black nationalists shared this view. For example, Huey Newton, one of the founders of the Black Panther Party, attacked the homophobia of the black power movement and thought that the Panthers should ally

themselves with the Gay Liberation Front. For a discussion of Newton's iconoclastic view of homosexuality, see Savran, *Communists, Cowboys, and Queers*, 154.

37. For an important critique of the homophobia underlying Mailer's and Cleaver's racist construction of black masculinity, see Wallace, "Black Macho," 34–69.

38. Eldridge Cleaver, *Soul on Ice* (New York: Dell, 1992), 100. Hereafter all references are to this edition and will be cited by page number.

39. See Tomas Almaguer, "Chicano Men: A Cartography of Homosexual Identity and Behavior," *differences* 3, no. 2 (summer 1991): 75–100.

40. It is also important to point out that Cleaver's argument converged with and inadvertently legitimated Daniel Patrick Moynihan's notorious claims in his "Report on the Negro Family" (1965). Although Cleaver stressed the role of racism, he claimed, like Moynihan, that the obstacles black men faced were exacerbated by the supposedly matriarchal structure of the black family. For a detailed critique of the masculinism underlying Cleaver's argument, see Wallace, "Black Macho," 51–69.

41. Mailer's racism was attacked even by Cold War liberals such as Norman Podhoretz. For a discussion of these attacks, see Jumonville, *Critical Crossings*, 89–93, and Ross, *No Respect*, 84–85.

42. Quoted in Ross, *No Respect*, 89. Ross also discusses Kerouac's reaction to Mailer's essay, 88–89.

43. For a detailed discussion of *On the Road*'s reception, see Ann Charters, introduction to *On the Road* (New York: Penguin, 1991), vii–xxx. See also Jumonville, *Critical Crossings*, 187–90.

44. Quoted in Charters, introduction, xvii.

45. Jack Kerouac, *On the Road* (New York: Penguin, 1991), 21. Hereafter all references are to this edition and are cited by page number.

46. This is not to minimize the homoeroticism of Sal's pursuit of an "authentic" masculinity. As we saw in the introduction, the difference between desire and identification was particularly difficult to locate in the Cold War era, when male homosocial bonds were objects of intense scrutiny and suspicion. Indeed, contemporary critics tended to see Sal's bonds with other men as homoerotic rather than identificatory. Still, it seems important at this juncture to distinguish Sal's desire to be the cowboy described in this passage from the gay macho style, which as we will see in chapter 5 did *not* entail an identification with heteromasculinity.

2 *Resisting the Lure of the Commodity:* Laura *and the Spectacle of the Gay Male Body*

1. The other films Frank identified as films noirs were *The Maltese Falcon* (John Huston, 1941), *Murder, My Sweet* (Edward Dmytryk, 1944), *Double Indemnity* (Billy Wilder, 1944), and *The Woman in the Window* (Fritz Lang, 1944). The release of these

films had been delayed because of the war, which may explain why Frank was so quick to seem them as signaling a new trend, despite the fact that they were hardly representative of postwar Hollywood cinema.

2. For a detailed account of the controversy surrounding the casting of Webb, see Rudy Behlmer, "The Face in the Misty Light: *Laura,*" in *Behind the Scenes* (Hollywood: Samuel French, 1990), 177–99. See also Vito Russo, *The Celluloid Closet: Homosexuality in the Movies,* rev. ed. (New York: Harper & Row, 1987), 45–46.

3. Otto Preminger, *Preminger: An Autobiography* (Garden City, N.J.: Doubleday, 1977), 73.

4. On the treatment of homosexuality in classical Hollywood film before and after the establishment of the Production Code, see Russo, "Who's a Sissy? Homosexuality according to Tinseltown," in *The Celluloid Closet,* 4–59. For a more general discussion of the code, see David Bordwell, Kristin Thompson, and Janet Staiger, *The Classical Hollywood Cinema: Film Style and Mode of Production to 1960* (New York: Columbia Univ. Press, 1985), 102–4.

5. Rick Altman has recently argued that the homogeneity and uniformity of the classical system has been greatly exaggerated. He has also shown that the roots of the cinematic apparatus lay in nineteenth-century melodrama and other forms of popular entertainment rather than in the realistic novel, as film historians have tended to claim. See Rick Altman, "Dickens, Griffith, and Film Theory Today," *South Atlantic Quarterly* 88 (spring 1989): 321–59. My use of the term *classical system* merely refers to the paradigm that governed the production of films in the era of the studio system and is not meant to suppress the diversity and heterogeneity of classical Hollywood cinema. To be sure, the classical system was not monolithic or totalizing and clearly permitted a range of deviation. But, as we will see, potentially subversive modes of cinematic discourse such as film noir tended to accede to the dominance of the classical system, even as they offered spectators a transgressive form of visual pleasure.

6. On the resemblance between "primitive" cinema and the variety show and other forms of popular entertainment, see Tom Gunning, "The Cinema of Attractions: Early Film, Its Spectator, and the Avant-Garde," in *Early Cinema: Space, Frame, Narrative,* ed. Thomas Elsaesser (London: British Film Institute, 1990), 56–62. Gunning uses the term *cinema of attractions* to refer to the direct mode of address deployed by early cinema. He shows that early cinema was unabashedly exhibitionistic and subordinated narrative to spectacle in order to capitalize on the popularity of fairgrounds, vaudeville, and other forms of commercialized leisure.

7. For a discussion of the cinematic apparatus that provides an important alternative to the dominant paradigms in film studies, see Anne Friedberg, *Window Shopping: Cinema and the Postmodern* (Berkeley and Los Angeles: Univ. of California Press, 1993), 15–38. Friedberg argues that moviegoing and the shopping mall share a visual logic that can be traced to the mobile and ambulatory gaze promoted by *flanerie* and other forms of nineteenth-century visual culture.

8. For a discussion of the similarities between theatrical and early cinematic experience, see Miriam Hansen, *Babel and Babylon: Spectatorship in American Silent Film* (Cambridge: Harvard Univ. Press, 1991), 93–101.

9. For a discussion of the way in which classical Hollywood cinema continued to mobilize the sort of visual pleasure offered by early cinema, despite its subordination of spectacle to narrative, see Gunning, "The Cinema of Attractions." Gunning argues that with the emergence and consolidation of the classical system, the "cinema of attractions" does not disappear but "goes underground, both into certain avant-garde practices and as a component of narrative films" (57).

10. For a detailed discussion of the tension between spectacle and narrative in classical Hollywood cinema, see Jane Gaines, "The Queen Christina Tie-Ups: Convergence of Show Window and Screen," in "Female Representation and Consumer Culture," ed. Jane Gaines and Michael Renov, *Quarterly Review of Film and Video* 11, no. 1 (winter 1989): 35–59.

11. In legitimating voyeurism and fetishism as acceptable modes of spectatorship, classical Hollywood cinema did not discriminate against women, despite the tendency of feminist film critics to claim otherwise. On the way in which Hollywood encouraged the eroticization of the female gaze, see Hansen's discussion of the cult of Valentino: "Male Star, Female Fans," in *Babel and Babylon*, 245–68.

12. For a discussion of the way in which the cult of the star, by fostering a fetishistic relation between spectator and screen, tended to prevent classical Hollywood cinema from achieving its goal of telling a story, see Gaines, "The Queen Christina Tie-Ups." See also Hansen, *Babel and Babylon*, 245–68. For a general discussion of the star system and the sort of gaze it fosters, see Richard Dyer, *Stars* (London: British Film Institute, 1990).

13. For a particularly useful discussion of the way in which the commodity form encouraged a gaze that became easily distracted by the element of spectacle in classical Hollywood cinema, see Mary Ann Doane, *The Desire to Desire: The Woman's Film of the 1940s* (Bloomington: Indiana Univ. Press, 1987), 22–33. See also Jeanne Allen, "The Film Viewer as Consumer," *Quarterly Review of Film Studies* 5, no. 4 (fall 1980): 481–99; Charles Eckert, "The Carole Lombard in Macy's Window," *Quarterly Review of Film Studies* 3, no. 1 (winter 1978): 1–21; and Gaines, "The Queen Christina Tie-Ups."

14. On working-class immigrant women and subcultural forms of spectatorship, see Hansen, *Babel and Babylon*, 60–125; Judith Mayne, *Private Novels, Public Films* (Athens: Univ. of Georgia Press, 1988), 69–94; Kathy Peiss, *Cheap Amusements: Working Women and Leisure in Turn-of-the-Century New York* (Philadelphia: Temple Univ. Press, 1986); Elizabeth Ewen, "City Lights: Immigrant Women and the Rise of the Movies," *Signs* 5, no. 3, Supplement (spring 1980): S45–S65; and Gaines, "The Queen Christina Tie-Ups."

15. Rachel Bowlby, *Just Looking: Consumer Culture in Dreiser, Gissing, and Zola* (New York: Methuen, 1985), 4.

16. On women and department stores, see especially Susan Porter Benson, *Counter-Cultures: Saleswomen, Managers, and Customers in American Department Stores, 1890–1940* (Urbana: Univ. of Illinois Press, 1986). See also Bowlby, *Just Looking,* and Gaines, "The Queen Christina Tie-Ups."

17. For a definition of camp that is particularly relevant to the mode of spectatorship I am attributing to gay men, see Jack Babuscio, "Camp and the Gay Sensibility," in *Gays and Film,* ed. Richard Dyer, rev. ed. (New York: New York Zoetrope, 1984), 43. Babuscio defines camp as "an emphasis on sensuous surfaces, textures, imagery and the evocation of mood as stylistic devices—not simply because they are appropriate to the plot, but as fascinating in themselves."

18. Important discussions of gay male spectatorship are Richard Dyer, *Heavenly Bodies: Film Stars and Society* (New York: St. Martin's, 1986), 141–95; Janet Staiger, "The Logic of Alternative Readings: A Star Is Born," in *Interpreting Films: Studies in the Historical Reception of American Cinema* (Princeton: Princeton Univ. Press, 1992), 154–77; and Jane Feuer, "Gay Readings," in *The Hollywood Musical* (Bloomington: Indiana Univ. Press, 1993), 139–43. In attributing to gay male spectators a gaze that hovered over the surface of the image, I do not mean to suggest that there were not other forms of gay male spectatorship that can also be understood as oppositional. Obviously, many gay male spectators may have allowed themselves to become absorbed in the diegesis but rejected the heterosexual subject-position it made available to them by giving the film a gay inflection or by interpreting it in ways that were grounded in their own personal histories. For a discussion of gay male forms of spectatorship that depended on the gay male spectator's willing absorption in the diegesis, see Staiger, "The Logic of Alternative Readings." Staiger argues that when it was initially released in 1954, gay men interpreted Vincente Minnelli's *A Star Is Born* as though it depicted Judy Garland's own unhappy life as a star. Staiger's argument is compelling, but she minimizes the degree to which the mode of spectatorship she ascribes to gay men was limited primarily to white, lower-middle-class gays.

19. On the popularity of the musical in postwar urban gay male communities, see Feuer, "Gay Readings." On the popularity of the melodrama, see Staiger, "The Logic of Alternative Readings."

20. On the diversity and heterogeneity of early film audiences, see Hansen, *Babel and Babylon,* 60–89, and Douglas Gomery, *Shared Pleasures: A History of Movie Presentation in the United States* (Madison: Univ. of Wisconsin Press, 1992), 18–56.

21. For a detailed discussion of the classical system as a set of strategies designed to anticipate and control the reception of Hollywood films, see Bordwell, Staiger, and Thompson, *The Classical Hollywood Cinema,* 157–240.

22. The feminist scholarship challenging masculinist theories of spectatorship is

too vast to cite here, but particularly important and influential examples are Teresa de Lauretis, "Desire in Narrative," in *Alice Doesn't: Feminism, Semiotics, Cinema* (Bloomington: Indiana Univ. Press, 1984), 103–57, and Doane, *The Desire to Desire*, 1–37.

23. "The New Pictures," *Time*, 30 October 1944, 54.

24. Russo, *The Celluloid Closet*, 94. According to Russo, for many gay male spectators, Webb's classic portrayal of a gay man was not Lydecker but Elliot Templeton, an aging male spinster who dies in *The Razor's Edge* (Edmund Goulding, 1946).

25. Not all reviewers were distracted by the film's lush visual style and failed to note its lack of narrative coherence. Manny Farber, for example, described the film as "boring," complaining that the action was not sufficiently motivated. Despite this criticism, however, Farber allowed his gaze to become distracted by the element of spectacle in the film. He was transfixed by Webb's performance and singled it out for praise: "The best part of the picture is its description of a Brahmin columnist, named Waldo Lydecker, played with great pleasure by Clifton Webb, whose snobbishness and fastidiousness are about the only facts studied in any detail; his perfumed literary style of talking expresses a lot of auntyish effeminacy and his values get across with some force." Manny Farber, "Murdered Movie," *New Republic*, 30 October 1944, 568.

26. Bosley Crowther, "A Big Hello," *New York Times*, 22 October 1944, sect. 2, p. 1.

27. For a useful discussion of the set of conventions that distinguishes film noir from other forms of classical Hollywood cinema, see Christine Gledhill, "*Klute* 1: A Contemporary Film Noir and Feminist Criticism," in *Women in Film Noir*, ed. E. Ann Kaplan (London: British Film Institute, 1978), 6–21. See also Frank Krutnik, *In a Lonely Street: Film Noir, Genre, Masculinity* (London and New York: Routledge, 1991), 15–29.

28. On the way in which film noir threatened to undermine the classical system, see J. P. Telotte, *Voices in the Dark: The Narrative Patterns of Film Noir* (Urbana and Chicago: Univ. of Illinois Press, 1989). See also Dana Polan, *Power and Paranoia: History, Narrative, and the American Cinema, 1940–1950* (New York: Columbia Univ. Press, 1986), 193–249. Many film scholars do not accept the argument that film noir constituted a subversive form of cinematic discourse and instead stress its conformity with the classical system. See, for example, Bordwell, Staiger, and Thompson, *The Classical Hollywood Cinema*, 74–77.

29. For an especially good discussion of the differences between film noir and the detective genre, see Krutnik, *In a Lonely Street*, 33–44.

30. On film noir's distinctive narrative structure, see Gledhill, "*Klute* 1," 6–21. See also Polan, *Power and Paranoia*, 193–248, and Krutnik, *In a Lonely Street*, 33–44.

31. On this aspect of film noir, see Gledhill, "*Klute* 1."

32. Lee Edelman, "Imagining the Homosexual: *Laura* and the Other Face of

Gender," in *Homographesis: Essays in Gay Literary and Cultural Theory* (New York: Routledge, 1993), 192–241.

33. Robert J. Corber, *In the Name of National Security: Hitchcock, Homophobia, and the Political Construction of Gender in Postwar America* (Durham, N.C.: Duke Univ. Press, 1993).

34. For a more detailed discussion of the way in which the discourses of national security manipulated the Kinsey report's findings, see Corber, "Reconstructing Homosexuality: Hitchcock and the Homoerotics of Spectatorial Pleasure," in *In the Name of National Security*, 56–82.

35. On the increasing visibility of gay men in the realm of political representation, see especially John D'Emilio, *Sexual Politics, Sexual Communities: The Making of a Homosexual Minority in the United States, 1940–1970* (Chicago: Univ. of Chicago Press, 1983).

36. For a particularly good discussion of gay men's strategic appropriation of the stereotype of the effeminate homosexual as a means of increasing their visibility, see Richard Dyer, "Seen to Be Believed: Some Problems in the Representation of Gay People as Typical," in *The Matter of Images: Essays on Representations* (London and New York: Routledge, 1993), 19–51.

37. On the femme fatale's potentially transgressive role in film noir, see especially Janey Place, "Women in Film Noir," in *Women in Film Noir*, 35–54. See also Elizabeth Cowie, "*Film Noir* and Women," in *Shades of Noir*, ed. Joan Copjec (London: Verso, 1993), 121–65. For a more general discussion of the femme fatale in classical Hollywood cinema that also stresses her transgressive role, see Mary Ann Doane, *Femmes Fatales: Feminism, Film Theory, Psychoanalysis* (New York: Routledge, 1991).

38. Place, "Women in Film Noir," 36.

39. For a reading of film noir that stresses its oppositional content, see Sylvia Harvey, "Woman's Place: The Absent Family of Film Noir," in *Women in Film Noir*, 22–34. See also Brian Neve, *Film and Politics in America: A Social Tradition* (London and New York: Routledge, 1992), 145–70.

40. For a particularly good discussion of the way in which film noir registered the postwar decline and abandonment of the city, see David Reid and Jayne L. Walker, "Strange Pursuit: Cornell Woolrich and the Abandoned City of the Forties," in *Shades of Noir*, 57–96.

41. Susan Sontag, "Notes on Camp," in *Against Interpretation and Other Essays* (New York: Farrar, Straus, & Giroux, 1966), 284.

42. Quoted in Russo, *The Celluloid Closet*, 46.

43. On the function of commodity aesthetics in capitalist social formations, see W. F. Haug, *Critique of Commodity Aesthetics: Appearance, Sexuality, and Advertising in Capitalist Society* (Minneapolis: Univ. of Minnesota Press, 1986).

44. Quoted in Susan Buck-Morss, *Dialectics of Seeing* (Cambridge: MIT Press,

1989), 110. It goes without saying that Mark's "dream-sleep" has none of the utopian connotations inscribed in Benjamin's use of the term.

45. Haug, *Critique of Commodity Aesthetics,* 50.

46. Ibid., 19.

47. See especially Kristin Thompson, "Closure within a Dream: Point of View in *Laura,*" in *Breaking the Glass Armor: Neoformalist Film Analysis* (Princeton: Princeton Univ. Press, 1988), 188–91.

48. Thompson, "Closure within a Dream," 162–94.

3 *"Real American History":* Crossfire *and the Increasing Invisibility of Gay Men in the Cold War Era*

1. Quoted in Rudy Behlmer, "The Face in the Misty Light: *Laura,*" in *Behind the Scenes* (Hollywood: Samuel French, 1990), 190.

2. Vera Caspary, *Laura* (Boston: Houghton Mifflin, 1942), 9. Hereafter all references are to this edition and are cited by page number. Significantly, this allusion to Lydecker's homosexuality was included in the original script of the film version but was deleted at the request of the Breen office as a violation of the Production Code.

3. Caspary discusses her membership in both the Communist party and the League of American Writers in her autobiography, *The Secrets of Grown-ups* (New York: McGraw-Hill, 1979).

4. For an important revisionist history of the "woman question," as it was addressed by the Communist party, see Barbara Foley, *Radical Representations: Politics and Form in U.S. Proletarian Fiction, 1929–1941* (Durham, N.C.: Duke Univ. Press, 1993), 213–46. Foley shows that the marriage between Marxism and feminism was more happy in the thirties than it is today. For a more critical view of the Communist party's treatment of the "woman question," see Paula Rabinowitz, *Labor and Desire: Women's Revolutionary Fiction in Depression America* (Chapel Hill: Univ. of North Carolina Press, 1991).

5. Caspary addressed working-class female experience more directly in her short story "The Gardenia," originally published in *Today's Woman* in 1952, although her focus remained issues of female subjectivity. The story was later made into *The Blue Gardenia* (Fritz Lang, 1953), a film noir starring Anne Baxter. The film emptied the story of its feminist content and thus provides yet another example of the tendency of left-wing directors to suppress the most progressive aspects of their sources. (Lang was a member of the Anti-Nazi League, which was investigated by HUAC, and he was briefly blacklisted in the early 1950s.) For more on the relation between the film and the story, see Janet Bergstrom, "The Mystery of *The Blue Gardenia,*" in *Shades of Noir,* ed. Joan Copjec (London: Verso, 1993), 97–120.

6. See Foster Hirsch, *Film Noir: The Dark Side of the Screen* (New York: Da Capo,

1981); and Frank Krutnik, *In a Lonely Street: Film Noir, Genre, Masculinity* (London and New York: Routledge, 1991). Hirsch and Krutnik carefully map the similarities between film noir and the hard-boiled detective novel, but they show little interest in the differences between them. Nor do they show much interest in the political content of the hard-boiled detective novel and how it did and did not influence film noir.

7. For a detailed discussion of Scott's and Dmytryk's political histories, see Larry Ceplair and Steven Englund, *The Inquisition in Hollywood: Politics in the Film Community, 1930–1960* (Berkeley and Los Angeles: Univ. of California Press, 1979), 325–60. See also Brian Neve, *Film and Politics in America: A Social Tradition* (London and New York: Routledge, 1992), 145–70. Dmytryk was eventually able to work again as a director. One of his projects following his political rehabilitation was *Walk on the Wild Side* (1962), a film noir adapted from a Nelson Algren novel, in which the villain is not a gay man but a lesbian played by Barbara Stanwyck.

8. Although space does not permit me to discuss it in detail, it is worth noting that *Murder, My Sweet* provides another example of the tendency I am trying to clarify in this chapter. On the one hand, the film included an explicitly marked gay male character, Lindsay Marriot (Douglas Walton), and thus acknowledged that the gay male subculture was an integral part of American society. On the other hand, Scott and Dmytryk eliminated the racial subplot of *Farewell, My Lovely* (1941), the Raymond Chandler novel from which the film was adapted. In the novel the police halfheartedly investigate the murder of a black bar owner because it occurred in a "colored" section of Los Angeles and they know it will never make it into the newspapers. In the film, the bar owner is white, and thus the police's lack of enthusiasm for investigating his murder cannot be attributed to racism.

9. Quoted in Ceplair and Englund, *The Inquisition in Hollywood*, 317.

10. Nor can it be claimed that they were afraid of violating the Production Code, which as I noted in chapter 2 prohibited the explicit treatment of homosexuality. *Murder, My Sweet* retains the homosexual subplot of the Raymond Chandler novel virtually intact.

11. Ceplair and Englund, *The Inquisition in Hollywood*, 453. Ceplair and Englund reprint the memo as an appendix.

12. It is worth noting that Brooks had a distinguished career as one of Hollywood's most progressive screenwriters and directors. He wrote the script for *Brute Force* (Jules Dassin, 1947), a film noir that sympathetically portrays a prison uprising, and he collaborated with John Huston on the script for *Key Largo* (John Huston, 1948). He wrote and directed *Deadline USA* (1952), which starred Humphrey Bogart as a newspaper reporter who staunchly defends the freedom of the press, and he directed *The Blackboard Jungle* (1955), a social-problem film that was partially inspired by a recent Supreme Court ruling, *Brown v. Board of Education.*

13. For more on this reversal of strategy, see Walter Kalaidjian, *American Culture*

between the Wars: Revisionary Modernism and Postmodern Critique (New York: Columbia Univ. Press, 1993), 59–159. In focusing on the problems with the category of the "common man," I do not mean to ignore the political achievements that its adoption enabled. The adoption of the Popular Front as the official policy of the Communist party in 1935 significantly extended the party's influence on American political and cultural life. Moreover, the category of the "common man" informed some of the most important and influential cultural criticism of the thirties and forties, most notably F. O. Matthiessen's *American Renaissance.* On the relation between Matthiessen's achievement in *American Renaissance* and the party's reversal of strategy, see Jonathan Arac, "F. O. Matthiessen and American Studies: Authorizing a Renaissance," in *Critical Genealogies: Historical Situations for Postmodern Literary Studies* (New York: Columbia Univ. Press, 1989), 157–75.

14. Michael Kazin has recently shown how, through carefully orchestrated appearances on television programs such as *Meet the Press,* in which he addressed reporters by their first names and mixed dire warnings about Communist subversion with seemingly guileless humor, McCarthy was able to position himself as a man of the people. According to Kazin, McCarthy was seen as an idealistic small-town boy who, like the Jimmy Stewart character in Frank Capra's *Mr. Smith Goes to Washington* (1939), had come to the nation's capital to clean it up. Michael Kazin, *The Populist Persuasion: An American History* (New York: Basic, 1995), 183–93.

15. Feminist critiques of the logic of abstraction that governs American citizenship include Jean Bethke Elshtain, *Public Man, Private Woman* (Princeton: Princeton Univ. Press, 1981); Anne Norton, *Reflections on Political Identity* (Baltimore: Johns Hopkins Univ. Press, 1988); and Carole Pateman, *The Sexual Contract* (Stanford: Stanford Univ. Press, 1988).

16. On the relation between bodily abstraction and participation in the political public sphere, see in particular Nancy Fraser, "Rethinking the Public Sphere: A Contribution to the Critique of Actually Existing Democracy," in *Habermas and the Public Sphere,* ed. Craig Calhoun (Cambridge: MIT Press, 1992), 109–42. See also Michael Warner, "The Mass Public and the Mass Subject," in the same volume, 377–401.

17. Richard Brooks, *The Brick Foxhole* (New York: Harper, 1945), 23. Hereafter all references are to this edition and are cited by page number.

18. Donald Webster Corey, *The Homosexual in America: A Subjective Approach* (New York: Greenberg, 1951), 120–21.

19. For a discussion of Myrdal's influence on Corey's study, see Toby Marotta, *The Politics of Homosexuality: How Lesbians and Gay Men Have Made Themselves a Political and Social Force in Modern America* (Boston: Houghton Mifflin, 1981), 6–7.

20. For more on Myrdal's highly influential study, see Michael Omi and Howard Winant, *Racial Formation in the United States: From the 1960s to the 1980s* (New York: Routledge, 1986), 16–21.

21. On the influence of Corey's minoritarian approach to the question of gay male identity on the postwar gay rights movement, see John D'Emilio, *Sexual Politics, Sexual Communities: The Making of a Homosexual Minority in the United States, 1940–1970* (Chicago: Univ. of Chicago Press, 1983), 167–68; and Marotta, *The Politics of Homosexuality*, 4–7.

22. Ceplair and Englund, *The Inquisition in Hollywood*, 453.

23. Hirsch, *Film Noir*, 104.

24. For an interesting comparison between Ryan and other actors who played psychopaths in films noirs, see Hirsch, *Film Noir*, 157–65.

25. See Neve, *Film and Politics in America*, 98–99; and Krutnik, *In a Lonely Street*, 209–10.

26. Dana Polan, *Power and Paranoia: History, Narrative, and the American Cinema, 1940–1950* (New York: Columbia Univ. Press, 1986), 66–68.

27. Siegfried Kracauer, "Those Movies with a Message," *Nation*, June 1948, 569.

28. Kracauer, "Those Movies with a Message," 572.

29. I want to be clear that in claiming that Scott and Dmytryk tended to exaggerate the courage required in making a film about anti-Semitism, I am not arguing that racism was a more serious problem than anti-Semitism, or that Jews have been less oppressed than blacks. My point is simply that in the late 1940s when the horrors of the Nazi death camps were coming to light, audiences would have been more receptive to a film about anti-Semitism than to one about racism.

30. For a good discussion of the social-problem film as it evolved in the forties and fifties, see Jackie Byars, *All That Hollywood Allows: Re-Reading Gender in 1950s Melodrama* (Chapel Hill: Univ. of North Carolina Press, 1991), 112–31. For a discussion of the social-problem film as it evolved in the sixties and seventies, see Michael Ryan and Douglas Kellner, *Camera Politica: The Politics and Ideology of Contemporary Hollywood Film* (Bloomington: Indiana Univ. Press, 1988), 87–95.

31. I have taken the figures in this and the following sentence from Byars, *All That Hollywood Allows*, 113.

32. It is worth noting that when social-problem films were adapted from novels in which homosexuality figures as a theme, the controversial material was suppressed. In *The Lost Weekend* (Billy Wilder, 1945), for example, the alcoholism of the Ray Milland character is attributed to writer's block, but in the Charles Jackson novel from which it was adapted it is caused by a false accusation that he had a homosexual relationship with a fraternity brother. On the relation between the film and the novel, see Vito Russo, *The Celluloid Closet: Homosexuality in the Movies*, rev. ed. (New York: Harper & Row, 1987), 96–97.

33. Susan Sontag's essay "Notes on Camp," originally published in *Partisan Review* in 1964, provides a concrete example of the way in which camp, in aestheticizing homosexuality, enabled it to enter the public sphere not as a "problem" but as an object of admiration and respect. Although it tended to empty camp of its political

content, Sontag's celebration of the practice included the gay male subculture from which it had sprung. Sontag's essay is reprinted in her *Against Interpretation and Other Essays* (New York: Farrar, Straus, & Giroux, 1966), 277–93. Important discussions of Sontag's essay include Andrew Ross, "The Uses of Camp," in *No Respect: Intellectuals and Popular Culture* (New York: Routledge, 1989), 135–70; and David Bergman, "Strategic Camp: The Art of Gay Rhetoric," in *Gaiety Transfigured: Gay Self-Representation in American Literature* (Madison: Univ. of Wisconsin Press, 1991), 103–21.

34. For more on this aspect of camp, see Ross, "The Uses of Camp." Although Ross argues persuasively that camp allowed gay men to distance themselves from the conventional morality and taste of the middle class, he does not adequately consider the extent to which in the forties and fifties this "distance" expressed opposition to the suburbanization of American culture.

35. Film noir's affirmation of gay male identity and experience was not limited to camp but included the gay macho style. In *The Big Sleep* (Howard Hawks, 1946), Geiger's lover, Carroll, stages his homosexuality through a theatrically masculine appearance. In attributing to him a theatrically masculine appearance, the film adhered to the Raymond Chandler novel on which it was based. Not surprisingly, in the novel Philip Marlowe is even more contemptuous of the macho Carroll than he is of the effeminate Geiger. Carroll's hard-boiled manner is not the "real thing" and thus it threatens to expose Marlowe's as similarly inauthentic. At one point when Carroll punches him, Marlowe remarks contemptuously: "It was meant to be a hard one, but a pansy has no iron in his bones, whatever he looks like." Raymond Chandler, *The Big Sleep,* in *The Raymond Chandler Omnibus* (New York: Knopf, 1964), 61.

36. I do not want to exaggerate the degree to which the gay macho style circumvented the policing of gay male sexuality. Needless to say, one of the consequences of the AIDS epidemic has been a backlash against the public display of gay male sexuality, licensing a remedicalization of the gay male body. My point is simply that in the seventies before the AIDS crisis, commodity culture acknowledged gay male sexuality in ways previously unimaginable, promoting the gay macho style through the production, distribution, and mass marketing of products designed specifically to appeal to the so-called gay clones who lived and socialized in urban gay ghettos.

37. In addition to Clifton Webb in *Laura,* there are also the examples of Sidney Greenstreet and Peter Lorre in *The Maltese Falcon* (John Huston, 1941); George Macready in *Gilda* (Charles Vidor, 1946); Clifton Webb in *The Dark Corner* (Henry Hathaway, 1946), in a reprise of his role in *Laura;* and Robert Walker in *Strangers on a Train* (Alfred Hitchcock, 1951).

38. Andrew Ross shows how the emergence of television as the dominant form of mass communication triangulated the hierarchical relationship between Broadway and film. Through television, film displaced Broadway as the hegemonic mode of

cultural production, further marginalizing it. Just as actors who had appeared on Broadway were once reluctant to act in films, so actors who had become stars through film were now reluctant to act on television. See Ross, "The Uses of Camp," 137–38.

This explains, I think, why playwrights such as Clifford Odets, Lillian Hellman, and Arthur Miller, who had strong ties to the Left, were more insulated from the McCarthy witch hunts than were Hollywood screenwriters and directors with similar ties. The national-security apparatus clearly made investigating Hollywood its priority, even though the influence of the Popular Front on Broadway was arguably greater. Broadway directors such as Elia Kazan who were aggressively investigated by HUAC were best known as Hollywood directors.

39. For this reason, camp and the gay macho style should be seen as two sides of the same oppositional coin, at least as they were deployed in the Cold War era. Both camp and the gay macho style provided gay men with a means of staging their opposition to the suburbanization of postwar American culture.

4 Tennessee Williams and the Politics of the Closet

1. See in particular Edward A. Sklepowich, "In Pursuit of the Lyric Quarry: The Image of the Homosexual in Tennessee Williams' Prose Fiction," in *Tennessee Williams: A Tribute,* ed. Jac Tharpe (Jackson: Univ. Press of Mississippi, 1977), 525–44, and John M. Clum, "'Something Cloudy, Something Clear': Homophobic Discourse in Tennessee Williams," in *Displacing Homophobia: Gay Male Perspectives in Literature and Culture,* ed. Ronald R. Butters, John M. Clum, and Michael Moon (Durham, N.C.: Duke Univ. Press, 1989), 149–67. See also David Savran, *Communists, Cowboys, and Queers: The Politics of Masculinity in the Work of Arthur Miller and Tennessee Williams* (Minneapolis: Univ. of Minnesota Press, 1992), 111–14.

2. Tennessee Williams, "Hard Candy," in *Collected Stories* (New York: Ballantine, 1986), 359. Hereafter all references are to this edition and are cited by page number.

3. See Sklepowich, "In Pursuit of the Lyric Quarry," and Clum, "'Something Cloudy, Something Clear.'"

4. This is not to suggest that gay male critics were happy about Williams's revelations in his *Memoirs.* Whereas earlier Williams had concealed too much, now he concealed too little. He discussed his experiences of cruising for sex after the death of lover, Frank Merlo, *too* openly and in *too* much detail. On the reception of Williams's *Memoirs,* see Savran, *Communists, Cowboys, and Queers,* 131 and passim.

5. Harold Beaver, "Homosexual Signs," *Critical Inquiry* 8 (August 1981): 99–119.

6. Ibid., 105.

7. Beaver limits his discussion of gay male semiosis to camp. On the gay macho style as another important form of gay male semiosis, see Richard Dyer, "Getting

over the Rainbow: Identity and Pleasure in Gay Cultural Politics," in *Silver Linings: Some Strategies for the Eighties*, ed. George Bridges and Rosalind Brunt (London: Lawrence & Wishart, 1981). See also chapter 5 below.

8. In emphasizing the changes that have occurred in urban gay communities since Stonewall, I do not mean to legitimize the received narrative of postwar gay male politics. Although contemporary urban gay communities are less closeted and more politicized than earlier ones, I hope to show that in the fifties gay male resistance was not limited to camp, which is to say that there were gay men who were political before Stonewall.

9. This sentence, which is emphasized in the original and concludes the story, is clearly meant to function as a kind of punch line. Only the reader who is willing to read as a gay man will fully appreciate its humor, with its pun on choking and hard candy.

10. For a discussion of the epistemological structures of the closet and the way in which they continue to govern gay male experience, see Eve Kosofsky Sedgwick, *Epistemology of the Closet* (Berkeley and Los Angeles: Univ. of California Press, 1990), esp. 67–90.

11. D. A. Miller has written compellingly about the double bind Enlightenment constructions of the subject place gay men in when extended to them. See D. A. Miller, "Secret Subjects, Open Secrets," in *The Novel and the Police* (Berkeley and Los Angeles: Univ. of California Press, 1988), 192–220.

12. At the same time, however, it is also important to stress that precisely because they occur in a public place, Mr. Krupper's sexual activities transgress the privatization of sexuality, its confinement to the bedroom, and help to colonize public space for gay men.

13. On the history of the Mattachine Society, see John D'Emilio, *Sexual Politics, Sexual Communities: The Making of a Homosexual Minority in the United States, 1940–1970* (Chicago: Univ. of Chicago Press, 1983), and Toby Marotta, *The Politics of Homosexuality: How Lesbians and Gay Men Have Made Themselves a Political and Social Force in Modern America* (Boston: Houghton Mifflin, 1981).

14. Quoted in Jonathan Katz, *Gay American History: Lesbians and Gay Men in the U.S.A.* (New York: Harper & Row, 1976), 410.

15. On the way in which the Mattachine Society compromised its own founding principles by attempting to propitiate a hostile suburban mainstream, see Savran, *Communists, Cowboys, and Queers*, 84–88.

16. For a fuller discussion of the way in which the subaltern's fragmented relation to identity can be enabling rather than disabling from a political perspective, see Chela Sandoval, "U.S. Third World Feminism: The Theory and Method of Oppositional Consciousness in the Postmodern World," *Genders* 10 (spring 1991): 1–24.

17. Recent critiques of essentialism have tended to minimize the role the stabiliza-

tion of minority identities has played in the consolidation of political collectivities. For an important defense of the strategic use of essentialism in contemporary theory and politics, see Diana Fuss, *Essentially Speaking: Feminism, Nature, and Difference* (New York: Routledge, 1989). See also Katie King, "Local and Global: AIDS Activism and Feminist Theory," *Camera Obscura* 28 (January 1992): 80–98.

18. See Sklepowich, "In Pursuit of the Lyric Quarry," Clum, "'Something Cloudy, Something Clear,'" and Savran, *Communists, Cowboys, and Queers,* 81–84.

19. What is disturbing about this argument is that it does not differ significantly from the virulently homophobic critique of Williams's plays that first emerged in the late fifties when it became widely rumored that Williams was gay. According to this critique, Williams did not express his homosexuality in his plays directly but indirectly. It surfaced most fully in his creation of strong female characters who were really gay men in drag. Critics dubbed Williams's strategies of indirection the "Albertine strategy," after Albertine, the sexually ambiguous lover of the narrator in Marcel Proust's *A la recherche du temps perdu.* For an example of this critique, see Stanley Edgar Hyman, "Some Trends in the Novel," *College English* (October 1958): 1–3. Hyman's criticism of Williams recalls the Cold War construction of "the homosexual" in that it positions Williams as the enemy within who must be exposed because he is secretly undermining the nation's morality.

20. See, for example, Lee Barton, "Why Do Playwrights Hide Their Homosexuality?" *New York Times,* 23 January 1972, 27.

21. Quoted in Savran, *Communists, Cowboys, and Queers,* 81–82.

22. For a more detailed discussion of the problems with this understanding of the closet, see Sedgwick, *Epistemology of the Closet,* 67–90. As Sedgwick notes, although coming out of the closet can be a powerful and disruptive act, its effectiveness as a political strategy is limited. To begin with, the closet is a structure that is imposed on gay people, not one they have created to protect themselves from an intrusive public gaze. Even the most openly gay people find reasons for reentering the closet when they apply for a job or a bank loan, petition the courts for visiting or custody rights, or encounter a homophobic authority figure who is in a position to determine a job promotion or a salary raise. Moreover, individual acts of disclosure necessarily have a limited effect on structures that are institutionally embodied and collectively enforced.

23. Clum, "'Something Cloudy, Something Clear,'" 154. It is not at all clear to me in what way Mr. Krupper's sexual activities might be considered exploitative. After all, the six quarters he gives to the young men he encounters at the Joy Rio are hardly a large sum (even by postwar standards). The purpose of the quarters seems to be to provide an alibi that allows the young men to engage in a forbidden activity they find pleasurable without feeling guilty.

24. Ibid., 158.

25. Ibid., 159.

26. See Clum, "'Something Cloudy, Something Clear,'" 159, and Savran, *Communists, Cowboys, and Queers*, 100–101.

27. Tennessee Williams, *Cat on a Hot Tin Roof* (New York: Signet, 1985), 84. Hereafter all references are to this edition and are cited by page number.

28. Williams's emphasis on the "unspoken" here and elsewhere in *Cat on a Hot Tin Roof* provides another important link between it and "Hard Candy." As in "Hard Candy," Williams's evasions seem meant to position the spectator as a gay man. To understand fully the play's meaning, the spectator must master gay male reading practices, that is, fill in the blanks and read between the lines.

29. In stressing that the patriarchal injunction to multiply is economic as well as biological, I mean to foreground the way in which patriarchal capitalism instrumentalizes the male body, in particular the penis and the anus, which it relegates to the status of use-value. For a discussion of the way in which homosexuality violates the *biological* injunction to multiply under patriarchal capitalism, see Beaver, "Homosexual Signs."

30. Luce Irigaray, "Women on the Market," in *This Sex Which Is Not One,* trans. Catherine Porter (Ithaca: Cornell Univ. Press, 1985), 172.

31. Ibid.

32. Luce Irigaray, "Commodities among Themselves," in *This Sex Which Is Not One,* 193.

33. Ibid.; emphasis in the original.

34. See Eve Kosofsky Sedgwick, *Between Men: English Literature and Male Homosocial Desire* (New York: Columbia Univ. Press, 1985), 21–27, and Diana Fuss, *Essentially Speaking*, 48–49. Many critics writing from an antihomophobic or gay affirmative perspective have identified Irigaray's work as the *locus classicus* of a recent strand of feminist theory that conceives of authoritarian regimes as even more homosexual than gay male culture. See, for example, Eve Kosofsky Sedgwick, *Epistemology of the Closet*, 154, and Lee Edelman, *Homographesis: Essays in Gay Literary and Cultural Theory* (New York: Routledge, 1993), 130–31. This rejection of Irigaray's work strikes me as a particularly costly theoretical move because her understanding of homosexuality as a form of male bonding in which the penis does not operate symbolically can be used to distinguish between patriarchal and nonpatriarchal forms of homosexuality, as I am doing here in my discussion of the differences between Brick and Big Daddy.

35. Sigmund Freud, *Three Essays on the Theory of Sexuality,* in *The Standard Edition of the Complete Psychological Works of Sigmund Freud,* ed. James Strachey et al., 24 vols. (London: Hogarth Press and the Institute of Psychoanalysis, 1953–74), vol. 7.

36. Sigmund Freud, "On Transformations of Instinct as Exemplified in Anal Eroticism," in *The Standard Edition of the Complete Psychological Works,* 17:127–33.

37. For a fuller discussion of the way in which gay male desire exceeds the

heterosexual mapping of the body and thus has the potential to disrupt patriarchal capitalism, see Guy Hocquenghem, *Homosexual Desire,* trans. Daniella Dangoor (Durham, N.C.: Duke Univ. Press, 1993), esp. 93–112. See also Gilles Deleuze and Felix Guattari, *Anti-Oedipus: Capitalism and Schizophrenia,* trans. Robert Hurley, Mark Seem, and Helen R. Lane (Minneapolis: Univ. of Minnesota Press, 1983).

38. See in particular Savran, *Communists, Cowboys, and Queers,* 106–10.

39. In this respect, Maggie's attempt to intervene in Brick and Skipper's relationship represents an interesting variation on the triangulation of male desire Sedgwick maps in *Between Men.*

40. For a discussion of the impact of Kazan's testimony on his reputation both on Broadway and in Hollywood, see Peter Biskind, *Seeing Is Believing: How Hollywood Taught Us to Stop Worrying and Love the Fifties* (New York: Pantheon, 1983), 169–82. See also Brian Neve, *Film and Politics in America: A Social Tradition* (London and New York: Routledge, 1992), 188–98.

41. See Michel Ciment, *Kazan on Kazan* (New York: Viking, 1974).

42. For a fuller discussion of *On the Waterfront* as a kind of apologia for Kazan's controversial testimony, see Biskind, *Seeing Is Believing,* 169–82.

43. Maria St. Just, *Five O'Clock Angel: Letters of Tennessee Williams to Maria St. Just, 1948–1982* (New York: Knopf, 1990), 56.

44. See in particular Savran, *Communists, Cowboys, and Queers,* 102–10.

45. Although Miller's opposition to McCarthyism was courageous—unlike Kazan, he refused to name names when he appeared before HUAC in 1956—he does not seem to have understood or been troubled by the way in which the discourses of national security contained resistance to the Cold War consensus by linking questions of gender and sexual identity directly to issues of national security. Nor did he express opposition to the Cold War construction of "the homosexual" and "the lesbian" as security risks.

46. In the present context, it seems particularly telling that Kazan refused to acknowledge the political content of Williams's plays. In the early seventies, he told an interviewer who asked him to compare Williams to Arthur Miller: "Williams, by the way, is political in the sense that he supports any cause that is truly liberal, in every way he can. But it's always pure, it's always immediate, it's not calculated. And it's always personal." Michel Ciment, *Kazan on Kazan,* 79. In other words, Williams's political commitments were stereotypically feminine. They were intuitive rather than intellectual and thus remained at the level of the "personal." Unlike the macho Miller, he was supposedly incapable of engaging in a systematic analysis of Cold War America. Thus his treatment of the closet in *Cat on a Hot Tin Roof* could not possibly have a political resonance that extended beyond the merely personal.

47. Quoted in Donald Spoto, *The Kindness of Strangers: The Life of Tennessee Williams* (New York: Viking, 1986), 319.

48. See in particular Clum, " 'Something Cloudy, Something Clear,' " 151–52.

5 Gore Vidal and the Erotics of Masculinity

1. "Donald Webster Corey" is the pseudonym under which Edward Sagarin published his work on gays and lesbians. I have chosen to refer to him by his pseudonym because he did not reveal his true identity until he repudiated his work in the sixties and began to claim that homosexuality and lesbianism constituted pathologies. On Corey's transformation into Sagarin and the disavowal it entailed of his former identity as a gay rights activist, see John D'Emilio, *Sexual Politics, Sexual Communities: The Making of a Homosexual Minority in the United States, 1940–1970* (Chicago: Univ. of Chicago Press, 1983), 167–68, and Toby Marotta, *The Politics of Homosexuality: How Lesbians and Gay Men Have Made Themselves a Political and Social Force in Modern America* (Boston: Houghton Mifflin, 1981), 19–21.

2. Donald Webster Corey, *The Homosexual in America: A Subjective Approach* (New York: Greenberg, 1951), 94. Hereafter all references are to this edition and are cited by page number.

3. Gore Vidal, *The City and the Pillar Revised* (New York: Signet, 1965), 156. Hereafter all references to the afterword are from this edition and are cited by page number.

4. For an important reassessment of Vidal's place in American literary history that situates the controversy surrounding the publication of *The City and the Pillar* in relation to the homophobic categories of Cold War political discourse, see Donald E. Pease, "Citizen Vidal and Mailer's America," in *Gore Vidal: Writer against the Grain,* ed. Jay Parini (New York: Columbia Univ. Press, 1992), 247–77.

5. Leslie Fiedler, "Come Back to the Raft Ag'in, Huck Honey!" in *The Collected Essays of Leslie Fiedler,* 2 vols. (New York: Stein & Day, 1971), 1:142–52.

6. Teresa de Lauretis, "Sexual Indifference and Lesbian Representation," *Theater Journal* 40 (1988): 155–77.

7. Claude Summers, "*The City and the Pillar* as Gay Fiction," in *Gore Vidal,* ed. Parini, 67.

8. The term *gay macho style* usually refers to a set of practices adopted by many gay men in the seventies and eighties to indicate their participation in the gay male subculture. These practices included bodybuilding, growing beards and mustaches, and wearing certain clothing (leather, denim jeans and jackets, flannel shirts, and leather boots). Postwar gay macho icons have included Montgomery Clift, James Dean, Marlon Brando, the Marlboro Man, and the controversial disco group popular in the late seventies, the Village People.

9. For a discussion of Vidal's influence on the gay liberation movement, see Dennis Altman, *Homosexual: Oppression and Liberation* (New York: New York Univ. Press, 1993 [1971]).

10. For important examples of gay liberation writing, see Altman, *Homosexual;*

Out of the Closets: Voices of Gay Liberation, ed. Karla Jay and Allen Young (New York: New York Univ. Press, 1992); and *The Gay Liberation Book,* ed. Gary Noguera and Len Richmond (San Francisco: Ramparts, 1973).

11. In this respect, the anti-essentialist project of the gay liberation movement can be said to have anticipated that of Queen Nation. For an important discussion of the postmodernist politics of Queer Nation and other contemporary gay and lesbian organizations, see Lauren Berlant and Elizabeth Freeman, "Queer Nationality," *boundary 2* 19 (1992): 149–80.

12. On the divisions within the postwar gay and lesbian rights movement, see D'Emilio, *Sexual Politics, Sexual Communities.* For a detailed discussion of the identity politics of the mainstream gay and lesbian rights movement, see Dennis Altman, *The Homosexualization of America* (Boston: Beacon, 1983), 108–45, and Jeffrey Weeks, *Sexuality and Its Discontents: Meanings, Myths and Modern Sexualities* (London: Routledge, 1985), 185–201.

13. Richard Dyer, "Getting over the Rainbow: Identity and Pleasure in Gay Cultural Politics," in *Silver Linings: Some Strategies for the Eighties,* ed. George Bridges and Rosalind Brunt (London: Lawrence & Wishart, 1981), 60–61.

14. Altman, *The Homosexualization of America,* 79–80.

15. Quoted in David Savran, *Communists, Cowboys, and Queers: The Politics of Masculinity in the Work of Arthur Miller and Tennessee Williams* (Minneapolis: Univ. of Minnesota Press, 1992), 163.

16. Leo Bersani, "Is the Rectum a Grave?" in *AIDS: Cultural Analysis, Cultural Activism,* ed. Douglas Crimp (Cambridge: MIT Press, 1988), 207.

17. Ibid., 209.

18. For critiques of the gay macho style that are similar to Bersani's, see Jamie Gough, "Theories of Sexual Identity and the Masculinization of the Gay Man," in *Coming on Strong: Gay Politics and Culture,* ed. Simon Shepherd and Mick Wallis (London: Unwin Hyman, 1989), 119–36, and Don Mager, "Gay Theories and Gender Role Deviance," *Sub-stance* 46 (1985): 32–48.

19. Bersani, "Is the Rectum a Grave?" 212.

20. Ibid.

21. For an important discussion of the problems with this kind of thinking about gender and sexuality, see Judith Butler, *Gender Trouble: Feminism and the Subversion of Identity* (New York: Routledge, 1990). See also Gayle Rubin, "Thinking Sex: Notes for a Radical Theory of the Politics of Sexuality," in *Pleasure and Danger: Exploring Female Sexuality,* ed. Carole S. Vance (Boston: Routledge & Kegan Paul, 1984), 265–319. For an important elaboration and application of Rubin's argument, see Eve Kosofsky Sedgwick, *Epistemology of the Closet* (Berkeley and Los Angeles: Univ. of California Press, 1990), 1–63.

22. Richard Dyer, "Getting over the Rainbow," 61.

23. On the Gay Liberation Front's troubled relation to the New Left, see D'Emilio, *Sexual Politics, Sexual Communities,* 223–39. For a more detailed discussion of the macho posturing of the leaders of the New Left, see Alice Echols, "We Gotta Get out of This Place: Notes towards a Remapping of the Sixties," *Socialist Review* 22 (1992): 9–33, and Savran, *Communists, Cowboys, and Queers,* 147–54.

24. On the psychoanalytic theory of fantasy, see Jean Laplanche and Jean-Bertrande Pontalis, "Fantasy and the Origins of Sexuality," in *Formations of Fantasy,* ed. Victor Burgin, James Donald, and Cora Kaplan (London: Routledge, 1989), 5–34.

25. For an important application of the psychoanalytic theory of fantasy to lesbian camp, which has inspired my understanding of the gay macho style, see Teresa de Lauretis, "Film and the Visible," in *How Do I Look?: Queer Film and Video,* ed. Bad Object-Choices (Seattle: Bay Press, 1991), 223–64. For a slightly different reading of lesbian camp, which sees it as pure performance, see Sue-Ellen Case, "Towards a Butch-Femme Aesthetic," *Discourse* 11 (1988–89): 55–73.

26. Gore Vidal, *The City and the Pillar* (New York: Dutton, 1948), 91. Hereafter all references to the novel are to this edition and are cited by page number.

27. Summers, "*The City and the Pillar* as Gay Fiction," 61.

28. See, for example, Gilbert Herdt, "'Coming Out' as a Rite of Passage: A Chicago Study," in *Gay Culture in America: Essays from the Field,* ed. Gilbert Herdt (Boston: Beacon, 1991), 29–67. Herdt's ethnographic study of gays and lesbians who came out in Chicago in the 1980s is particularly troubling because its main point of comparison is the gay subculture of the 1950s, which it characterizes as secretive, unhealthy, and sex-obsessed, the very terms the discourses of national security used to stigmatize it.

29. For an important critique of teleological understandings of the construction of subjectivity, see Teresa de Lauretis, *Alice Doesn't: Feminism, Semiotics, Cinema* (Bloomington: Indiana Univ. Press, 1984), 158–86.

30. In this respect, Jim's attitude toward homosexuality differs markedly from that of the other gay male characters in the novel, who constantly complain about the supposedly pernicious influence of women on American society. In blaming this influence for the prevalence of homosexuality in American society, these complaints bear a striking resemblance to the contemporary discourses of momism. Significantly, Vidal deleted many of the passages in which these complaints occur when he revised the novel for publication in 1965.

31. The limitations of Corey's minoritarian model may reflect the influence of Gunnar Myrdal's classic study of race relations, *The American Dilemma* (1944), on his understanding of the gay male subculture. For more on this subject, see the discussion of Corey in chapter 3.

32. Kaja Silverman, *Male Subjectivity at the Margins* (New York: Routledge, 1992), 339–88.

6   A Negative Relation to One's Culture: James Baldwin and the Homophobic Politics of Form

1. For a discussion of the critical reception of *Another Country,* see Mike Thelwell, "*Another Country:* Baldwin's New York Novel," in *Black American Writers,* vol. 1, ed. C. W. E. Bigsby (Deland, Fla.: Everett/Edwards, 1969), 181–98. Thelwell's essay is an important exception to the overwhelmingly negative response to the novel. See also Daryl Dance, "James Baldwin," in *Black American Writers,* vol. 2, ed. M. Thomas Inge et al. (London: Macmillan, 1978), 73–120.

2. Irving Howe, "Black Boys and Native Sons," *Dissent* 10 (autumn 1963): 354–68. Hereafter all references are to this version and are cited by page number.

3. Fern Marja Eckman, *The Furious Passage of James Baldwin* (New York: M. Evans, 1966), 168–69.

4. Lyall H. Powers, "Henry James and James Baldwin: The Complex Figure," *Modern Fiction Studies* 30 (winter 1984): 651–67.

5. See in particular James's preface to the New York edition of *The Wings of the Dove,* reprinted in Henry James, *The Art of the Novel: Critical Prefaces,* ed. R. P. Blackmur (New York: Scribner, 1962), 288–306. On the importance of *The Wings of the Dove* to Baldwin's project in *Another Country,* see Powers, "Henry James and James Baldwin," 252–54.

6. Other postwar writers who willingly acknowledge a debt to James include Lionel Trilling, whose *The Middle of the Journey* (1947) was in part inspired by *The Princess Casamassima,* but none of these writers equaled Baldwin in stature.

7. On the tendency of "major" postwar writers to reject James as a model, see Thomas Hill Schaub, *American Fiction in the Cold War* (Madison: Univ. of Wisconsin Press, 1991), 53–54.

8. Ralph Ellison, "Brave Words for a Startling Occasion," in *Shadow and Act* (New York: Vintage, 1973), 53–54.

9. I have borrowed the term *creolizing* from postcolonial studies. See in particular Paul Gilroy, *The Black Atlantic: Modernity and Double Consciousness* (Cambridge: Harvard Univ. Press, 1993), 1–40. See also Kobena Mercer, "Diaspora Culture and the Dialogic Imagination: The Aesthetics of Black Independent Film in Britain," in *The Media Reader,* ed. Manuel Alvaredo and John O. Thompson (London: British Film Institute, 1990), 25–35, and Stuart Hall, "The Whites of Their Eyes: Racist Ideologues and the Media," in the same volume, 8–23.

10. On the importance of racializing whiteness, see Hazel Carby, "The Multicultural Wars," *Radical History Review* 54 (fall 1992): 7–18. See also her "The Politics of Difference," *Ms.,* Sept.–Oct. 1990, 84–85.

11. Several contemporary reviewers recognized that Baldwin tried to imitate James's style and praised him for refusing to use the naturalistic mode of narration.

Elizabeth Hardwick, for example, in a review of *Nobody Knows My Name* (1961), praised Baldwin for being "a Negro writer who has modeled his style on Henry James, rather than on the naturalistic American style that has always appeared so suitable and so near at hand for the expression of the ugly facts of our life, of Negro life, and through Negro life, all our American lives." Elizabeth Hardwick, "The New Books," *Harper's Magazine* 224 (January 1962): 94.

12. Richard Chase, "A Novel Is a Novel," *Kenyon Review* 14 (autumn 1952): 679. Hereafter all references are to this version and are cited by page number.

13. Lionel Trilling, *The Liberal Imagination* (New York: Viking, 1950), 212. Hereafter all references to Trilling's essays are to this edition and are cited by page number.

14. On the narrative Cold War liberals constructed in order to justify the growing conservatism of their cultural politics, see Schaub, *American Fiction in the Cold War*, 1–24.

15. On the rehabilitation of James by Cold War liberals, see Schaub, *American Fiction in the Cold War*, 40–41. On the relegation of James to the genteel tradition of American letters, see William E. Cain, "Criticism and Politics: F. O. Matthiessen and the Making of Henry James," *New England Quarterly* 35 (June 1987): 136–86.

16. This is not to suggest that several other critics had not already begun the work of reviving scholarly and critical interest in James. F. O. Matthiessen, for example, published *Henry James: The Major Phase* in 1944. Matthiessen's project to rehabilitate James, however, should not be confused with that of Trilling and Chase, whose interest in James reflected the growing conservatism of their cultural politics. For a discussion of Matthiessen's ambivalence toward James, see Cain, "Criticism and Politics."

17. Richard Chase, *The American Novel and Its Tradition* (Garden City, N.J.: Doubleday-Anchor, 1957), 10. Hereafter all references are to this edition and are cited by page number.

18. For more on Trilling's distortion of Parrington's cultural politics, see Jonathan Arac, "F. O. Matthiessen and American Studies: Authorizing an American Renaissance," in *Critical Genealogies: Historical Situations for Postmodern Literary Studies* (New York: Columbia Univ. Press, 1989), 157–75.

19. Robert J. Corber, *In the Name of National Security: Hitchcock, Homophobia, and the Political Construction of Gender in Postwar America* (Durham, N.C.: Duke Univ. Press, 1993), 26–31.

20. For a more detailed discussion of the link between Communism and homosexuality in the postwar period, see my *In the Name of National Security*.

21. For an important discussion of the relation between this distinction and Cold War political discourse, see Geraldine Murphy, "Romancing the Center: Cold War Politics and Classic American Literature," *Poetics Today* 9, no. 4 (1988): 737–47. See also Russell Reising, *The Unusable Past: Theory and the Study of American Literature* (New York: Methuen, 1986), 124–27.

22. See in particular Murphy, "Romancing the Center." See also Sacvan Bercovitch, *The Rites of Assent: Transformations in the Symbolic Construction of America* (New York: Routledge, 1993), 1–28.

23. On the reemergence of a consensus model of American history in the postwar period, see Richard Pells, *The Liberal Mind in a Conservative Age: American Intellectuals in the 1940s and 1950s* (Middletown, Conn.: Wesleyan Univ. Press, 1988), 147–62, and David W. Noble, "The Reconstruction of Progress: Charles Beard, Richard Hofstadter, and Postwar Historical Thought," in *Recasting America: Culture and Politics in the Age of Cold War* (Chicago: Univ. of Chicago Press, 1989), 61–75.

24. For a discussion of the *Menorah Journal* and Trilling's brief involvement with it in the thirties, see Alan M. Wald, *The New York Intellectuals: The Rise and Decline of the Anti-Stalinist Left from the 1930s to the 1980s* (Chapel Hill: Univ. of North Carolina Press, 1987), 27–50. On Trilling's ambivalence toward his Jewish identity, see in particular Daniel T. O'Hara, *Lionel Trilling: The Work of Liberation* (Madison: Univ. of Wisconsin Press, 1988), 29–66. See also Neil Jumonville, *Critical Crossings: The New York Intellectuals in Postwar America* (Berkeley and Los Angeles: Univ. of California Press, 1991), 116–27.

25. Murphy, "The Politics of Reading *Billy Budd*," *American Literary History* 1 (summer 1989): 361–82. Curiously, Murphy does not include the Marxist critic C. L. R. James among those who participated in the postwar struggle to define Melville's political legacy. Yet his *Mariners, Renegades, and Castaways: The Story of Herman Melville and the World We Live In* (1953) engaged in a counter-hegemonic reading of Melville that challenged the Cold War consensus. For a discussion of James's use of Melville to critique the Cold War consensus, see Henry Louis Gates Jr., "Criticism in the Jungle," in *Black Literature and Literary Theory*, ed. Henry Louis Gates Jr. (New York: Methuen, 1984), 1–24.

26. Important examples of readings of *Billy Budd* from the perspective of myth criticism are Newton Arvin, *Herman Melville* (Westport, Conn.: Greenwood, 1972), and R. W. B. Lewis, *The American Adam: Innocence, Tragedy and Tradition in the Nineteenth Century* (Chicago: Univ. of Chicago Press, 1955), 147–52.

27. Richard Chase, *Herman Melville: A Critical Study* (New York: Hafner, 1971 [1949]), 269. Hereafter all references are to this edition and are cited by page number.

28. Richard Chase, "Art, Nature, Politics," *Partisan Review* 12 (1950): 590–91.

29. Ibid., 591.

30. Although Matthiessen was not openly gay, his homosexuality was apparently common knowledge among left-wing academics. The left-wing economist Paul Sweezy in the biographical sketch of Matthiessen that he wrote for a collection of Matthiessen's writings published posthumously described Matthiessen's living arrangement with his lover, the painter Russell Cheney. Paul M. Sweezy, "A Biographical Sketch," in *F.O. Matthiessen (1902–1950): A Collective Portrait*, ed. Paul M. Sweezy and Leo Huberman (New York: Henry Schuman, 1950), x. See also David Bergman,

Gaity Transfigured: Gay Self-Representation in American Literature (Madison: Univ. of Wisconsin Press, 1991), 85–102.

31. James Baldwin, *Notes of a Native Son* (Boston: Beacon, 1955), 15. Hereafter all references are to this edition and are cited by page number.

32. On the relation between New Criticism and Cold War political discourse, see Mark Walhout, "The New Criticism and the Crisis of American Liberalism: The Poetics of the Cold War," *College English* 49 (December 1987): 861–71.

33. For a discussion of the tendency of white male left-wing intellectuals to romanticize a criminalized black male identity, see Alice Echols, "We Gotta Get out of This Place: Notes towards a Remapping of the Sixties," *Socialist Review* 22 (1992): 9–33. See also Van Gosse, *Where the Boys Are: Cuba, Cold War America, and the Making of a New Left* (London: Verso, 1993).

34. Baldwin himself encouraged critics to read his criticisms of Wright as an Oedipal struggle. In "Alas, Poor Richard," for example, he explained that he deliberately tried to spark a quarrel with Wright in order to bring about a reconciliation with him: "I think, in fact, that I counted on this [reconciliation] coming about in some mysterious, irrevocable way, the way a child dreams of winning, by means of some dazzling exploit, the love of his parents." James Baldwin, "Alas, Poor Richard," in *Nobody Knows My Name* (New York: Vintage, 1993), 190.

35. Richard Wright, "Blueprint for Negro Writing," in *The Black Aesthetic*, ed. Addison Gayle Jr. (Garden City, N.J.: Doubleday-Anchor, 1972), 315. Hereafter all references are to this version and are cited by page number.

36. Baldwin, *Nobody Knows My Name*, 217.

37. Ibid., 220.

38. On Baldwin's rejection by black nationalist intellectuals, see Henry Louis Gates Jr., "The Welcome Table," in *Lure and Loathing: Essays on Race, Identity, and the Ambivalence of Assimilation*, ed. Gerald Early (New York: Viking-Penguin, 1993), 144–62, and Michele Wallace, *Black Macho and the Myth of the Superwoman* (London: Verso, 1990), 56–62.

39. Consider, for example, the following passage from *Black Boy* (1946): "Whenever I thought of the essential bleakness of black life in America, I knew that Negroes had never been allowed to catch the full spirit of Western civilization, that they lived somehow in it but not of it. And when I brooded upon the cultural barrenness of black life, I wondered if clean, positive tenderness, love, honor, loyalty and the capacity to remember were native with man." Richard Wright, *Black Boy* (New York: Harper Collins, 1993), 56. On Wright's attempts to reconcile the contradictions of the Communist party's approach to the "Negro question," which was at once separatist and integrationist, see Barbara Foley, *Radical Representations: Politics and Form in U.S. Proletarian Fiction, 1929–1941* (Durham, N.C.: Duke Univ. Press, 1993), 170–212.

40. On the hybridization of identity, see Homi K. Bhabha, "The Other Ques-

tion: Difference, Discrimination, and the Discourse of Colonialism," in *Out There: Marginalization and Contemporary Cultures,* ed. Russell Ferguson, Martha Gever, Trinh T. Minh-ha, and Cornel West (Cambridge: MIT Press, 1990), 71–87. See also Gilroy, *The Black Atlantic,* 1–40.

41. James Baldwin, *Another Country* (New York: Vintage, 1993), 375–76. Hereafter all references are to this edition and are cited by page number.

42. On the impact of *The Feminine Mystique* on postwar white middle-class housewives, see Elaine Tyler May, *Homeward Bound: American Families in the Cold War Era* (New York: Basic, 1988), 209–17.

43. William A. Cohen, "Liberalism, Libido, Liberation: Baldwin's *Another Country,*" *Genders* 12 (winter 1991): 9. Although space prohibits me from responding fully to Cohen's reading of *Another Country,* I feel compelled to comment on his failure to situate Baldwin's novel historically. Cohen's biggest complaint about *Another Country* is that it "cannot sustain a gay black subject—the one we might expect from so outspoken a gay black writer" (17). The problem with this critique is that it assumes that it was possible in the postwar period for black men to identify fully as gay. As I noted in chapter 1, gayness was largely a white middle-class construction. On the obstacles black men continue to face in identifying as gay, see *In the Life: A Black Gay Anthology,* ed. Joseph Beam (Boston: Alyson, 1986), and *Brother to Brother: New Writings by Black Gay Men,* ed. Essex Hemphill (Boston: Alyson, 1990).

44. For an important critique of kinship models of political solidarity, see Iris Marion Young, "The Ideal of Community and the Politics of Difference," in *Feminism/Postmodernism,* ed. Linda J. Nicholson (New York: Routledge, 1990), 300–323. See also Cindy Patton, *Inventing AIDS* (New York: Routledge, 1990), 5–24; Biddy Martins and Chandra Talpade Mohanty, "Feminist Politics: What's Home Got to Do with It?" in *Feminist Studies/Critical Studies,* ed. Teresa de Lauretis (Bloomington: Indiana Univ. Press, 1986), 191–212; and Gilroy, *The Black Atlantic.*

45. James Baldwin, "Here Be Dragons," in *The Price of the Ticket* (New York: St. Martin's/Marek, 1985), 690.

46. Gates, "The Welcome Table," 162. Gates mistakenly refers to the title of Baldwin's essay as "Here Be Monsters."

47. Ibid.

48. Ralph Ellison, "The World and the Jug," in *Shadow and Act,* 137.

Conclusion: The Work of Transformation

1. On the ascendancy of the civil rights model within the gay rights movement, see Dennis Altman, *The Homosexualization of America* (Boston: Beacon, 1983), 108–45, and Jeffrey Weeks, *Sexuality and Its Discontents: Meanings, Myths, and Modern Sexualities* (London: Routledge, 1985), 185–201.

2. On the exclusions and suppressions the creation of Stonewall as a gay and lesbian Independence Day required, see in particular Toby Marotta, *The Politics of Homosexuality: How Lesbians and Gay Men Have Made Themselves a Political and Social Force in Modern America* (Boston: Houghton Mifflin, 1981), 291–303. Many of the leaders in the Gay Liberation Front and the Lesbian Liberation Committee, the groups primarily responsible for organizing the annual commemoration of Stonewall, strongly objected to the presence of street queens, transvestites, and female impersonators as demeaning to women and reinforcing negative stereotypes.

3. Indeed, as I was preparing this manuscript for submission, the U.S. Court of Appeals for the Sixth Circuit declared constitutional a referendum amending the Cincinnati City Charter, originally passed in November 1993, to exclude gays and lesbians from civil rights protections. Dealing a serious setback to the gay rights movement's pursuit of the status of suspect class for gays and lesbians, the court ruled:

"Those persons having a homosexual 'orientation' simply do not . . . comprise an identifiable class. Many homosexuals successfully conceal their orientation. Because homosexuals generally are not identifiable 'on sight' unless they elect to be so identifiable by conduct (such as public displays of homosexual affection or self-proclamation of homosexual tendencies), they cannot constitute a suspect class or a quasi-suspect class. . . . Those persons who fall within the orbit of legislation concerning sexual orientation are so affected not because of their orientation but rather by their behavior which identifies them as homosexual, bisexual, or heterosexual."

Equality Found. of Greater Cincinnati v. City of Cincinnati, nos. 94–3855/94–3973/94–428 (6th Cir. 17 May 1995). Online, University of Utah Lib., Lexis, p. 9.

4. The refusal of the courts to grant gays and lesbians status as a suspect class has led several legal theorists to argue for the need to devise legal strategies that do not depend on either the equal protection clause or the right to privacy. See for example Kendall Thomas, "Beyond the Privacy Principle," *Columbia Law Review* 92 (1992): 1431–516. Thomas contends that anti-gay legislation should be challenged on the grounds of the Eighth Amendment, which prohibits cruel and unusual punishment. Other legal theorists are less willing to abandon the traditional strategies but have argued that they should be revised so that they incorporate poststructuralist understandings of identity. See for example Janet Halley, "The Politics of the Closet: Towards Equal Protection for Gay, Lesbian, and Bisexual Identity," *UCLA Law Review* 36 (1989): 915–76.

5. For a discussion of the founding of Queer Nation and its political agenda, see Allan Berube and Jeffrey Escoffier, "Queer Nation," *Out/Look: National Lesbian and Gay Quarterly* 11 (winter 1991): 12–23.

6. Berube and Escoffier, "Queer Nation," 15.

7. For a detailed discussion of these strategies, see Lauren Berlant and Elizabeth Freeman, "Queer Nationality," *boundary 2* 19 (1992): 149–80. Berlant and Freeman brilliantly deploy poststructuralist theory, but surely their very generous assessment of the cultural politics of Queer Nation and its offshoots is a projection of their own political fantasies. For a more balanced assessment of Queer Nation's tactics and aims, see Rosemary Hennessy, "Queer Visibility in Commodity Culture," *Culture Critique* 29–30 (winter 1994–95): 31–76.

8. For a detailed discussion of outing and the controversy it spawned in the gay and lesbian communities, see Larry Gross, *Contested Closets: The Politics and Ethics of Outing* (Minneapolis: Univ. of Minnesota Press, 1993). Michelangelo Signorile, who devised the strategy while a columnist for the gay weekly *Outweek*, provides a powerful defense of outing in *Queer in America: Sex, the Media, and the Closets of Power* (New York: Random House, 1993).

9. Although much of this scholarship was indebted to the work of Michel Foucault, it was also influenced by the groundbreaking work of the sociologist Mary McIntosh, whose 1968 article "The Homosexual Role" helped to shift attention away from explaining gay and lesbian identity to understanding how homosexuality came to be seen as the defining condition of some men and women. For a detailed discussion of McIntosh's influence on gay and lesbian scholarship, see Weeks, *Sexuality and Its Discontents.*

10. For a critique of gay and lesbian identity politics that exemplifies this perspective, see Diana Fuss, *Essentially Speaking: Feminism, Nature, and Difference* (New York: Routledge, 1989), 97–112.

11. Perhaps the most influential example of a critique of gay and lesbian identity politics written from a poststructuralist perspective is Judith Butler, *Gender Trouble: Feminism and the Subversion of Identity* (New York: Routledge, 1990). See also her "Imitation and Gender Insubordination," in *Inside/Out: Lesbian Theories, Gay Theories,* ed. Diana Fuss (New York: Routledge, 1991), 13–31.

12. Sedgwick, *Epistemology of the Closet* (Berkeley and Los Angeles: Univ. of California Press, 1990), 1.

13. Some important discussions of the tactical advantages of the term *queer* are Lisa Duggan, "Making It Perfectly Queer," *Socialist Review* 22 (1992): 11–31; Teresa de Lauretis, "Queer Theory: Lesbian and Gay Sexualities," special issue of *differences* 3, no. 2 (summer 1991): iii–xviii; and Judith Butler, "Critically Queer," *Bodies That Matter: On the Discursive Limits of "Sex"* (New York: Routledge, 1993), 223–42.

14. For a more detailed discussion of this problem with queer theory and activism, see Lisa Duggan, "Queering the State," *Social Text* 12, no. 2 (summer 1994): 1–14.

15. An important exception to this blindness in queer theory can be found in Sedgwick, "Introduction: Axiomatic," *Epistemology of the Closet,* 1–63.

16. I do not mean to suggest that in the so-called Information Age cultural

representation has not become a crucial site of political intervention and struggle. My point is simply that heterosexuality as an institution is also reproduced at the political and economic levels and that we ignore those levels at our peril.

17. Although the Christian Coalition's recently disseminated "Contract with the American Family" does not explicitly target gays and lesbians, it contains a number of clauses that have disturbing implications for the gay rights movement. For example, the clause in support of "parents' rights" seem directed against policies permitting gay and lesbian adoptions. The clause calling for "family-friendly tax policies" could conceivably encourage legislation banning domestic-partner benefits. For a more detailed discussion of the implications of the "Contract" for gays and lesbians, see Gabriel Rotello, "Contract on Gays," *Nation*, 19 June 1995, 872–73.

INDEX

Almaguer, Tomas, 48
Altman, Dennis, 142, 143–44
American exceptionalism, 168
American studies, 24–25, 166, 205 n. 2,
206 n. 8. *See also* Chase, Richard;
Trilling, Lionel
Arac, Jonathan, 25, 207 n. 19
Arvin, Newton, 163

Baldwin, James, 3–5, 16, 17–18, 47–48,
103–4, 114; *Another Country,* 177–90;
on black nationalism, 177; on James,
Henry, 160–61; on Mailer, Norman,
176; on Wright, Richard, 172, 173–74;
on *Uncle Tom's Cabin,* 173
Beaver, Harold, 108–9
Behlmer, Rudy, 79
Benjamin, Walter, 26, 69, 206 n. 9, 215
n. 44
Bersani, Leo, 142–44, 158
Bowers v. Hardwick, 193
Bowlby, Rachel, 58
Brick Foxhole, The, 84, 87–93
Brooks, Richard, 15, 86–87, 217 n. 12
Brown, Norman O., 4

Capra, Frank, 12
Camp: definition of, 18, 59, 102–3,
204 n. 41, 213 n. 17; relation to film
noir, 14–15; relation to gay macho
style, 221 n. 39. *See also* Film noir;
Ross, Andrew; Sontag, Susan; Spectatorship

Caspary, Vera, 79–81, 216 n. 5. *See also*
Communist party
Chase, Richard, 162–63; on *Billy Budd,*
169–70; on James, Henry, 164; on
Matthiessen, F. O., 171–72; on novel
as form, 162–63; on romance, 167;
on Wallace, Henry, 171
Christian Coalition, 193, 236 n. 17. *See
also* Christian Right
Christian Right, 4, 192. *See also* Christian Coalition
Cleaver, Eldridge, 47–49, 176, 210
n. 40
Closet, the: as epistemological structure, 109, 223 n. 22; as trope in *Cat
on a Hot Tin Roof,* 17, 132–33; as trope
in "Hard Candy," 110–13; in relation
to Cold War, 115–16, 131–33
Clum, John, 116
Cohen, William, 188, 233 n. 43
Cold War consensus, 2–4; and American studies, 24–25, 166–72; and domestic model of masculinity, 5–6;
and film noir, 9–10, 13–14, 66–67;
and homosexualization of left-wing
politics, 2–3, 10–11, 165–66, 169–72;
and suburbanization, 8. *See also*
Masculinity; Suburbanization
Communist party: and "woman question," 16, 216 n. 4, 216 n. 5. *See also*
Caspary, Vera
Corey, Donald Webster, 91–92, 226 n. 1;
on Gore Vidal, 135–36; 156–57, 192

win, 160–62. *See also* Chase, Richard; Ellison, Ralph; Parrington, V. L.; Trilling, Lionel
Jameson, Fredric, 28

Kazan, Elia, 130–33, 220 n. 38, 225 n. 46; criticisms of *Cat on a Hot Tin Roof,* 130–31; testimony before HUAC, 131. *See also* Williams, Tennessee
Kennedy, Elizabeth, 19, 204 n. 42
Kerouac, Jack, 49–53
Kinsey report, 10, 63
Kormer, Charles, 86
Kracauer, Siegfried, 97, 100

Laura, film version of, 55–56, 59–78; novel version of, 80–84
Lauretis, Teresa de, 138
LeMaire, Rufs, 55

Male homosexual panic, 11–12. *See also* Fordism
Mailer, Norman, 173, 176, 185; "The White Negro," 44–49
Marcuse, Herbert, 4, 139
Masculinity: domestic model of, 6–7, 200 n. 10; oppositional forms of, 8–9, 31–32, 44–53, 145; Popular Front representation of, 42, 209 n. 29. *See also* Cleaver, Eldridge; Gay macho style; Mailer, Norman; Mills, C. Wright; Organization man, rise of
Mass culture, theories of, 25–26, 31–36, 206 n. 8, 206 n. 9
Mattachine Society, 19, 113–14, 209 n. 30
Matthiessen, F. O.: homosexuality of, 171–72, 231 n. 30; influence on American studies, 25, 206 n. 7; left-wing politics of, 171, 217 n. 13; on *Billy Budd,* 169, 170–71; on Henry James, 230 n. 16. *See also* Chase, Richard
McCarthy, Joseph, 87, 218 n. 14
McCarthyism, impact on Hollywood, 13, 95, 101, 220 n. 38

Menorah Journal, 168
Miller, Arthur, 36–43, 133, 209 n. 31, 209 n. 32, 225 n. 45
Mills, C. Wright, 6, 30–36; macho image of, 31–32, 207 n. 19; relation to New Left, 31–32
Minelli, Vincent, 59, 213 n. 18
Moynihan, Daniel Patrick, 201 n. 21, 210 n. 40
Mulvey, Laura, 71
Murder, My Sweet, 85, 217 n. 8
Murphy, Geraldine, 169, 231 n. 25
Myrdal, Gunnar, 91–92, 201 n. 21; influence on gay rights movement, 91–92, 228 n. 31

New Deal, 13, 96–98
New Left, 7, 9, 29

Odets, Clifford, 36
On the Waterfront, 131
Oppositional consciousness, definition of, 4, 199 n. 5
Organization man, rise of, 5–7, 71–72

Parrington, V. L.: Lionel Trilling's criticisms of, 164–65; on Henry James, 164
Paxton, John, 85
Pease, Donald E., 206 n. 12
Playboy, 8–9
Polan, Dana, 95–96
Political preconscious, definition of, 29, 206 n. 12
Polonsky, Abraham, 10
Popular Front, 13, 86–87, 217 n. 13; and Hollywood, 12, 13, 28; relation to film noir, 9–10
Preminger, Otto, 55–56
Production Code, 55–56, 67, 211 n. 4

Queer Nation, 193, 227 n. 11

Reich, Wilhelm, 4
Riesman, David, 6

Robert J. Corber is an independent scholar and author of *In the Name of National Security: Hitchcock, Homophobia, and the Political Construction of Gender in Postwar America.*

Library of Congress Cataloging-in-Publication Data

Corber, Robert J.

Homosexuality in cold war America : resistance and the crisis of
masculinity / Robert J. Corber.

p.   cm. — (New Americanists)

Includes index.

ISBN 0-8223-1956-x (cloth : alk. paper). —

ISBN 0-8223-1964-0 (paper : alk. paper)

1. Gays in popular culture—United States.   2. Masculinity in popular
culture—United States.   3. Homosexulity in motion pictures—United
States.   4. Film noir—United States—History and criticism.   5. Gay
men's writings, American—History and criticism.   6. Masculinity in
literature.   7. Homosexuality in literature.   I. Title.   II. Series.

HQ76.3.U5C65   1997

306.76'6'0973—dc21   96-53408